Throwing frisbees at the sun
A book about Beck
Rob Jovanovic

A Jawbone book
First edition 2015
Published in the UK and the USA by
Jawbone Press
2a Union Court,
20–22 Union Road,
London SW4 6JP,
England
www.jawbonepress.com

ISBN 978-1-908279-60-6

JACKET DESIGN Mark Case

Printed by Everbest Printing Co Ltd, China

1 2 3 4 5 19 18 17 16 15

Contents

Introduction: Que Onda?   6

CHAPTER 1 'She was in bed, dressed like Jean Harlow.'   9

CHAPTER 2 'Try to turn something disposable into something   17
beautiful.'

CHAPTER 3 'There were still chickens running around in the street.'   25

CHAPTER 4 'She gave me a key that didn't work and I never   39
saw her again.'

CHAPTER 5 'All we had was an acoustic guitar and energy.'   49

CHAPTER 6 'I was expecting my shoes to get stolen.'   60

CHAPTER 7 'I was lost in my own little world.'   74

CHAPTER 8 'I nailed my earlobe to the speaker.'   87

CHAPTER 9 'I wasn't prepared for any kind of success at all.'   104

CHAPTER 10 'I thought it would be a disaster.'   119

CHAPTER 11 'You hear it and it immediately attacks your   141
immune system.'

CHAPTER 12 'We had to run out in the rain and put him in a town car.'   150

CHAPTER 13 'In the end it worked itself out.'   168

CHAPTER 14 'It was a reunion of sorts.'   184

CHAPTER 15 'I think it meant something at some point.'   197

CHAPTER 16 'It's something else.'   209

CHAPTER 17 'You get an idea and go with it. There's no great plan.'   216

CHAPTER 18 'These songs are meant to be pulled apart.'   225

Endnotes   240
Discography   244
Index   249
Acknowledgements   254

INTRODUCTION
Que Onda?

Even in the twenty-first century, a long-distance line to Denver, Colorado, can be pretty crackly. Through the intermittent static, I had been passed from publicist to publicist, and now I had Beck Hansen on the line.

'I'm sorry if the tape recorder puts you off,' I told him. 'It will keep beeping.'

'It beeps?' he replied.

'Yes, it's a legal thing to let the other person know that I'm recording them.'

'OK!' he laughed. 'A little espionage!'

I was perched at the bottom of my stairs, hoping that my tape recorder was working properly, while Beck regaled me with stories of his home, life, and music. Though I couldn't see him, I knew he was eating an apple for his lunch.

Our chat covered lots of ground, and is peppered throughout this book. Apparently, he still set his alarm clock on some Sunday mornings to get down early to the swap meets so that he could battle through the hoards of shoppers and riffle through the stacks of old vinyl, hoping to find an obscure old folk collection, or some Tropicalia that he'd never heard of.

He was just as I'd expected.

* * *

Wednesday, July 7th, 1993. Beck is at the KCRW studio in Los Angeles for his first live radio session. That night, he'll be playing another show at his mother's venue, Café Troy, but for now the airwaves are filled with Woody Guthrie's voice:

> All these people, seeing how they lived, outside, like coyotes. Around in the trees and under the bridges and all along the railroad tracks and in their little shack-houses that they built out of cardboard and coal sacks and old corrugated iron that they got out of the dumps. It just struck me that I should write this song called 'I Ain't Got No Home In This World Anymore'.

It was quite an introduction. Beck's own song followed: a slide guitar riff, a backing tape, a shambolic drum beat in the studio, opening up a song that would become the sound of late 1993: 'Loser'.

It's all here in these few stolen moments: the genius songwriter, a very deliberate nod to his influences, a mother on the fringes of the art house music scene, and an incredibly infectious song.

* * *

Beck is arguably the most important, original force in contemporary music, matching critical acclaim and ever growing sales figures. His rock/rap/folk albums *Mellow Gold* (with hit single 'Loser') and *Odelay* came to define the mid-90s American cutting edge, while introspective albums like *Mutations* and *Sea Change* gained him a whole new audience. He returned to the sublimely distinctive mix of rap, rock, and Latino beats on *Guero* and *The Information*, before the precise half-hour of *Modern Guilt* preceded a six year recording hiatus—at least as far as new albums were concerned. In 2014, he released the acclaimed *Morning Phase*, an album rooted in the Californian vibes of his upbringing.

During his break from releasing albums, Beck had undertaken numerous production duties, put out cover versions of entire albums via his website, published a collection of sheet music, and much more. All this cemented the long-held view that Beck is truly an original in an age when originality is at an all-time low.

* * *

Another meeting with Beck. At the end of the last century I'd been sent a strange invitation, and was dispatched to the West Coast of America by a magazine editor in order to produce a Beck travelogue. I spent a week in the desert. The month of May was especially hot and walking down the strip in Las Vegas became almost unbearable during the day. However, in the cool of the evening, it was comfortable to be outside, as the heat dissipated across the desert from the rotten oasis. I made my way to the Tropicana, an old-school casino opposite the plastic splendour of Luxor and New York, New York. Beck was mixing bizness with pleasure that night in a dinner-theatre setting, dropping his lobotomy beats to the banks of curved booths and red leather seats.

The sold-out crowd slowly made their way in. The atmosphere was exquisite, with local hipsters and the travelling hardcore from LA mixing happily with the nonchalance of the city itself. The few hundred souls-in-the-know witnessed the then-unknown Tenacious D play a support set, and then it was time for the main event. The opening chords rippled out from behind a velvet curtain, and slowly the barrier was raised and the band revealed. Bass guitar, dark and heavy: Justin Meldal-Johnsen. Cymbals frying: Joey Waronker. Beat suffocating. 'Novacane'. Snare drums echoing like breaking glass. Beeps from Casio calculators invading the mix then faded away: Roger Manning Jr. 'Novacane'. Turntables scratch, drums break: DJ Swamp. Guitars cackle and hiss: Smokey Hormel. Brass section complete. 'Novacane'.

The show was ingenious. The genius was centre stage. After the show, Beck was surrounded. An English accent, mine, broke through the scrum. Beck's eyes alighted, looking for the speaker.

'Did you like the show?' he asked.

I sure did.

It's what led me to write this book.

CHAPTER 1

'She was in bed dressed, like Jean Harlow.' (1915-72)

The SS *Potsdam* was a German-built, steam-driven ocean liner dating back to 1900. In 1915, it had been sold to the Swedish-American Line and renamed the SS *Stockholm* as it began transporting thousands of Swedes across the North Atlantic to the USA. During the late 19th and early 20th centuries, more than 1.3 million Swedes made the journey. Most continued on to the Midwest where the weather, logging opportunities, and farms reminded them of home.

By late 1915, with the Great War raging across Central Europe, the number of people making the trip had decreased, the sinking of the *Lusitania* in May having sent shockwaves around the world. But despite the risks involved, nineteen-year-old Olaf Gabriel Ostlin boarded the SS *Stockholm* in Gothenburg in December and began his journey to the USA.[1] He arrived at Ellis Island on December 26th and was processed into the country, ready to start a new life.

Rather than head across the continent, Ostlin settled in New York. There he found work with the American Can Company and met and married Sadie Rosenberg, who came from a family of Russian-Polish Jews and was one of twelve children of Abraham and Fanny Rosenberg.[2] Olaf and Sadie had two children: Robert, born in 1921, and Audrey, born in 1929. Sadie committed suicide at the age of thirty-five, leaving Olaf to raise the children alone.

Audrey Ostlin was a real free spirit. During World War II, she fell in with the Beats and bohemians around Union Square. She danced, stripped, appeared on TV, and wrote poetry. In 1949, the petit Audrey appeared in a stage show that required her to have green hair. After one performance, she headed down to Greenwich Village, wearing just a raincoat, a green G-string, and a pair of emerald green sequinned pasties. At around three in the morning, she entered the Waldorf Cafeteria, a dreary place that had become the preferred hangout for painters and sculptors. Across the bar sat a group of Beats and artists. One of them, Alfred Earl 'Al' Hansen, was transfixed as she walked over in her green high-heels. 'I'm going to marry that cunt,' he was heard to mutter.[3]

Like Ostlin, Hansen (two years her senior) also came from Scandinavian stock. His grandfather, Nicholas Sr., had hopped on to a Schooner from his native Norway and relocated to Queens, New York. His father, Nicholas Jr., was born in a shack in the yard of a dry dock in Greenpoint, Brooklyn, where Nick Sr. worked. Nick Jr. served in World War I as a motorcycle messenger, and from then on was an avid motorcycle enthusiast. On the eve of the Depression, Nick Jr. started a small construction company, which did well throughout the downturn. Later on, he bought a few gas stations. One was right next door to the family home in Jamaica, Queens. His wife, Katherine, worked for the Democratic Party; she was a 'ward heeler' and politically well connected.

Al grew up with a love of art, and had spent much of his childhood drawing. One of his earliest projects was a hand-made newspaper, the *Daily Flash*, which he produced with his brother, Gordon, and a friend, Jimmy Breslin.[4]

During the war, Al became Private Al Hansen of the 508th Parachute Infantry Regiment and was sent to Europe. He didn't drop in—he arrived by boat on the French coast. This was the tail end of World War II. A few weeks later, Hansen and his comrades had worked their way across France and Belgium and arrived in Frankfurt, Germany. The city had taken a tremendous bombing over the previous months and was littered with partially destroyed buildings, collapsed walls, and piles of bricks where homes once stood.

Hansen's regiment was charged with working its way across the city on a building-by-nondescript-building basis, looking for any last pockets of resistance. It was potentially dangerous work, but so far it had thrown up little excitement or real danger. One afternoon, with the last of the day's sunshine casting long shadows that made every nook and cranny a potential hidey-hole, Hansen spied it: a grand piano on the fifth floor of a building just ahead, visible because the sidewall of the block had disintegrated into a pile of bricks and rubble.

Hansen was gripped by a compulsive urge. While the rest of his group sat around, he carefully made his way over to the building. His temerity led him up flight after flight of stairs before he opened the door into what had once been an opulent-looking living room. He put down his rifle and moved slowly over to the instrument, taking the weight with his lower legs and pushing with all his might. The piano started to edge slowly toward the precipice and then flipped, almost in slow motion, as it toppled out into the German evening.

The piano seemed to take an age to reach the ground below. As it travelled through the still air, Hansen felt a strange calm until the very last moment before the piano hit the bricks below. A moment of exquisite silence. And then chaos. A deafening crunch of the wooden casing exploding against the rubble, echoing from the surrounding buildings like a gunshot, followed by the sound of the keys and strings splitting into a hundred thousand pieces. Hansen was elated. The falling German piano was just the first of many 'happenings' he would perform.

Back in the USA, Al Hansen would forge a reputation among the avant-garde, but first he would use the GI Bill to fund his attendance of an art course at Tulane University in New Orleans. Then, on his return to New York, he met Audrey at the Waldorf Cafeteria. They hit it off immediately. They went on the road, just like the rest of the Beats, hitchhiking down to Miami Beach. Audrey tried to dye her green hair brown, but the mixture of chemicals turned it purple.

Later in the year, Al and Audrey were married. They decided to settle back in Manhattan, and in 1953, Audrey gave birth to a daughter. They named her Bibbe. She grew to be the spitting image of her mother.

Bibbe's parents had divorced by the time she turned three. Al went back to studying art, and Audrey remained in New York. 'My mother was originally supposed to play *Sabrina* in the movie,' she recalled. 'She was a dancer on the old Perry Como Show, the one who did the *Thumbelina* dance, and she was in those old commercials that were done live. One of the famous ones was the one she goofed up. The girl comes onscreen in elegant profile and gets her cigarette lit. Then she turns to the camera to exhale and coughs half a lung out. She could be very silly and fun.'

Growing up with Audrey was a challenge. 'My mother was a heroin addict,' Bibbe told the *Independent*'s Luiza Sauma in 2008. 'But she took me to the opera and imparted a great love of literature and theatre.'

Bibbe found herself living in a variety of situations. She was sent to Nova Scotia for a time, and then returned to New York to be cared for by one of her mother's lesbian admirers. Later, she was rooming with Jack Kerouac's daughter, Jan, when they were both aged thirteen. Inspired by The Beatles, they started a band called The Whippets with another friend, Charlotte Rosenthal, and soon, after a chance meeting with a producer, they were recording a single for the Laurie Records label. 'I Don't Want To Talk To You' b/w 'Go Go Go With Ringo' made the charts in Canada in 1964.

Later, when Al returned to New York, Bibbe moved back in with him. Al had got to know the Andy Warhol entourage, and was dating Valerie Herouvis. Bibbe would accompany him to the Factory on East 47th Street, and was chosen to appear in *Prison* with Edie Sedgwick. Warhol asked her to take part in the film because of her recent experiences. She'd been picked up as a runaway and truant and taken to the Manida Street Youth House, which housed up to 120 troublesome girls.

According to Beck, Bibbe was involved 'very briefly' with Warhol, and appeared in 'one or two' of his short films. 'They would just set somebody up and film them for five minutes and call it a movie. I think, to her, The Factory was just a bunch of grown-ups. It wasn't really where she was at. From everything she's told me, it was just a bunch of speed freaks hanging around, and sometimes someone would bring out a camera. I don't think it was as crazy as it seems now, looking back. You know, that time period—anything in the 1960s, but especially something like that scene—is always blown up into this larger-than-life thing.'

Splitting her time between being with Al at the Factory and around Audrey's new partner, a prominent Jew by the name of Jimmy Shapiro, provided a unique environment for the teenage Bibbe. Jimmy was a pilot, and had served in the Navy Air Force during the Korean War. His mother, Rose, owned 50 percent of the Fabergé cosmetics company with her half-brother, Sam Rubin. Jimmy was stationed for a while at Point Judith, Rhode Island, and for a while Audrey and Bibbe lived in a small beach cottage there in Breakwater Village. When Jim left the service, the three of them moved to Saranac Lake, New York, where they started an air taxi service called North Country Airways and managed the nearby Lake Clear Airport.[5]

Back in New York, Audrey continued to lead an interesting life, as Bibbe recalled:

> My mother started hanging out at society nightclubs like the 21, the Pompeii Club, the Stork Club. She was meeting all these characters, and one of them was Charlie Walker, the heir to the Hiram Walker whiskey fortune. He was hilarious, and he moved in with us for a while. My mother would be off in Boston, scoring cocaine for Uncle Charlie, and he would babysit me. He was always sloshed out of his mind. Constantly inebriated.
>
> She met so many thieves, degenerates, and gangsters. One of the lasting images I have as a child is waking up early one morning to go to school and hearing music in the distance. I went down the hall and saw my mother's door ajar, and I peered in and she was in bed dressed like Jean Harlow. She was saying, 'If you

listen right here, and listen very carefully to this part, it sounds like a beer bottle going through the window.' And at the foot of her bed there were four thugs sitting in straight-back chairs. It's seven in the morning, and she was giving music appreciation lessons to these guys. They were trying so hard to stay awake and pay attention.

In August 1968, the fast living took its toll, and Audrey died at the age of thirty-seven. Her obituary, penned by Daniel List, was published in the *Village Voice*, who wrote that she had 'lived a life that might burn up any two other people [before] finally [coming] to roost in the West Village, where she had fallen in with an assortment of scurves, hop heads, and, unaccountably, some angels. ... Life being the shit house that it is, the scurves won out over the good guys, and Audrey just plain burnt out.'

* * *

Al Hansen's artistic explorations had led him to the heart of the Fluxus movement, and he'd crossed paths with John Cage and Yoko Ono. He signed up for a course given by Cage and hooked up with several artists who took the same course. He was driven by a sense of artistic spontaneity.

Al found art in everyday garbage, working with everything from candy wrappers to cigarette butts. His was an unusual chaos of style and material. This meshed perfectly with Fluxus, which was inspired by Marcel Duchamp and the idea that art need not come from a skilled artist, and that everyday items could be incorporated to make art—an ethos that Al would follow for the rest of his life.

In 1965, Al published a book about his artistic beliefs entitled *A Primer Of Happenings & Time Space Art*. He began churning out thousands of collages, many of them based around the image of the Venus de Milo. And he was on the scene when Andy Warhol was shot. 'He actually ran into Valerie Solanas as she was on her way out of the Factory from shooting Warhol,' Beck later explained. 'He made a book about it called *Why Shoot Andy Warhol?* It's really beautiful.'

14

Al Hansen became the catalyst for many Fluxus and Pop Art events, and his enthusiasm encouraged those around him to go on to greater things. 'He was the life and soul of the Fluxus party,' Beck later recalled. 'He would hook up everybody together. At his funeral, all the Fluxus people were there, and all the Pop art people, and they all talked about how mischievous he was. He didn't really play the game, though. He would get drunk and insult the gallery owner's wife and get banned. He was the Bukowski of the scene.'

One day, Al gave his teenage daughter Bibbe a couple of dollars to go to the corner store. She never came back. The following weeks involved 'sex scandals, a drug bust, and some very dicey stuff'.

By the age of seventeen, Bibbe was living in Los Angeles, where she met an aspiring violin player named David Campbell. Campbell was born in Toronto, Canada, in 1948, and moved to Seattle at the age of nine. He was a tall, softly spoken man, and in later years Beck would develop a very close facial resemblance to him, leading father and son to be described as 'two peas in a pod'.

David started playing the violin at the age of nine, and later studied at the Manhattan School of Music. He moved to Los Angeles in the late 1960s, and began studying the music of The Beatles, The Rolling Stones, and Leonard Cohen. He would earn pocket change by playing their tunes on his violin to the cinema queues in Westwood Village.

David and Bibbe were married in 1969. Their first son, Bek David Campbell, was born on July 8 1970 in Los Angeles.

* * *

Beck has a unique family tree—one that juxtaposes artistry with relative poverty, and that involved him from an early age in a series of cultural shifts that would have an inevitable influence on the eclectic nature of his work. But while some critics would portray him as somebody who emerged into a life of art and privilege, his early life would be spent bouncing around between his mother and grandparents.

Neither household was particularly prosperous. Beck had to learn how to fend for himself from an early age, while also helping to support his family, and that independence would no doubt help him—if only subconsciously—to make up his own musical mind and not follow trends or movements. The reality of his own Los Angeles upbringing ensured that he did not fit into the clichéd idea of California, and he has always been keen to stress that he grew up in East LA among immigrants from Mexico and Central America.[6]

By the time of Beck's birth, the hippie idealism of 60s California was as shot and faded as flower power. The Beatles had split up, and the spectre of Vietnam cast a long shadow across the country. The explosion of pop and rock music that had left its imprint so memorably on the previous decade had also produced casualties. Jimi Hendrix died just after Beck was born; a month later, Janis Joplin passed away in nearby Hollywood; and within a year, Jim Morrison was dead in Paris. The 1970s would be a very different decade.

CHAPTER 2

'Try to turn something disposable into something beautiful.' (1973-80)

By the early 1970s, Los Angeles had long established itself as *the* epic suburban sprawl, truly the city of the motorcar. For English architectural critic Reyner Banham, 'One of the greatest sights on earth is the aerial view of the intersection of the San Diego and Santa Monica freeways.'

LA was also strengthening its position as one of the world's great musical centres. Carly Simon and Jackson Browne were holed up in Laurel Canyon, and the Eagles would soon dominate the airwaves. Of course, LA is famously the city with no real centre. It's so large that it is, in fact, many smaller cities merged into one. Though Beck has spent much of his adult life living in and around the 'bohemian enclave' of Silver Lake, within about ten miles lay Koreatown, Little Ethiopia, Hollywood, and the Central American neighbourhoods he lived in as a child. All of these neighbourhoods push up against each other, bursting with 14 million people—most of whom have come from elsewhere to call LA home.

It might be a cliché, but it is also true, to say that Beck synthesized all manner of musical styles into his own unique brew. This came about in no small part because of the myriad of cultures that surrounded his formative years. Beck, as musical entity, could hardly have broken through in the way he did at any other time in history. It was his interaction with Los Angeles—with the people who lived there and the people who arrived during the 1970s and early 1980s—that shaped his view of the world.

'I completely take for granted what I've grown up around, as I think everybody does,' he admitted. 'I have such a fondness for the Armenian neighbourhood and the Korean neighbourhood, Monterey Park where there are hundreds of thousands of Chinese straight from Hong Kong, Guatemalan neighbourhoods. Even as an outsider, it's something nostalgic for me.'[7]

* * *

Things began to look up for the Campbell household around 1971–72. David had managed to find some work playing with Jackson Browne, and he performed in Carole King's touring band before arranging the strings on her album *Rhymes & Reason*, which went to #2 on the *Billboard* charts. This set him on his way. That same year, 1972, a second son, Channing Campbell was born.

While David was able to take advantage of so much music being made in Los Angeles, the young Beck didn't take much notice of his father's work. 'I heard him play here and there,' he said, 'but it wasn't like I went into the living room and people were jamming or anything. I just remember that he was always working. I liked what he played, but it wasn't like I went out and picked up an instrument and started playing myself. It wasn't until a lot later that I picked up an instrument.'

By the autumn of 1974, Beck started school in Los Angeles, and was immediately tagged as an enigma by the authorities there. 'When I first started school, I was four or five—the administrators and the teachers, and the certifiers, the paper-registering people of the world gave the *c* to me. I don't think they could deal with *b-e-k*. It would always become *b-e-c-k*, and I guess I got tired of saying, *no, b-e-k*. So I just went with it. Somehow I think it gave me a little more weight. I thought maybe as a kid—I was a small kid—with a name like that I was going to float away.'

Soon after starting school, Beck gave his first onstage performance … as a donkey. It almost scarred him for life. 'All I remember is that one kid was the goat, one was the horse, and one was the giraffe. I had to get up to the front and say, *The donkey goes eeyore*. Everybody started laughing, and

I thought I'd done something really wrong. I was horrified. It turned me off performing for a long time.'

Beck spent a lot of time during the summer months in Kansas with his paternal grandparents, Noreen and D. Warren Campbell, a Presbyterian minister. He enjoyed staying with them because they did all the things grandparents can get away with, like giving him cookies and letting him watch TV. Looking back, though, he felt they weren't sure what was going on. 'I had a kind of weird home,' he said. 'I think they were kind of concerned.'

It was in Kansas that Beck was really opened up to a lot of music for the first time—by the unlikely influence of listening to Presbyterian hymns. 'That music influenced me a lot,' he said, 'but not consciously. There's something biblical and awkward and great about all those lyrics.' Later, after he had discovered the blues and its links to the rhythms of rap, he tied it all back to the religious songs of his past. 'The religious energy of a minister in front of his congregation is pretty similar to rock'n'roll energy. The grunt and the groan and the punctuation of a sermon is similar to the grunt and the groan of a soul singer or rapper. It's all connected to the blues.'

It was around this time that Beck began seeing more of his maternal grandfather, who would occasionally stay with Bibbe on his trips to the West Coast. The first time they met, Al gave him an unusual present—a machete. He surely deserves some of the credit for some of Beck's unique lyrical styles. 'When I was about five, I was trying to get my grandfather to explain what rhyming was,' he recalled. 'He explained it to me, and *pull down your pants and do the hot dog dance* was my first lyric. My grandfather got a kick out of that.'

As well as his performance pieces, Al Hansen was now working on bizarre sculptures, often prepared by recycling garbage. Years later, in an interview with *Rolling Stone*, Beck told a story that offers a good example of their artistic closeness:

He was this strange phenomenon, you know, who'd come from

out of nowhere. I remember he came to stay with us when I was about five, and he brought with him bags full of junk and magazines, cigarette butts—all sorts of refuse and materials that he would use for his art pieces. I had some old toys that had broken and didn't work stored in the back room somewhere. He found an old rocking horse, the kind you buy at K-Mart, made out of plastic with springs on it. And he offered me five bucks for it, which, for me, was an unheard-of quantity of money. I immediately said yeah, he could have it. But I couldn't understand what he would do with it, what use he could have for it.

So I came back from school one day and saw this thing sitting at the side of the house, vaguely familiar but somehow completely unrecognisable. He had taken the thing and glued cigarette butts all over it, severed the head off and spray-painted the whole thing silver. It was this metallic headless monstrosity. I think I was interested, but something within me recoiled as well. It was, it was so raw: something so plain and forgotten suddenly transformed into this strange entity.

Beck realised that, to many, his grandfather might seem like a homeless person, carrying around bags full of old magazines and smoked cigarettes. 'At the time, it was more of a curiosity to me. But in retrospect, I think things of that nature gave me the idea, maybe subconsciously, that there were possibilities within the limitations of everyday life, with the things that we look at that are disposable. Our lives can seem so limited and uneventful, but these things can be transformed. We can appoint ourselves to be, to be alchemists, turning shit into gold. So I always carried that with me.'

Although he got a certain amount of artistic inspiration from his grandfather, the young Beck seemed uninterested in music. His father's playing and arranging didn't immediately inspire him, and the various other influences he was exposed to also had little or no effect on him at the time. The first music he can remember hearing at home was, he said, 'likely to have been a musical comedy, one of those Broadway pieces of rubbish that my mother listened to at the house. There were very few records at our house and there were some absolute horrors with melodies that made me want to vomit. The first record I really adored was "Ruby Tuesday" by the Stones. I knew nothing about them, not even that they were English. It was that song that I loved, that simple melody.' He also recalled listening to *Rubber Soul* at the age of five, 'though I'm not sure how that's filtered into what I do now. And I remember hearing "Hot Child In The City" while driving to school'.

In the light of Beck's upbringing, it is easier to understand his claims not to have been aware of a lot of 1970s music. Listening to a Beck record, one is tempted to jump to the conclusion that he absorbed a lot of popular music from that time. The truth is very different.

It's sort of strange for me because I totally missed the 1970s. Sometimes there's this notion that I'm this encyclopaedia of 1970s culture, which isn't really true—I know much less than anyone else in the band. I wasn't even aware of most of the music in the 1970s ... maybe Blondie and Devo. You know, sometimes people will say, *hey, that sounds exactly like so and so, you must have listened to a lot of their stuff*—and often I haven't even heard of them. I don't think I even heard Black Sabbath until I was nineteen or twenty. I just wasn't exposed to it—it just wasn't in our house. My mum would just play show tunes and stuff like that all the time.

After a few short stays, Al Hansen moved in with his daughter for a longer spell toward the end of the 1970s. 'He lived in the garage for a couple of years,' Beck later told *Request* magazine. 'This was probably about 1977. I didn't have a lot of contact with my grandfather, but seeing how he worked gave me a lot of confidence. Seeing the way he worked, I never felt that I had to have schooling in order to create. He was this presence; he got people excited about the scene.'

Al would take Beck and Channing on scavenging missions along Sunset Boulevard in search of materials to use in his art. 'He used specific materials—cigarette butts, matches, Hershey Bar wrappers,' Beck told VH1. 'My art is a little less focused. I tend to use ephemera from computers, diskettes; there's imagery from muscle building. Instead of all those things ... that you'd throw in the dustbin, I keep them, and my grandfather would keep them as well—try to turn something disposable into something beautiful.'

While Al would take trash and turn it into art ('turning shit into gold', as Beck put it), his grandson has been credited with doing something similar in his music, by taking many different styles and combining them into one song. Beck agreed with the principle—to some extent. 'On a certain level that's right on,' he told *Request*, 'but when you say *recycling*, it cheapens the aesthetic a bit and makes the music sound second-class. I think the process has a gracefulness and a dignity to it, so I like to say my music is orchestrated—an organisation of disparate elements.'

* * *

Times were becoming hard in the Campbell household, and some things other kids took for granted were no longer available to Beck and his brother Channing. 'We stopped having Christmas when I was very young,' he recalled, 'because we couldn't afford it. I remember one year my brother and I made a Christmas tree out of cardboard. We cut it out and stuck it on the wall. It was a traditional sort of thing, but it was depressing. It always is if you haven't got any money.

Asked by *Q* magazine about whether his family had been poor, Beck was evasive. 'You could say that,' he replied. 'I don't want to talk about it. Where I come from financially doesn't inform my music.' Throughout this time, Beck and Channing remained close. When they were not hanging out with Al, they would be left to their own devices, while Bibbe was out working. She believed in a hands-off approach to parenting. 'She's just a chain-smoking, make-your-own-dinner kind of mom,' Beck said. To her credit, Bibbe has never tried to claim any of Beck's musical abilities to be part of his upbringing. 'He's an original,' she said. 'He did it all completely on his own. I wouldn't have a clue as to how *Bek* became *Beck*.'

22

With little or no money to hand, the two brothers had to make up their own entertainment. 'When I was little, we used to have these missions,' Beck recalled. 'We'd strip down to our underwear and have a destination—like the supermarket eight blocks away. We had to make it there and back without getting arrested or beaten up or pregnant.'

It was a time of adventure and discovery. 'As kids, me and my brother always had to fend for ourselves,' Beck told the *Times Metro* in 1997. 'We had to learn how to cook and to feed ourselves all the time—I started cooking pretty young. It was kind of a necessity really. My parents would be working, my dad would be off for a week somewhere, and you'd get hungry. You'd think, *I want a hamburger*, but then you'd think, *How do you make a hamburger?* So you sort of figure it out. I remember when I was a teenager going to shows, and me and my brother were the youngest ones there. We were the only kids around.'

The latter half of the 70s saw a new musical entity arrive on the West Coast: a strange new beast called punk. Al Hansen saw something in this new music that appealed to his artistic nature, and soon became involved in it. 'My grandfather was into that whole Masque scene,' Beck recalled. 'He hipped my mom to bands like The Screamers and The Bags and The Plugz.'[8] Soon, Bibbe was involved in the scene as well, playing mother to a whole host of young punks who needed a place to sleep for the night. Beck wasn't overly keen on this situation. 'I wish she'd done all that stuff when she was a teenager,' he explained. 'There seems to be a point—and this is true for a lot of my friends too—where their mothers reach their mid forties and turn into freaks. They become teenagers again. She's definitely become more open-minded. My brother and I were sort of left to our own devices. Again, it was the same with a lot of people my age. They weren't very *parented*. In fact, almost everybody I know was like that. It wasn't an LA thing, more a 60s/70s thing. That generation was definitely ... I don't want to say self-centred, but maybe self-focused.'

Beck found it difficult to get used to walking into the kitchen in the morning and finding a punk or two at the breakfast table. 'I just remember all these people sprawled about looking like thrashed parrots,' he recalled. 'Very colourful and debauched, but very sweet, too. They were normal people—they just smelled a little funny. She would let punks stay at our house who didn't have a place to stay. She claims that Darby Crash [lead singer of The Germs] crashed out a few times on our living room sofa. She was older but felt kind of sorry for them.'

For Bibbe, punk was a breath of fresh air: 'It was like the best thing I'd heard in years, so there was always a peanut butter and jam sandwich and a couch.' Her involvement in the punk scene eventually led to her playing guitar in the Los Angeles ensemble Black Fag with Vaginal Creme Davis, a 6ft 7in African American drag queen and performance artist.

David and Bibbe divorced in 1984, and Beck went through a series of rented homes in multicultural settings. In 2004, he told *Filter*:

Something typical of the neighbourhood I lived in would be a store that was a butcher, but they also sold cassette tapes, and somebody on the back would do your income taxes. That's a certain mentality that's just fluid. It's open. I think that's a big aspect of how I see music-making. There was a time, maybe when I was younger, where I wished everything were just one thing or just sort of a normal, what-you-see-on-TV kind of thing. I remember going to London and seeing all these row houses, and there was a certain uniformity that said, *This is London, This is England*—and there's nothing like that in LA. It's just this amazing collision—complete randomness—and you eventually just embrace it.

After splitting with David, Bibbe felt as she was returning to her 'old self' for a while. 'I wanted to know what it was like,' she explained. 'I was a Hollywood wife back then. I always had a wild streak, but I was in wild recovery, living with my staid husband—a wonderful musician, arranger, and composer. I needed a rest from being a maniac wild child. I had my own children, and things were very calm for me for about five or six years.'

That calmness was about to vanish into the Los Angeles night.

CHAPTER 3

'There were still chickens running around in the street.' (1980-87)

Things were changing for Beck. After spending the late 1970s in Los Angeles, Al Hansen moved to Cologne in Germany, and Bibbe met Sean Carrillo, a Mexican artist, whom she would later marry. Carrillo's parents had moved from the northern Mexico town of El Paso to Los Angeles, where he was born in 1960, one of nine children. He was a member of the Asco art collective, a Chicano group based in East LA. 'When I met Bibbe, I was just this kid,' he told *Index* magazine in 1999. 'She already knew everything about me and the Chicano art movement at that time. She knew where we came from, what we were about. She's with the trends before they happen.'

As a result of his mother's new relationship, Beck suddenly had a new, half-Mexican family. 'Even now, I feel more comfortable being around Mexican people than anyone else,' he said. 'Half my family was Mexican. It's just the way of life that was around me growing up. It's very natural with them. I can feel out of place with other people, but not with them.'

For a while, Beck and his new family lived in Hollywood, back in the days when it was still affordable, just prior to the 1980s property boom. The area had been in decline for a while, as he recalled, in an interview with *Rolling Stone*:

I spent my childhood watching the decline of Hollywood

Boulevard, watching the dying embers, the final light of the Hollywood era, fade into decay. I remember certain relics of the 40s and 50s Hollywood eras still around when I was growing up.

They had the lunch counters, shoeshines, and family-owned businesses, which have now turned into rock-poster shops and bad souvenir shops. We lived near Tiny Naylor's, which was a monument from the age of the 50s drive-in coffee shops. It was just a megalopolis of hamburgers and milkshakes, that whole— you drive up, and the waitress puts the tray on your car. They still had that up into the 70s. And right next to that was Ali Baba's, a Middle Eastern restaurant with belly dancers, and on top of it was a two-to-three-storey statue of Ali Baba.

Then, in the early 80s, all that was suddenly gone. The developers came in and tore it all down and turned it into giant condominiums and block apartments. I remember seeing LA just transformed within a couple years. All of a sudden there were mini-malls everywhere. The 80s came and conquered. And it erased a lot of the heritage of that city. It's not the same city at all.

At one time, the family rented Marlon Brando's old home, set on different levels, with a dozen staircases snaking in and around the property. Beck would spend his weekends riding his bike around Hollywood Boulevard, where he'd see the break-dancers and hear Grandmaster Flash. 'My funk came from being eleven years old on a Saturday night, hanging out on Hollywood Boulevard with all the break-dancers,' he said.

Shortly after that, the family moved to South Vermont Avenue. The apartments they inhabited were fairly small, and Beck never had a room to himself. 'When I was growing up, I used to share the living room with my little brother—he slept on the couch, I slept on the floor. He liked to listen to Leonard Cohen's *Songs From A Room* while he fell asleep, but it was so dark and creepy, it gave me nightmares. Especially the song where he takes his son, Isaac, up to the mountain and kills him.'

Later on, he recalled, he had to sleep in a sleeping bag under the kitchen table. The next move was downtown—to Hoover & Ninth Street, and a neighbourhood populated largely by Koreans and Salvadoran refugees—where once again Beck had to change school. By now, he was buying music for himself during the family's trips to LA thrift stores, which gave him the chance to pick up some cheesy second-hand albums. 'I was really into easy-listening records,' he recalled. 'I had all the Mancini records and Jobim. It was the early 80s, so it wasn't really campy or retro—I just had a genuine affection for the music. The second-hand store would have a bin of records, Mancini and stuff like that. It was five records for a dollar. You went to the Salvation Army and there'd be some elderly person who'd just passed away, and you'd end up buying all their junk. There wasn't any Top 20 stuff.'

Beck's favourite part of the city was Carroll Avenue. The houses there were originally sited at an area near Bunker Hill, which was torn down in the 1930s. It looks like San Francisco, a series of Victorian houses on steep hills. 'I watched, in my lifetime, whole neighbourhoods be completely flattened and obliterated,' he said. 'So it's a little glimpse of the original LA.' The neighbourhoods Beck lived in around East Hollywood were filled with slightly run-down Spanish style houses. 'You could walk off Hollywood Boulevard and you'd be in these beautiful streets,' he recalled. 'It was definitely urban, but there were these great old houses you could get for $150 a week. Now all that stuff's gone, and it's Beirut-style apartment buildings.'

His family's financial circumstances would improve, but during the early 1980s, things were still pretty tight.

It was a little rough. By the time I was a teenager, we were living on the edge of things. I would say we were economically depressed—we were basically living in a ghetto. But I wouldn't want to sell myself as some kind of rags-to-riches story, because that reduces it to something soulless. It was an impoverished childhood, but it was rich in other ways. Where I grew up wasn't your typical, homogenised, one-track frame of mind. There were a lot of other things going on. Everyone was outside all the time; there were mariachi bands, animals running down the middle of the street. We lived in a one-bedroomed apartment, five of us in a tiny space. If you're thirteen or fourteen, all you want is to be alone. So I would go to the library and spend days there. I just stumbled onto a lot of stuff, got into some different books, but then there are a lot of other ones that I've just totally missed.

The family apartment had a steel security door with numerous bolts to keep it secure, but one night, someone crowbarred it off. The would-be thieves must have been disappointed on entering the apartment—all they found were second-hand books and records; nothing of any real value.

While Beck's somewhat unconventional upbringing would stand him in good stead to look after himself in the future, his schooling left a lot to be desired, and by the age of fourteen, in fact, he had given up going to school at all. He had never wanted to drop out, but his circumstances had made things difficult—and dangerous, as he explained to the *Daily Telegraph* in 2014:

I would never want to give the idea that I left because I didn't think school was important. It was just the circumstances that I was in. ... When you're a teenager, you want space—you want time alone. Also, the part of Los Angeles where I was going to school, it wasn't exactly the safest. It was a hardcore school— there were lots of hardcore gangs. I was the only white guy in my neighbourhood, which was fine by me, but not for some.

It was just that five percent were pretty hardcore. ... That was a little bit of a problem. So I had to keep a low profile, just for my own survival. A lot of them had been in [Salvadoran] death squads. Our gang-bangers weren't just local kids—they were trained killers. One particular gang used to have crosses tattooed on their foreheads. The high school near to us was the first in America to put metal detectors on the entrance. I was pretty much the only white kid there and I stopped going when I was fourteen. It wasn't safe for me.

Beck had an idealised view of school in part because it wasn't readily available to him. After dropping out of high school he applied to an art school, but his application was turned down. He felt that the education system just wasn't open to him. 'The education system in America depends on where you grow up,' he explained. 'In my part of LA, it was completely backward. I remember being in an English class, being taught the same thing year after year. It never went anywhere, and there was nothing interesting. But I knew there were interesting things out there, and I knew there were possibilities.'

In later years, Beck would be repeatedly asked whether he harboured any regret about dropping out of school so early. 'Oh, yeah, definitely,' he told *Rolling Stone*. 'More than anything, I envy my friends that got to go to college. I thought maybe I would work for a few years and save money to go to college, but that never worked out. I went to New York instead and was playing music. I thought I would eventually go back to school, but I never have.' He was also memorably quoted as saying, in his best Groucho Marx voice, 'I'm sure there's something good about high school, but not any of the ones I went to.'

Something of a loner, Beck struggled to relate to his peers, and would mainly hang out with his brother and other much older people. And it wasn't just at school where he felt like the odd man out. As one of the only white kids in his East LA neighbourhood, he would find himself in some hairy situations on an almost daily basis. There was, he recalled, some 'pretty badass shit going on. Getting chased by kids with lead pipes every day.'

Having to frequently escape from these sorts of incidents turned Beck into something of an athlete. 'I guess it made me tougher, but I'm not tough for tough's sake. I don't really have the mass. I've been in fights. I've been in chases more. I'm a pretty fast runner, I think I was the fastest runner in my neighbourhood.' He also had to contend with living in the epicentre of a crack epidemic during the 1980s. His day-to-day life meant he'd see fourteen-year-old kids out of their minds on crack trying to smash down street signs, and others lying in the street, destitute.

Beck found himself caught in something of a cultural Catch-22. Living in a half-Mexican family excluded him from white culture, but at the same time the colour of his skin excluded him from the local gangs. 'I felt completely alienated from suburban white culture, even intimidated by it,' he said. 'I couldn't relate to kids my own age and colour because I didn't live the way they did, but at the same time I couldn't hang with the Salvadoran gangs on my street, 'cos to them I was the *Whetto*—the weird white kid.'

He was also being exposed to a mixture of religious influences. Bibbe Hansen had given her sons a vaguely Jewish upbringing. Her own mother, Audrey, and stepdad, Jimmy, were Jewish, and she had faced anti-Semitism while growing up.[9] Beck's stepfather, Carrillo, was Catholic, and attended confession every week, while David Campbell (whom Beck saw little of during this period) had been involved with Scientology since the 1960s.

Bibbe too had also taken some Scientology courses in the early 1970s, while Beck himself would attend a series of courses in his mid teens, including *How To Achieve Your Goals* and *How To Handle Problems*, and would later defend it against some of the common criticisms it has received in recent years. 'The only time I ever hear anything negative about it is in interviews,' he told *Spin* in 2008. 'In the real world, people I know—they don't give a shit. I was raised celebrating Jewish holidays, and I consider myself Jewish. But I've read books on Scientology, and drawn insights from that. There were years when I wasn't involved, but it didn't mean that it wasn't a part of what I grew up with. It's books— it's not a belief system. It's only true if it's true for you. That's the way anything is.'

He has also spoken of the Jewish side of his upbringing. He didn't have a bar mitzvah, but only because his mother couldn't afford it— something she would gripe about 'for years'. 'I went to Hebrew school for a while, though. I got some of the Jew knowledge—I just didn't get the ceremony. I remember my friends getting bar mitzvah'd, though.'

The first time Beck got drunk was one Passover, when his mother invited some non-Jewish friends over to the apartment. 'They brought a party atmosphere with them,' he recalled. 'There's serious parts at Passover, but there's celebratory parts, too. I used one of the prayers from Passover in a song I did on a Christmas jam I did. It was a Hanukkah interpretation of "The Little Drummer Boy".'

* * *

In his free time, before he discovered blues and folk, Beck immersed himself in *Star Wars*—he claims to have watched the original trilogy about fifty times—and James Bond films. Both of these would have indirect effects on his music. He could often be seen in his Stormtrooper mask, which in later years he would wear in the 'Loser' video and onstage. The James Bond connection, meanwhile, would indirectly inspire his love of noise and punk after he was encouraged to buy a Pussy Galore record by the band's name.[10] 'Pussy Galore was a James Bond character so I bought it,' he recalled. 'I was a total Bond freak. It was so distilled and pure, it had all the elements, just turned up.'

It wasn't 'noise' that started Beck on his current path, though. It was folk and blues. The story of how he first connected to these genres has been told many times, and each time, the facts are slightly different. So here is an all-encompassing version of the tale, which you can cut and paste to suit your own preference: at the age of {fifteen, sixteen, seventeen}, Beck {stumbled upon, found, was given} an old record by Mississippi John Hurt.[11] This happened at {the library, a friend's house, his aunt's, his parent's}.

It was shrink-wrapped. It hadn't even been opened, and it was this insane close-up of his face, sweating, this old, wrinkled face, and I took it. I was going to return it, but I didn't. I loved the droning sound, the open tunings, the spare, beat down-tone. And

31

his voice was so full. He just went through so much shit, and it comes across really, really amazing. This wasn't some hippie guy fingerpicking in the 1970s, singing about rainbows. This was the real stuff. I stopped everything for six months and was in my room fingerpicking until I got it right.

Prior to this, the only things Beck had really listened to were 'trucks going by outside, and helicopters with spotlights looking for criminals'. He didn't relate to the plastic synthetic sounds of many of the bands of the day.

By being a kid in the 1980s and seeing how fake and artificial all the music was, and feeling disconnected from it—all this Huey Lewis & The News stuff didn't make an impression on me—and stumbling across Blind Willie Johnson, Woody Guthrie … this kind of stuff is really potent and pure. It kind of shook me up. It all seemed so possible. None of the pop music in the 80s seemed like you could be part of it. You just had it inflicted on you. Now I hear music on the radio, and it's guitars. It sounds a little more possible. Hearing Woody Guthrie, it's like, *Oh, that's guitar.* He's just sort of talking. He's just a person.

Inspired by his find, Beck immersed himself in listening to as much of this stuff as he could afford. He also got a guitar and taught himself to play. 'I got a nylon stringed guitar, and that's what I learned to play on. I remember saving up for a while and I finally got an old Gibson— the same model that Woody Guthrie used. It didn't sound good when I tried to play a pop song, but it sounded good when I tried to play a folk song.'

Folk and blues sounded so pure to Beck—especially when compared with the phoney, fake-sounding music on the radio. Prior to that, he hadn't even liked the blues. 'I'd never liked the blues before,' he said. 'I thought it was all just hoochie-coochie Chicago stuff. Oh God, really boring. Then I heard Son House, and it was the most lonesome, strange, really sparse, heavy wooden-sounding music ever.'[12]

He was really taken by the tradition and honesty of the songs he was learning and hearing. 'I was very uninspired to make music until I stumbled upon Mississippi John Hurt, Woody Guthrie—those kinds of musicians. It was just a guitar, and I liked the sound of it. It was really simple, the antithesis of the 80s. Once I discovered this traditional folk music, country music, Delta blues, I had a whole world to get lost in.'

Beck felt that Los Angeles, as a city, had no roots; it was a city assembled under false pretences. Now, gravitating toward folk and blues, he wanted to get to the essence of the music—not the later exponents, but the pure sound as he saw it:

I dig Leadbelly. He's like the most powerful twelve-string player. You can't copy his music, you can't even play it, because it's coming from hands that are three times bigger than normal hands, you know. I never really got into Pete Seeger. There's a sort of grandfather quality to him that's sweet but it seems a little corny. I never really got into Arlo Guthrie, either.

I was more interested in Woody Guthrie because he was more stripped-down, more connected with traditional music. Early Arlo Guthrie music had a 60s kind of reality about it. The 30s kind of reality of Woody Guthrie is more what I felt connected to.

Another fingerpicking inspiration was The Carter Family, whom he found to have a connection to the religious music he'd been exposed to ten years earlier at his grandparents' house in Kansas. 'There's this whole tradition of beautiful religious music that I love,' he said. 'Like The Carter Family, who came down from the hills of Bristol, Tennessee, to be recorded by Victor Alwords—they had these really strange, really beautiful harmonies.'

It wasn't until later years that he found that some of his contemporaries had similar musical loves. When Nirvana covered Leadbelly during their MTV *Unplugged* set, it came as a real shock:

> It was a strange moment to hear Cobain sing Leadbelly, because that was a song I'd been playing as a teenager. Leadbelly, Mississippi John Hurt, Woody Guthrie—anywhere I could, I was banging out those songs. And people wouldn't respond until maybe I'd accidentally play something Led Zeppelin had covered, and then people would recognise it as 'the Led Zep song'. I'd kind of finally given up on that music and started experimenting with drum machines when I heard Cobain do that. It was like, *What? Oh my God. Where was that audience before?* But it was good to have that music recognised.

Beck soon had a collection of all the blues, country, and folk greats: Guthrie, Hurt, the Carters, plus Jimmie Rodgers, Mississippi Fred MacDowell, Blind Willie Johnson, Son House, Blind Blake, Skip James … the list goes on. But one name is conspicuous by its absence. 'I was never drawn to Robert Johnson much,' he admitted. 'A lot of that stuff had a hyped-up, clichéd aspect. I was attracted to guys like Skip James. When he sings about the devil, you get a feeling of true evil.'

It wasn't too long before Beck started to see—or rather hear—the possibilities in the blues, even though it was a while before he would actually experiment with them. Mance Lipscomb, a relatively unknown Texas farmer-turned-guitarist, became one of his favourite performers:

> When I first got into Delta blues, I could hear the hip-hop beats in the music. It would just be Son House playing a slide guitar by himself, but there was this implied hip-hop beat in everything he was playing. Mance Lipscomb, too, had a lot of funk in him. I remember thinking it would be great some day to experiment with that. It's all related—it all goes back to the rhythm and the African influence. It's been filtered through so many different

times and genres, but it's still just as strong as ever. I fantasised about combining slide guitar and hip-hop music.

The first time I met somebody [Carl Stephenson] who had some equipment and knew how to loop up a beat, that's the first thing I did. It had been on my mind for years, and it was great to finally hear it.

'Loser', it seems, was just an accident waiting to happen.

If Beck had been born ten years later, this love of the blues might never have happened. He liked the fact that it was difficult to get the records—that they weren't just something that you could walk into the local chain record store and buy. 'I can't imagine dealing with the blues now,' he said. 'I remember when I was younger, you really had to search and dig the stuff up. It was all kind of obscure—you even had to find 78s. They didn't have the 3CD Son House reissue boxed set.'

* * *

With some basic songs under his belt, Beck began to experiment with some live performances in front of unsuspecting audiences. These consisted of blues and folk covers and goofy spoof songs that he made up on the spur of the moment. His primary venues were street corners, parks, and buses. 'I just carried my guitar everywhere. I was just kind of ready for any sudden jamboree that might befall me. I used to play down at Lafayette Park, near where I used to live as a kid, and all these Salvadoran guys would be playing soccer and I'd be practising a Leadbelly song. They would just be shaking their heads. Once in a while a ball would sail over my head.'

He also played at MacArthur Park—not exactly the safest of places— where David Bowie had filmed some scenes for *The Man Who Fell To Earth*. On the buses, he helped the public-transport loving minority of Los Angeles along on their journeys with some unusual sounds: 'I'd get on the bus and start playing Mississippi John Hurt with totally improvised lyrics. Some drunk would start yelling at me, calling me Axl Rose. So I'd start singing about Axl Rose and the levee and bus passes and strychnine, mixing the whole thing up.'

Many of these back-of-the-bus gigs took place while Beck was on his way to and from the Los Angeles Central Library downtown. He was devastated when arsonists targeted the building in April 1986. Around 400,000 books were destroyed and thousands more were damaged. Another big blow came in September of the same year when a second fire swept through the library's music department reading room.

With the library out of action, Beck took to making circuitous bus trips. He tended to choose longer routes so he didn't have to break up his 'set', with one of his favourites being the Vermont line down through south central LA and back around up to Hollywood. Other musicians would join him on occasion, but usually he was just left by himself to the stares and occasional abuse from the other passengers. He didn't make much money from these performances, but on reflection he felt he might have done if he'd changed his songs. 'It all comes down to "Hey Jude",' he said. 'I think the most successful street musicians I've seen in my time were the ones who just played "Hey Jude" all day and all night.'

At the same time as he was making these early forays into the live arena, Beck began trying out some crude home taping. By the age of sixteen, he was making tapes by recording on one cassette player, then playing along with that cassette and recording the results on another. He would repeat this until the sound was completely distorted; the screwed-up tape speed gave his voice a helium-like vocal effect (one that he occasionally still uses).

It wasn't until he was well into his teens that Beck began to understand what it meant that his mother had been around Andy Warhol and the Factory scene. 'I'd gotten into The Velvet Underground's first record, and I pulled it out and started looking at it,' he said. 'My mom saw that I was into it, and said, *I know them*. I said, *Tell me about that stuff*. I already sort of knew about it, but it hadn't really connected until then.'

Beck was becoming increasingly interested in a range of musical styles beyond just folk and blues. Footage has recently come to light showing a painfully young-looking Beck singing an impromptu jam containing the words 'We're all punkers now,' while his friend Lightfield Lewis plays the bongos.[13] It was also around this time that he met Justin Meldal-Johnsen, who a decade later would become a member of his band. 'I met Beck shortly after I met his dad,' Johnsen recalled. '[I met his dad] while I was working as a janitor in a recording studio, fresh out of high school. Beck and I were both seventeen or eighteen. We did some four-track jams back then too, and, Beck turned me on to lots of music.'

Outside of music, however, Beck's prospects looked pretty bleak. By now, he was receiving unemployment benefits, and would continue to do so for some time. He would hire himself out as a removal man on occasion, and sometimes found work at a local video store, but it was all pretty demoralising.

Amid the dreary day-by-day existence of hopping around LA with no money came one bright light. In the summer of 1987, Bibbe packed Beck off to Germany to spend some time with his grandfather. He had $150 spending money and the chance to explore a little of Europe. Al Hansen had spent time establishing the Ultimate Akademie, an art school that he set up with Lisa Gieslik. It was here that Beck began keeping notebooks of the collages that he put together. These would eventually form part of the exhibition *Playing With Matches*.

He found his time there 'very free':

Somebody would get the idea to start a band, and that night we'd be performing on the radio, and there'd be a local news crew interviewing us.

I think my grandfather influenced me like anybody in your life influences you. People's character and ideas tend to rub off on you, whoever you're around. It's not like he ever sat down and said, 'Here's how to make art.' He had a bottomless stream of plans and hustles and dreams, and he always had a lot of young people around him. He was always giving young artists advice, but I was a musician.

In the end, Beck saw Al not as a mentor but just one of many people who have shaped the way that he has evolved himself. 'I don't really think of Al as a teacher any more than anybody else in my life,' he explained. 'We all have relationships, friendships, that will eventually become pieces of who we are. It's hard for me to dissect what part of me is Al and what part of me is my friends from junior high. My other grandfather was a Presbyterian minister, so where that fits in, I don't know.'

On his return to Los Angeles, Beck found himself back in the same old depression that he'd left behind. He decided to take a chance before it was too late and so began a cross-country journey to the Big Apple to see whether his luck might change. But the trip would not go quite as smoothly as he had hoped. He was about to hit some trouble.

CHAPTER 4

'She gave me a key that didn't work and I never saw her again.' (1988-89)

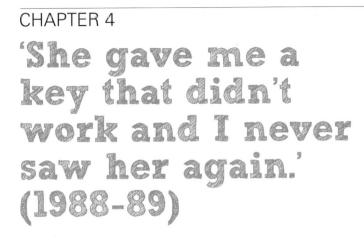

At the age of eighteen, Beck was a slight, skinny kid, but that didn't stop him taking on physical work if it meant a pay cheque—even a meagre one. At one time, he worked in a garment factory in Watts, a small neighbourhood in South LA. He was tasked with loading and unloading trucks. 'It was back-breaking work,' he recalled. 'I also worked doing yard work, I guess literally digging ditches.' He also worked as a dishwasher at a bakery, which was actually the most physically demanding of all the jobs he did, as he struggled to clean the industrial-sized steel mixing apparatus.

In order to escape from the rut into which he was sinking in California, Beck decided to make a drastic move before it was too late. Although he may have been planning his break for a while, when he actually got around to making a move, it was because he saw an advertisement for cheap bus tickets, and just went for it. He decided to take a chance, and with guitar in hand, he transported himself to New York with a view to expanding his musical sphere and experiencing the big city atmosphere.

Beck was slowly realising that he'd probably spend the rest of his life in low-paid employment, moving from job to job, never leaving Los Angeles. 'I didn't have rich parents to support me,' he told me. 'So I knew I was in for years of menial work. I decided to spend a few years seeing what was out there, before I was locked into a dead-end job.'

He chose New York because he wanted to sample the city that had been home for his mother and grandfather. Greyhound buses were offering a special promotion, allowing travel anywhere in the country for $30. New York was about as far from LA as possible, so he would be getting good value for his money. On the spur of the moment, he bought two tickets: one for himself and one for a girlfriend, who was hoping to study in New York and wanted to check out potential colleges.

Despite his blues education, Beck didn't really see going cross country as a romantic 'Beat' thing to do or as a means of 'riding the rails' in the traditional hobo style.

> There was no romanticism left in it by that time. As a teenager, I'd read all the Beat literature; I'd read all about the folk revival of the 1960s. I knew that was all gone. It wasn't about that. I was intensely into the blues, country blues, but I knew it wasn't a romantic thing. The blues came out of hardship, misery. I think in the 1960s it was romanticised, the wise-old-bluesman thing, but I didn't really have any illusions about it. You spend about two minutes in the downtown LA Greyhound bus station and your romanticism about taking a bus trip across America will be eradicated and exterminated immediately.

Beck was accustomed to low-budget, long-distance travel, having previously visited grandfather Al in Germany. 'I was used to going somewhere with no means, not really knowing anybody, sort of making my way through it. I was naive. I tend to trust people.'

If there were to be any sticky situations along the way, he felt that he'd had a good grounding in looking after himself in some of the more notorious areas of Los Angeles. 'At that point I'd seen some fucked-up shit: people machine-gunned on my front lawn; coming out in the morning and playing with the bandages when I was a little kid.'

Compared to this, a 3,000-mile bus trip with little or no money would have felt like a tea party. So, in mid 1988, Beck set off with his girlfriend, his guitar, a little cash, and nothing much else. 'It must have taken at least a week to get there,' he recalled. 'I stopped off here and there. Went through the South.'

One of the scarier moments came during that part of the journey, somewhere in West Texas, as the sun was going down. 'I realised that all the straight people, all the working people, had gotten off the bus, and everyone left was a drug fiend or an ex-con,' he recalled. 'I remember one of them whispering in my ear as soon as I fell asleep. He was going to slit my throat. I knew I was descending into the heart of America. I was discovering the heartland at that moment.'

He would later write a song entitled 'Heartland Feeling' that, while not about that exact encounter, was probably inspired by the many miles of nothingness he rode through across the country, and the feelings of vast open expanses, as depicted in songs by Springsteen and Mellencamp. His general plan was to eat food from vending machines, sleep on overnight bus hops from place to place, and spend the days in between wandering around each city before the following night's jaunt.

A decade later, he told *Mojo*'s Barney Hoskyns about how he had been 'immersed in stuff like *The Anthology Of American Folk Music*' in his youth. 'Of course, a certain amount of it was romantic and macabre and intriguing and fascinating,' he added. 'That faraway strange quality is definitely something I gravitated towards when I was younger. I guess travelling through America, I realised that a lot of strangeness is still out there, only maybe it's a little more frightening because it's alive here and now.'

If any of that 'strangeness' came too close to him, he would be sure to ward it away with a nifty little manoeuvre he learned along the way. 'Whenever anyone looking a little sketchy came my way,' he laughed, 'I'd start swinging my guitar around or start doing handstands or something. The best way to drive these people off is to pretend you're insane.'

Somewhere along the way, the bus drivers went on strike and almost scuppered Beck's plan of reaching the East Coast. This turn of events did, however, allow him a few free rides, as some kids taught him how to sneak on to a bus without paying. 'The guys who loaded the baggage were all driving the buses,' he explained. 'It was fairly chaotic, and the buses were all overcrowded, so it was pretty easy to sneak on.' He also hitchhiked for part of the journey when the buses were too overcrowded even to sneak on. But even that didn't match up to the romantic idea of hitching from coast to coast, as Beck ended up getting a ride from an optometrist. 'It's never like a movie,' he recalled. 'He just picked me up, we talked about laser-corrective eye surgery for an hour and a half, and then he dropped me off.'

Eventually, after a long and winding journey, the bus pulled into the Port Authority Bus Terminal in Manhattan—not the nicest of places at the best of times, but Beck arrived like a pauper in the promised land. 'It was the whole cliché,' he said. 'I had like $8 in my pocket, like a total idiot, with a guitar and nothing else.' He had his girlfriend, at least—or he thought he did. 'I think I got on the wrong subway train somewhere along the way,' he added. No sooner had they arrived than she dumped him.

With no place to stay, Beck had no option but to live rough for a while. He spent the summer looking for somewhere to live and working short-term jobs, such as checking in people's coats at a bookstore. With no money and no prospects, he just went with the flow. 'I just trusted that I'd find somebody who'd let me crash here or someone who knew about a job, and I'd get a job for a while,' he recalled. 'I never pushed to get anywhere. I just always trusted that I would end up where I was supposed to go. That was always my belief. And that would happen to greater or lesser degrees. If I ended up in a weird place, I'd just make the best out of it.'

One of the 'weird places' that he ended up in was the YMCA:

For a while I was working on the Upper East Side at the YMCA, taking ID photos—me and this Russian guy who didn't speak any English. We would just sit there every day, and they didn't need two people for the job. I'd press the button and he would pull the film out. It was really weird. We'd sit there for six hours just looking at each other like there was nothing to say. I'd be like, 'So where in Russia are you from?' He didn't know what I was talking about.

[We'd have], like, one person would come in every hour and ten minutes. There would be, like, this really hardcore forty-five-year-old Jewish lady—'I wanna see the picture.' And they freak out when they see the picture. They'll be like, 'No I have to get this done over again.' But we were told specifically: 'No matter how much they want their picture taken again, you don't take their picture again.' So we would have to deal with some chick, like, 'I cannot have a card where I look like this!' And I'd be trying to convince her—'Lady you look great.' And the Russian guy, he'd be looking wistfully off into the corner, thinking about Siberia or something.

Working these jobs did at least allow Beck to save up a little money—enough, he thought, to be able to rent a small place of his own. He saw somewhere advertised in a coffee shop and met a girl who gave him a key in exchange for his $600. When he arrived there, however, the key didn't fit the lock. He slept outside the building for a few nights, waiting for her to return, but he never saw her again. Eventually, he was told that she was a junkie, and that she'd skipped town with his hard-earned cash.

* * *

While Beck's living situation remained fraught, he was finding more luck on the artistic and musical scenes. He'd already done a little street-corner busking, and now began to trek further afield, jamming along with the freestyle rappers in Tompkins Square Park. 'That's where I first started rapping,' he recalled. 'There would be these homeless hip-hop freestyle things happening. We would get up there and do some folk-rap. The seeds of a lot of what I do now came out of that time.'

Beck was lucky to have arrived when he did and not a couple of weeks earlier. In August 1988, a riot erupted in Tompkins Square Park after local residents complained to the police about the number of homeless people sleeping there, and the noise they made, late into the night. A curfew was declared in the area, but when police tried to enforce it, fighting broke out.

Beck's stay in New York slowly began to take a positive turn. One day, he was hanging out around with his beat-up guitar on Avenue A, in the Alphabet City neighbourhood. 'I remember literally standing on the street and running into some people, and when they saw I had a guitar, they said, *here's an open-mic night—why don't you come?* I was scared to death to play.'

Despite his fears, this was just the invitation he needed, and he soon found himself in the midst of what he called the 'Lower East Side freak-out folk noise Delta blues Pussy Galore scene'. From then on, he'd busk during the day, play clubs at night … and little else besides. 'I didn't work,' he recalled. 'I just spent a couple of years sleeping on couches and being penniless. Just playing music. There's just all these people there making music and there's always a place to crash, and there's always something going on every night. I played on the streets for money. It's really hard to find work there.'

What Beck had stumbled upon, accidentally, became known as the 'anti-folk' scene. It had started with John S. Hall, a Brooklyn native who grew up in Greenwich Village, and his friend Lach, owner of the Chameleon. 'I started out in poetry readings and open mic nights as a spoken word artist,' Hall recalled. 'Then I went and got musicians to put music behind my work.'[14] He was unsure about the anti-folk scene itself. 'I couldn't really tell you much about anti-folk. It was something my friend Lach started in response to all the boring folk clubs that were thriving in New York but shutting out new artists.'

Another early member of the scene was Paleface. 'When I first arrived on the Lower East Side,' he recalled, 'the anti-folk scene was pretty small. The folk singers were sort of mixed together with the poets, painters, writers, and performance artists. Most people don't realise that anti-folk, as a term, was a joke started by artists in the East Village who were into punk but wanted to play acoustic. They couldn't get gigs in the West Village, at the folk clubs, so they started calling themselves the anti-folks.'

Paleface knew another stalwart of the scene, Daniel Johnston, who had been staying with Sonic Youth for a time before being 'kicked out for acting crazy.' He gave Johnston a place to sleep, and Johnston in turn encouraged him to write and record songs about his day-to-day experiences.

'I started writing a lot after that,' Paleface continued. 'I was also into all the new hip-hop coming out, so I started mixing the two, because I didn't give a fuck. Nobody else was doing that, so I got a lot of attention for it. Seymour Stein and Danny Fields came down to see me. That was a big deal, because the Ramones and the Stooges and the MC5 were legendary.'[15]

The visit from Stein and Fields was an exception; in the main, the growing scene was ignored by just about everyone outside of it. 'A few lucky neighbourhood people who happened to stumble on it were the audience. The *Village Voice* did what it usually does, and almost completely ignored it. They miss things that are right under their nose, maybe they don't have enough staff for music in the city but probably it's because *folk* music isn't street enough for them, or something equally hypocritical.'

Beck knew of Daniel Johnston but wasn't aware that he was making cassette albums at home and writing so many songs. He ended up covering one of Johnston's songs by mistake.

'I'd be just trading songs with different people,' Beck recalled, 'and I learned a couple of his. I thought they were old folk songs, and I had been performing them for a while when finally somebody told me, *No, no, no—that's a Daniel Johnston song*. These great songs were sort of almost like lost classics. So things like that were happening when I was there, I was more drawn to the folk stuff, though. I used to go see Dave Van Ronk and Ramblin' Jack Elliott.'

The overall aesthetic of anti-folk was exactly as the name suggests: a punkish, rowdy selection of folk songs delivered by performers who stomped and screamed around the stage. It was the total opposite of 1960s folk performers like Joan Baez and James Taylor who had, in the eyes of the anti-folk contingent, taken folk away from its raw roots. 'There was a real anti-Bob Dylan feeling in that scene,' Beck recalled. 'There was this need to move on and not linger in his shadow, which is a hard thing to do. I mean, anyone who picks up an acoustic guitar and a harmonica, immediately you're doing a Dylan. But we wanted to break through that. And that's where I started writing songs.'

45

Beck had been performing his old blues and folk standards with all the energy that he could muster, but he soon began adding his own lyrics to the original melodies before starting to write his own material from scratch. 'That scene was the whole punk-rock thing,' he said, 'which was right on for me. Punk was always sort of my favourite. But all I had was an acoustic guitar, and no one wanted to play with me. Here was this whole scene, with people with just acoustic guitars punking out really hard.'

Beck would 'punk out' every night and soon became friends with everyone in the scene. Michelle Shocked, Cindy Lee Berryhill, radio-host Kristin Johnson, Paleface, King Missile, Roger Manning, and Kirk Kelly all came through the same movement around the same time to achieve differing degrees of recognition on their own.

One of the most well known of these performers was Berryhill. Like Beck, she came from the West Coast, having been born in San Diego, and she too would return to California in the early 1990s. She had started out in a punk band before going solo as a singer-songwriter. Although she was involved in the anti-folk movement, she has not really carried its legacy with her in the music she's produced since. (Popular opinion is such that her 1987 debut album is still her best.)

Berryhill met Lach and Kirk Kelly almost as soon as she stepped of the bus to New York in the mid 80s. 'They gave me their cassette called *All Folked Up With Nowhere To Go*,' she recalled. 'I knew I'd found a couple of soul mates. I completely fell in love with everything about New York City.'

Berryhill got her first New York gig the same week, and was paid $200 for it. She was soon at the centre of the anti-folk scene, though at that point it didn't have a name. 'We were rattling around ideas for making our scene a thing,' she said. 'Lach had been doing shows at his loft on Rivington Street and had already done one folk festival, which he'd called something like New York New Folk Festival. I chimed in, [telling Lach] it'd be cool if he had an edgier name. I'd been playing at the AntiClub [in Los Angeles], a venue that booked outsiders and punks. So I suggested AntiFolk.'

The name stuck, and it continues to be used to this day to describe rough-edged folk music. Berryhill remembered seeing Beck around the time. 'I remember Beck and Paleface sitting outside of [the club] Chameleon, kind of a young Mutt and Jeff. One guy looking like a lanky Huck Finn, and Beck, the younger, shorter guy in a hoodie, sitting on the kerb drinking tall boys.'

Another female singer-songwriter on the scene was Michelle Shocked, whose father had introduced her to country bluesmen like Big Bill Broonzy and Leadbelly, as well as contemporary songwriters like Guy Clark and Randy Newman. From 1983 onward, she spent years travelling around between Texas, New York, and the Netherlands, honing her style of traditional folksiness with a strong post-modern feminist perspective and punk attitude. The latter dovetailed nicely with the scene that was blossoming at the decade's turn.

Beat poet Allen Ginsberg was also on the fringes of the anti-folk scene, and years later he had a conversation about it with Beck for *Shambhala Sun* magazine.

GINSBERG: Yeah, I knew some of them. I used to sing with them sometimes.

BECK: Well, I was playing the traditional stuff, and first I was really down with anti-folk. That's basically what the term was. It was separating themselves from all the new-age sounding stuff— the safe, watered-down stuff. That charged me up, and I came onto the idea of taking the traditional music and coming up with different words.

GINSBERG: That was my idea. Except I was too old to do it, and I didn't know how to play guitar.

BECK: To me it was incredible. Of course, I was only eighteen at the time, and it was all really new, and being in New York was really intense. I had a blast during that time. I was pretty much struggling, trying to play as much as possible. Lach and all these people took me right in y'know. They were so friendly.

As well as acoustic guitar, Beck would play banjo, harmonica and anything else that could get him on-stage. He fell in with poet and performer Mike Tyler, the publisher of *AIR*, aka the *American Idealism Rag*. 'He could get up onstage with somebody else and play the harmonica or the guitar or sing or hum or bang something and it just always seemed perfect,' Tyler recalled. 'All the false alternative hypocrisy just seemed to fade away when I saw him.'

Beck wanted to continue the tradition of the original folk music but put his slant on it. 'I wasn't trying to do anything like what Dylan did with the original music. That was part of the anti-folk idea, to keep the basic style but not to write typically, you know ... singer-songwriter songs. I was trying to keep my songs cut down, tight, not like Dylan's half-poetic style.'

He soon overcame any initial stage fright to become a regular at clubs like ABC No Rio, the Chameleon, and the Pyramid. 'It gave me a chance to play the music, and everybody in the scene would come to the shows. It was a little bit of support.'

Everyone would support everyone else, and being around like-minded individuals made it easy to hang out, see free shows, and try out new things. It was an invaluable musical education. On one occasion, Beck went to see the anarchic industrial group Missing Foundation and then tried 'to get some of that energy off an acoustic guitar.'

Onstage, Beck was becoming something of a dervish, and he didn't need a band or technology to help him. 'Before I had a drum machine,' he recalled, 'I had my foot. I would just stomp the thing. It was an insular scene, but there was a lot of space within there to do almost anything you wanted. I remember going in and getting as drunk as possible and getting up and playing a few tunes. We could take our cue from KRS-One: rewrite an old Woody Guthrie song, make it something totally different. It felt powerful because we didn't need guitars, amps, a practice space or anything—everyone was a one-person band.'

CHAPTER 5

'All we had was an acoustic guitar and energy.' (1990)

In New York, Beck wrote early versions of several songs he'd re-work later, including 'Pay No Mind', 'Cut 1/2 Blues', 'Totally Confused', and 'The Fucked Up Blues'. Without even hearing the songs, the titles give a feel for his outlook on life at the time.

It was around this time that Beck put together his first tape of original material: a set of songs for banjo and harmonica titled—surprise, surprise—*Banjo Story*. Three of those songs—'Let's Go Moon Some Cars', 'Goin' Nowhere Fast', and 'Sucker Without A Brain'—would also end up on *Fresh Meat And Old Slabs*, the tape Beck made for his mother's birthday years later, but would never be officially released. The songs on *Banjo Story* are really the lowest of the lo-fi, mixing traditional country and blues arrangements with the bizarre lyrical twists that would become Beck's trademark. Copies still circulate among fans today.

'A couple of years ago, someone gave me a fifth-generation copy of one of these tapes,' Beck recalled, around the turn of the millennium. 'And you know, by the fifth generation, it's kind of sped-up, so it was like the chipmunk version. It was ridiculously high. Most of the bootlegs I've heard from those early tapes are sped up.'

The cover of the tape was designed by a mysterious individual by the name of Marcel and shows a bald-headed person (possibly a baby) riding on the back of a centipede. The opening track, 'Let's Go Moon

Some Cars', is the epitome of hillbilly-country, featuring just Beck and his banjo. After the title phrase, he suggests going to 'steal some beer', 'set something on fire', and 'shoot some pigs'. The next song, 'Goin' Nowhere Fast', has Beck lamenting his impoverished position and could easily be mistaken for a mid-period Woody Guthrie song.

'Talkin Demolition Expert' had a real down-home feel to it, and could almost have been by one of any number of 1950s country singers— if you ignore the lyric, that is. 'I got all kinds of devices that I'm gonna detonate,' Beck sings, as he tells the story of quitting his office job, killing his boss, and going on a *Rambo*-style rampage. 'I got bazookas, hand-grenades'.

'Sucker Without A Brain', which describes a horrific bus crash, has an almost waltz-like feel. 'Here comes that bus / Right into your face,' he sings. 'The driver tried to swerve / But he just didn't see ya / Now you're buried b'neath the wheel / Just like a tortilla.'

Other highlights include 'Chewin' Like Gilligan', which starts with Beck stomping and hitting what sounds like the lid of a biscuit tin before talking his way through a jumbled story about leaving town with a travelling show. 'You Can Be So Careless' is one of the stronger efforts on the tape: a longer song with a lengthy harmonica solo, and a sign of the better things to come. *Banjo Story* closes with 'Hell', not a song at all but a short spoken piece by an uncredited girl who sounds about nine years old. 'You could stay in hell for about fifteen years,' she says, 'and they wouldn't even let you.'

* * *

Another figure on the fringes of the anti-folk scene was Julian Summerhill, then going by the name Victor.[16] He remembers Beck dropping by one day to play him his first cassette of original songs.

'There must have been twenty or more songs on that tape, each one more generic and unremarkable than the last,' he recalled. 'The thing that was a bit startling about this was his process: it was extremely diligent and tenacious behaviour for someone just starting out. Someone else might have become bored with this lacklustre early output and moved on to something else, but he had an absolutely fierce determination to succeed, and I think this is what carried him through.'

Armed with his tape, Beck grew in confidence, while at the same time the scene itself was beginning to gather some momentum. Everyone was getting into the spirit of 'claiming back folk music', and as far as Beck was concerned, if Leadbelly had been there, he would have been stomping and yelling with the best of them. 'We were going back to the roots of country blues and the original Woody Guthrie, Jack Elliott-type folk of the 50s,' he explained. 'It was our reaction to the whole 60s and 70s folk thing, which ended up as James Taylor and Cat Stevens and all those women with quivering voices who sang about white birds and unicorns. We were taking back the folk music that had got such a bad name, living out our fantasies of putrid homelessness and distilled malt liquor.'

Beck and his peers on the anti-folk scene were reviving the real essence of 'alternative' music—long after everyone else had forgotten what it meant. 'I guess you could say that was a time of realisation or derealisation, forgetting what you know and starting over. It still felt that something was possible, that there was no way it was going to get turned into something commercial, that it would always remain true, that you wouldn't be able to work a formula out for it. There was a feeling that *we will not be fooled*. It was innocent in the sense that it wasn't a post-post-post-post-thing, you know?'

The songs could be about absolutely anything: one memorable (or forgettable, depending on your taste) tune was about a packet of potato chips. Beck himself had an early, unrecorded song about a train that went around the country destroying everything in its path. 'We were writing about really mundane things,' he explained, 'and trying to get to the essence of them. We were singing songs and getting over what it's like to be *here right now*. I remember thinking it was great, because there were all these people playing folk music really aggressively. I'd always thought folk music had a bad rap, being cracked up to be this overwrought, really

51

sensitive muck. It was great to hear people shouting and yelling. It was like the music was supposed to be.'

Having previously rejected synthetic mid-80s pop in favour of the raw, ragged feel of the blues, this folk-attack was right up his street. He'd begun writing the songs for *Banjo Story* because it was the only way to get a whole night at the Chameleon club. 'Lach wouldn't book me for a whole night unless I wrote my own songs. So I said OK, and I went and got a pen and wrote five songs about things like pizza or waking up after having been sawn in half by a maniac—stuff like that. He finally gave me a Friday night.'

He especially liked the fact that the scene had some history. 'The whole scene inspired me to add something to the tradition. It should just become your own song. That's what I like about folk music: it's just everybody's songs, and everybody can take a song and reinterpret it their own way and change the words. Music's become unhealthy. It used to be a communal thing. Now you go and watch a couple of people do it. I think that's why all these kids start moshing, cos that's the only thing that they can give back.'

* * *

Sadly, the anti-folk scene was not well documented, and most of the performers who went on to any kind of fame did so without taking much of the anti-folk sound with them. There are no live tapes in general circulation, no videos, and little in the way of official releases from the time. This lack of documentation is not helped by the fact that the music press of the day paid virtually no notice to what was going on, and as such live reviews or interviews are non-existent.

The best way to hear what Beck's music might have sounded like back then is to listen to early tapes like *Banjo Story*, *Golden Feelings*, or *Fresh Meat And Old Slabs*, although the latter two were recorded after he had returned to Los Angeles. Word of mouth is the only route back into the anti-folk scene, and it is thanks to the recollections of those who were there at the time that we know that Beck could sometimes be seen onstage in his Stormtrooper mask, or writhing around on the floor playing a harmonica, or jumping about playing percussion on whatever was in range for him to hit.

Beck embraced the punk aesthetic and mixed it into a roots style. He also realised that there were no restrictions when it came to subject matter or songs, and it was this that set him on the course he has followed throughout his career. Having spent a few years learning to copy old blues songs, he was now confident enough to add noise, bizarre percussion, and wacky vocals to his songs. The songs he was writing didn't have to follow any traditional patterns or structures, and his lyrics could be about absolutely anything that he dreamt up. All the limits usually put on popular music had been removed, and Beck was free to follow his heart to whatever strange places it would take him and his music. The breaking of these boundaries was the trigger for Beck to start writing songs at an ever-increasing rate, and he would follow these 'anti-rules' on everything from crude homemade tapes to major-label albums sold the world over.

The fact that a lot of the artists had little money made the punk ethic of doing your own thing with whatever you had ring truer than ever. 'A lot of us were playing folk music because we couldn't afford all the instruments,' he recalled. 'And, Jesus, it was New York, where were you going to rehearse with a band? All we had was an acoustic guitar and energy. It was cool, it was abstract, it was stand-up comedy and free-form lyrics. It was the time. It was a current of creative electricity.'

One of the people Beck really clicked with at the time was Paleface, a New York native and one of the earliest exponents of what became anti-folk who mixed booming acoustic guitar with clever lyrical plays on subjects like his disillusionment with the American dream. Once Beck started playing around the city, it was just a matter of time before the two got together. For a time, they were great friends, and Paleface let Beck sleep at his place for some time.

According to Paleface, they met for the first time on a street in the East Village: 'I saw this dude with a guitar over his shoulder, staring into a window, and walked up to him and introduced myself. That's how I was in those days: in tune and just looking for something to happen. I'd already been on the scene for five or six months, so I filled him in on all the places to go, and we immediately became best buds. We played together all the time, on the street and in the subway to make extra money. I was the one that played *Paul's Boutique* for Beck—he'd never heard it.'

Paleface introduced Beck to Daniel Johnston, while Beck taught his new friend a selection of old folk songs. 'Whenever I think of Beck, I think of those old folk songs,' he said. 'We sang them all the time. I remember I had a folk song called "Woa Is Me" that he sang really good. We felt that one because we were broke-ass anti-folk singers!' The duo would earn some change by singing in the subway and then go to the deli to buy a muffin to share. Sometimes they'd splash out and buy two hot dogs for 99 cents at Gray's Papaya on 6th Avenue.

Julian Summerhill also got to see Beck a lot during 1989–90.

I lived on the Lower East Side and was concerned primarily with writing poetry. I emerged from what you might call downtown avant-garde roots. In 1989, I decided to have a one-off art-band called The Faith Healers, and was invited to play the same venues as the anti-folk people. I would describe myself as *around* that scene but not of it. Beck seemed to just blow into town out of nowhere, like a will-o'-the-wisp, and began playing the downtown open mics. He was nineteen then, but looked about fourteen. I just remember being very fast friends, and sharing the stage with him often, both on his first early songs, and my own. He was fresh and very open to anything, musically.

Beck's background was a mystery to his new friends in New York. 'He was completely mute on the subject of his past,' Summerhill added. 'I once asked him where he was from, and he said simply *everywhere*. He presented himself as someone who maybe just stepped off a boxcar. But this was the whole point of being in New York at that time, for all of us, it was a place to reinvent yourself. Where's the fun in telling the truth?'

Summerhill and Beck often shared the same stage, and Beck's ability to mimic old folk songs was a revelation. 'I often asked him and Paleface to open those Faith Healers shows. It was clear to me that he was practicing in public, thrashing around to see if he might develop his style. He was an uncanny mimic at that time. He would memorize old folk songs and do them exactly like those guys—I mean spot-on exactly. It was disconcerting, really, those old voices coming out of such a jailbait-looking "runaway" kid.'

On February 21 1990, Summerhill set up a meeting.

I took Beck, Roger Manning, and Paleface on a kind of pilgrimage uptown to meet Arthur Stern. Arthur was an old friend and mentor of mine who was one of the original members of the Almanac Singers, which featured Pete Seeger and none other than Woody Guthrie. It was meant as a kind of summit—a kind of 'old guard meeting the new' type of deal.

After we settled in at Arthur's, I introduced everyone around. Arthur asked us each to play and sing something. We went around in a circle, and when it was Beck's turn, he chose to sing 'The 1913 Massacre', which was of course written by Woody Guthrie. Beck, true to form, sang it *exactly* like Woody did. I think Beck was thrilled to finally get a chance to do this song in front of someone who actually knew Guthrie. But when he finished, Arthur quickly admonished him for mimicking rather than reinterpreting Guthrie. His exact words were, 'Beck, you're just starting out, now you need to get your own style.'

I remember Beck turning crimson red and silently packing up his guitar. We immediately resumed talking, and went touring through Arthur's folk-museum of an apartment. When we turned to find Beck, he had disappeared from the place. Disappeared, I might add, from New York completely.

'Arthur kind of tore into Beck,' Paleface added. 'Told him to stop copying Woody Guthrie. Beck was visibly bummed and I felt a little uncomfortable for him. Arthur took us out for coffee and Beck disappeared around a corner without saying anything. We looked around and he was gone! We didn't speak about that after, as I remember. We just let it go.'

Shortly after that, Beck and Paleface went their separate ways. They had been good friends for a while, and Paleface had put Beck up for a while when, as he later put it, 'I couldn't find a place to live and couldn't hook up a job to save my life'. After a while, though, they had a falling out. 'I think after a few months it got a little tiring for him,' Beck recalled. 'I called him once and he just hung up on me. That was maybe 1991 or 1992. So I just kind of gave up. But I thought he was really talented—he was one of the best. I couldn't tell if he wanted me to hang out, or get out of his face.'

For Paleface, the crux of the matter was that 'the songs he started writing kind of sounded like my songs. Maybe if I'd been a little more mature, I would have handled it a little better, but I started to be kind of mean to him. I felt like he was trying to co-opt what I was doing. Shit, I had just done the same thing with Daniel [Johnston], but I felt like I was adding something else, something new to it. I just didn't have the perspective then.'

Another friend of Beck's from this era was acoustic punk fiend Roger Manning (not to be confused with Roger Manning Jr. from Beck's later touring band). Manning has been described as the 'spiritual leader' of the anti-folk movement, and was just about to release his debut LP on the legendary SST label when Beck arrived in New York. The two frequently crossed paths on open-mic nights at the Chameleon, and at casual all-night jams in Tompkins Square. When asked about Beck's early New York shows, which featured a lot of Mississippi John Hurt and Leadbelly covers, Manning describes it as 'like seeing the ghost of Woody Guthrie'.

Manning's views on what can and can't go into a song's lyrics are very similar to Beck's. 'People think lyrics have to be poeticised and formal, but my lyrics are the way I talk—if I wouldn't use a word in a conversation, I won't use it in a song.' He would describe his own songs as 'movies'. 'The words are the movie, and the music is the soundtrack,' he told the *San Diego Union-Tribune*. 'They're true movies about things that really happened, because life is the best story there is.'

Beck's own outlook on his early songwriting efforts was different. 'I just let whatever comes out, come out,' he told *Guitar Player* in 1994. 'Some of it I keep, some I toss out, some I turn into giant cigarettes and smoke 'em. Everybody's got their own songs, too. Everybody should turn off their TV machines and make up their own songs about whatever comes to mind: their couch, their friends, their loaves of bread. There should be so many songs out there that it all turns into one big sound, and we can put the whole thing into a pickup truck and let it roll off the edge of the Grand Canyon.'

Beck and Manning were both fond of lo-fi technology, too, although from a financial perspective, they didn't have much choice, given that they recorded their debut albums on four-track or eight-track machines. Another similarity was their love of low-budget acoustic guitars. 'I'd swear by any good-quality plywood guitar,' said Manning, who adorned his with a collection of stickers similar to Beck's legendary 'Jazzercise' guitar. For Beck, 'It's taking your guitar as a tool. It's not some priceless object. It's something you're supposed to make noise on.'

One of the downsides of the bohemian, 'sleep anywhere' lifestyle was the frequency of muggings and robberies. Beck was on the receiving end of more than his fair share of these during his time in New York. 'These gangs … just assume you must be some rich student because they see the guitar,' he recalled. 'Usually I'd only have about two bucks, which would just make them madder.' During the winter one freezing night, Beck was mugged on Avenue B. The attackers made off with six dollars, but Beck held on to his guitar for dear life, until the assailants were disturbed and ran off. A passer-by put Beck in a cab and paid his fare to the hospital.

The incident had a marked effect on him. 'He was a bit rattled,'

Paleface recalled. 'It was Mathew Courtney's prophecy come true. Mathew was the host of the open stage at ABC No Rio, the best in the city at the time. He used to complain to us that he didn't want to be our babysitter. We were quite young at the time and a bit wild, and he used to tell us to stay inside because the gangs would get us. The neighbourhood was pretty raw at the time.'

Beck himself admitted that he was 'pretty messed up' following the incident. 'I remember coming out of the hospital and the sky had this apocalyptic rust hue. The winters were very bitter there. Both my eyes were black, but you know I didn't have many options at the time. When I came out of hospital, a friend I was staying with kicked me out of his apartment with no word of explanation. It was January, and incredibly bleak. At which point, it felt like time to go home to Los Angeles.'

* * *

Looking back, Beck would admit that he 'didn't have a plan' when he first arrived in New York. 'LA at that point was just a cultural void,' he said. 'It's amazing to me that this whole hipster culture has emerged since the early 1990s. In New York there was a lot of really stimulating stuff happening, and I got right into it. After a while it was like I'd always been there.'

Although Beck had settled into New York and the anti-folk scene, it wasn't to be his permanent home. As the 90s dawned, he decided enough was enough and went back out West. 'I was tired of being cold,' he explained. 'Tired of getting beat up. It was hard to be in New York with no money, no honey, no thermostats, no spoons, no Cheerios. I kinda used up all the friends I had. Everyone on the scene just got sick of me. I really loved living in New York; if things had worked out differently, I would have stayed there.'

Whether Beck had always meant to return home after two years isn't clear, but that's what he did. He knew that his time in the Big Apple was up. The great adventure had come to an end. The anti-folk scene was breaking up, having run its natural course, and the artists that had contributed to it were slowly moving away from the scene—both figuratively and literally.

When Beck left the East Coast, he took with him an important education in both life and music. He had always been fairly independent, but his financial situation in New York had made him even more so. And he had become even more independent in his music.

Beck started on the next phase of his story by heading back to LA and moving in with his brother, Channing. By the time he got back home, he was making highly original music that would come as a slap in the face to those who heard it. He now mixed his folk and blues roots with noise and indie-rock influences, and his experiences in Tompkins Square Park paved the way for him to bring rap into the mix, too. These ingredients would later prove very fruitful, but he had a few more years of hardship ahead first.

CHAPTER 6

'I was expecting my shoes to get stolen.' (1990-92)

There are certain suburbs of Los Angeles where you can get a man to do each of your chores for you under the air-conditioned sun. A man to clean your car. A man to do your shopping. A man to clean your pool. A man to tend your garden. Some of these men gain a certain status of their own over time and then subcontract their chores to others further down the food chain. One of the chores seemingly below the remit of the gardener comes around every fall, when the trees shed their load and the leaves need to be removed from the lawns and pathways of the rich and famous. In Hollywood, rather than collect the leaves and put them in a bag, the gardeners' assistants use a leaf-blower—a kind of space-aged vacuum cleaner which, rather than sucking the leaves up, blows them away. Leaf-blowers would walk around the gardens and blow the leaves into the street or onto the neighbour's garden (thereby necessitating the need for the rest of the street to employ leaf-blowers of their own).

In the early 1990s, one of these leaf-blowers was Beck Hansen. He would later make reference to the job on his 1994 single 'Beercan' ('I quit my job blowing leaves / Telephone bills up my sleeves'), and would happily acknowledge the debt of this piece of garden machinery to his (and others') noise music. 'It's a very large population here, there's a leaf-blower contingent. There's no union that I know of so far, but there's certainly a spiritual brotherhood. They are the originators of noise music. It's like a cross between a Kramer guitar and a jet pack.'

Beck would work in jeans and an open plaid shirt with a Son Volt T-shirt underneath. With his limp blonde hair hanging about his face, he looked a little like a young Kurt Cobain, as did many youngsters up and down the West Coast at the time. But unlike the scores of other blowers, Beck spent his evenings distilling his streams of consciousness and a myriad of influences into songs with his battered old acoustic guitar and a primitive tape deck.

Beck had also been playing some shows since returning from his largely ill-fated trip to New York. These shows usually took place in Silver Lake or in the surrounding areas. He'd jump up onstage unannounced while the main act was setting up or taking a break. (Sometimes he'd ask the owner beforehand, sometimes he wouldn't.) Keen to get people to listen, rather than just ignoring him and talking through his mini-set, he began dreaming up ever-more-wacky songs that would at least make people laugh. Eventually, people did start to laugh, and then they started to listen, to this frenetic, raggedy kid with the beat-up acoustic guitar.

Over time, through word of mouth, Beck's performances at venues like Raji's, Jabberjaw, and Al's Bar would gain a dedicated following. And then there were his shows at Café Troy, owned by his mother and her second husband, Sean Carrillo. Every night was different. Every night he had a new song that he'd only just written. Every night he had a new story to tell. He'd keep people guessing as to how he'd take the stage in these small clubs and coffeehouses. Sometimes he'd emerge from an upright wooden coffin; sometimes he'd take the stage wearing his Stormtrooper helmet while a disco version of the *Star Wars* theme played over the PA. Sometimes he'd set fire to his acoustic guitar, or bring out his leaf-blower and clean up the stage, its jet-like roar causing feedback like no other as coasters and flyers were blown across the heads of the audience.

His songs told stories of being poor in LA; stories of working in burger bars, blowing leaves, of washing pots. Between the story-telling songs, he'd pause to tell stories without music. He was a cool, indie, one-man variety show. He had a great turn of phrase and a wicked, self-depreciating sense of humour. Before long, these now legendary shows were starting to catch the attention of record labels and talent spotters. Soon everyone was clamouring to hear Beck Hansen.

* * *

The road to vindication had been slow and hard. Back in East Los Angeles, Beck had reverted to his old routine of working small-time jobs by day and trying to get gigs by night. He was writing his own material at an ever-increasing rate, refining his lyrical skills and his humour. He had come to the conclusion that Los Angeles was his home, and he had to accept that. 'As an adult, I came to realise it was a part of me, if you hate it, you end up hating a part of yourself,' he said. 'So, eventually I was reconciled with the fact that this is me whether I like it or not.'

LA was where he felt comfortable, despite his lowly circumstances. 'It's like the family you grew up in: you don't agree with how it is, but it's your family.' Over time, he managed to save some money to buy a car, but his luck seemed to keep running out.

'I found a car in the newspaper for $100,' he recalled. 'I had it for one day, then the engine blew up on the freeway, and that was kinda shot, because if you don't have a car in LA, you spend more time waiting for a bus than you do at your job. Then someone gave me a bicycle, and it got stolen. Finally someone gave me a skateboard, but that went too. Then I was just reduced to my feet. I was expecting my shoes to get stolen.'

Despite the seemingly constant stream of setbacks, Beck continued writing new material and playing unannounced at other bands' gigs. Some nights, his whole set would be new songs, many of them based around in-jokes that made sense only to the small groups of friends who'd come along to see him. One of these friends was Steve Hanft, who was part of a group of CalArts students Beck had fallen in with, and would go on to direct Beck's breakthrough music video. They soon started talking about collaborating together.

'He was already famous in the underground café circuit of LA and New York when I met him,' Hanft recalled. 'People were like, *Oh, that's Farm Boy*. He had really long hair, really shitty boots, ripped-up pants. But I thought his songs were pretty cool, maybe I could use one of his songs in my film.' Hanft worked for years on a self-funded story about a racing driver called *Kill The Moonlight* and the eventual soundtrack used a trio of Beck tracks.

Another friendship forged in these days was with Ross Harris, whom Beck met through his brother, Channing. 'I threw a party at a house I had out in the valley,' Harris recalled. 'We were going to have a DJ and a band could play. Channing was like, *Hey, my brother is a really good musician, he plays Mississippi Delta blues and old folk songs, and do you mind if he comes and plays?* Beck showed up and just stomped out all of these amazing folk and blues tunes and original crazy stuff, right in my living room.'

For now, Beck was concentrating on the lyrics over the music. 'Words are the most important part to me,' he explained. 'If the words suck, then I can't listen to something … that's all I've had. I never had money to buy equipment and have a band with a big sound. All I had was an acoustic guitar, and you can only go so far [with that], so I had to make up everything else with words that would interest people.'

Beck moved from place to place during this time, from the shadow of the Griffith Observatory in Los Feliz to Echo Park and Silver Lake. He seemed to be constantly moving from Bibbe's to Channing's to various boarding houses and rental properties and back again. At one point, he is said to have lived in a downtown alley with just rats for company, although this is likely a story that has become more dramatic in the retelling. He did, however, live just off Sunset Boulevard for a while, behind Tang's Donut, where he would hang out until 4am, watching homeless guys play speed chess on the patio.[17]

Beck and his friends had a novel way of deciding how to spend an evening, based on the revolving sign outside a nearby podiatrist's. On one side of the sign was a cartoon of a foot with a set of crutches; on the reverse was a happy, smiling foot. At dusk, the gang would convene outside the store to see which way the sign was pointed when the owner switched it off for the night. If the happy foot faced the house, they'd head out for the night; if it was the other way around, they'd stay in.

The jobs that Beck endured during this period of his life were haphazard and soul sapping. 'I used to shift trash and unload trucks,' he recalled. 'I also did a bit of break-dancing in the street.' Another job he did for a while was painting various storefronts and interiors around East LA and Hollywood. 'I painted the inside of that place electric pink,' he explained, of a lingerie store near Victor Borge's star on the Hollywood Walk of Fame. 'We worked all night. For days, all I saw was electric pink.'

Just as had been the case when he was at school, Beck felt alienated from most of the people around him. Whereas in the past this had been because he was the only white kid on the block, now it came down to the fact that he hated watching the television—so didn't. 'I'd rather stare at a blank wall,' he claimed. The feeling of not quite fitting in with his workmates continued until one night, at a friend's house, he caught a glimpse of a sitcom. 'I suddenly realised: *Oh my God, everyone I'm working with is imitating a sitcom.* That's why I couldn't relate to them.'

One of the more painful jobs Beck undertook was to wear a little hat and work as a hot-dog waiter at a rich kid's birthday party in Brentwood that took place 'on a big tennis court turned into a roller skating rink', as he told *Details* in 1996. 'It was a lot of work, carrying the hot dogs and the cart with the umbrella up the endless stairs. The girls were seven or eight years old and real snooty—too snooty to even eat hot dogs. We got stiffed on the $15 pay, and stuck with 200 hot dogs'.

The never-ending stream of menial jobs included a stint in furniture removal, as well as a further period back at the video store. 'I was on the lowest rung of video-store employees,' he recalled. 'We weren't allowed to sit down, and we were only allowed to listen to this oldies radio that was piped in. They would play "Do Wah Diddy" at six o'clock every night. It was a little demoralising.'

Eventually, it all became a little too demoralising, and Beck began collecting unemployment cheques. The video-store job, for which he earned $4 per hour, would be the last entry on his eclectic resume. From now on, his sole focus was on playing the coffeehouse and punk-club circuits of Los Angeles and its environs, bashed-up guitar in hand, rope-strap dangling from its neck, harmonica in his pocket.

'I'd realised, when I heard that first Pussy Galore record, that ... fuck what you think music's supposed to be—just go do it!' he explained. 'People always say I came from the coffeehouses—and I [did] play there—but mostly I played in the punk-rock clubs and all-ages [venues]. ... In punk-rock clubs, there's a lot more energy.'

These venues were as colourful as they were diverse. Al's Bar on South Hewitt Street, on the edge of Little Tokyo in Downtown LA, has been described as the city's answer to the Cavern Club in Liverpool—meaning it was dark and underground. Raji's started life as a curry house before becoming a hard-rock club, playing host to the likes of Guns N' Roses and The Replacements.[18] A mile west on Hollywood Boulevard, restaurant-cum-coffeehouse Highland Grounds opened at the turn of the decade and played host to all manner of acoustic performers, Beck included. Club Spaceland was Beck's local venue on Silver Lake Boulevard, and was also a regular hangout for the Dust Brothers, who would play a key role in the Beck story further down the line. He also played downtown at the Onyx, at the Pik-Me-Up on West 6th Street, and at Fuzzyland in Highland Park. And then of course there was the Jabberjaw in Arlington Heights, where he would soon get his big break.

Beck's growing reputation as a live performer led to him being offered a support slot by rising San Francisco punks Green Day. More often than not, however, he was playing to small crowds of his own. Scott Cymbala of Fingerpaint Records, who would release Beck's *A Western Harvest Field By Moonlight* in 1994, remembers seeing an early performance at Café Troy around this time. 'There were like ten or twelve people there,' he recalled. 'It was great, because there were no expectations. It was pure and honest. He didn't have to live up to the crowd's expectations.'

Beck was starting to find other musicians on the LA scene with similar tastes and styles. With Martha Atwell, he formed a band called Ten Ton Lid to play covers of songs by The Carter Family and The Louvin Brothers. The band was shortlived, but they did have a memorable encounter with Mike Tyson, who at the time was training for his fight with Buster Douglas, at a gig up in Saugus, Santa Clarita. Tyson was so 'impressed' with what he heard, so the story goes, that he climbed up onstage in a Santa hat and relieved himself on the drum kit.

For Beck, finding people who shared his musical vision and tastes was paramount: people like Carla Bozulich of The Geraldine Fibbers, or the members of Possum Dixon. '[They] were really receptive, which is really a hard thing to find in LA. Most of the time there isn't a musical community, there isn't any kind of connection between bands, so when I met those people it was more of a family.'[19]

These encounters were few and far between, however, and most of the time Beck found himself being turned down for even the briefest of onstage performances.

Usually, they would just take one look and turn me flat down. At that time, acoustic music was associated with more of a 70s singer-songwriter scene that was out of fashion. It was a punk ethos—people playing on oil drums and being as loud and heavy as possible. Eventually, the bands took pity and said, 'Come and play while we set up.' I always had a guitar with me. I would play songs I had written over the last couple of weeks. They were novelty-esque compositions, so I'd get a laugh.

If you were around the scene in Los Angeles at that time, I was the least likely tipped for success. Every band I knew or played with had flyers and properly recorded demos and contacts. I couldn't even get a gig. I would try to talk bookers into letting me play twenty minutes on a Thursday night, and they still wouldn't go for it. That went on for years. I marvel at bands now who are playing the Wiltern after just nine months of existence.

Possum Dixon had been around for a couple of years when Beck met them in 1991. Lead singer Rob Zabrecky had experienced the same rounds of the LA clubs and was happy to help Beck along. When they first met, he recalled, Beck was 'a shy and soft-spoken waif-like guy about my age. He exuded a genuinely sweet sentiment and a great sense of humour. He was fun to be around'.

After they'd been chatting for a while, Zabrecky agreed to Beck's request to open at one of Possum Dixon's upcoming shows. 'His act didn't require any amp setup,' he recalled, 'so I agreed to have him open for us during our next show at the Pik-Me-Up. Onstage, he came alive while he played acoustic guitar and banjo and sang disjointed and surreal Dada-inspired lyrical melodies. Within a little time it became clear that Beck had the best songs of anyone from the local scene and the more I saw him, it became increasingly evident that he was wildly talented.'

The two acts would play numerous shows together like this over the next couple of years.

Beck also hung out with—and later recorded with—the girls from That Dog. Anna Waronker—the sister of Joey Waronker, who would later become Beck's drummer—was the band's chief songwriter and guitar player; sisters Petra (violin and vocals) and Rachel Haden (bass and vocals) were daughters of jazz legend Charlie Haden, who would later appear on *Odelay*. The third of the Haden triplets, Tanya, sometimes played cello with the band.[20]

By now, Beck was renting a place in Silver Lake, which now had a hub of musicians and artists. Rob Zabrecky remembers the area as 'hills and zigzagging streets with Latino families, a large gay community, and scattered proud hipsters who seemed to have been there since the beginning of time. Geographically, it was set in an amazing location that housed some of Los Angeles' steepest hills that had these distinctive little pockets that felt like the grittier parts of San Francisco.'[21]

Beck was now writing and recording music at a furious rate. 'I had a four-track,' he recalled, 'but one track was broken, so it was really a three-track.' He'd record a new cassette album every few months, make a dozen or so copies to sell at shows or give to friends, and then be 'off on the next thing. It was a way for me to have the process of writing and creating songs, and to have them put on a tape and have people hear them, it helped me have some perspective on it. It was my cut-rate version of making records, and I put out a handful of those tapes.'

A number of these tapes—which have titles like *We Like Folk … Who Cares … Destroy Us*, *Don't Get Bent Out Of Shape*, *Untitled 1992 Demos*, and *Beck, Like The Beer*—have survived to this day. The last of these contains unreleased songs such as 'Today', another 'list' song about what happened on a particular day, including finding 1,000 steaming hot dogs in his bathtub, which perhaps links back to that disastrous roller-skating party, and 'Watchtower Magazine', in which he finds out that his mother is a Jehovah's Witness. (Sample lyrics include 'Mom, I thought you were a Jew?' and 'Her prayers were much too frequent / After all that shock treatment'.) *Beck, Like The Beer* also includes fairly complete takes of 'Hollow Log' (later recorded for *One Foot In The Grave*), 'Gettin' Home' (from *A Western Harvest Field By Moonlight*), and 'Puttin' It Down' (from *Stereopathetic Soulmanure*).

Don't Get Bent Out Of Shape consists of around thirty-five songs spread across two tapes. Future releases such as 'Mexico', 'Aphid Manure Heist', 'Pay No Mind' and 'Fume' are included, alongside lots of rough acoustic gems that would otherwise have been lost. Among these are the Carter Family-esque 'That Highway Won't Get You To Heaven', 'In The Eyes Of The Lord', the understated melancholy of 'Why Can't I Believe In You', and 'Don't Believe The Joke They Put On You', which features characters such as Tom Joad and Daniel Johnston. Another tape, entitled *Feel The Bunny*, contains music recorded for a Steve Hanft project. It features 'I Went To The Liquor Store' and 'Big Stompin' Mama' between what seems to be dialogue from the film, and ends with Beck strumming and singing the theme from *The Dukes Of Hazard*.

Although there was no actual 'movement' in Los Angeles to compare with the anti-folk scene in New York, there was a bonding of likeminded bands and poets. Beck and his brother Channing produced a shortlived poetry booklet called *Youthless*, and could often be spotted at poetry readings by the likes of Exene Cervenka (of X) or Wanda Coleman. Beck also appeared in a documentary by French filmmaker Sophie Rachnal about the LA poetry scene. 'It was definitely good just to hang out,' said Scott Cymbala, who was also part of the scene. 'Everybody knew each other. There was always something going on, you could go see a show or a reading or a party.' You just had to know where to look. According to Beck, 'The clubs and parties may be many miles apart, but they were there if you could scratch the surface to see what was going on.'

A great diversity of musical styles was being thrown into the West Coast mixing pot—everything from mariachi to hip-hop, to go with the traditional folk, blues, and rock. 'That was my world,' Beck recalled. 'Still is.' For a time, he found himself 'rejecting so much new music, everything that is part of culture. Then … I just spun all around and decided to embrace it all. The machines, the rap, loud guitars, every sort of emotional level. And just go with it all.'

And just go with it all he did—'all' being the operative word. His unique brand of folk-blues-country drew on LA's mariachi and hip-hop scenes as well as his love of guitar-based indie rock, all topped off with his keen sense of observational humour, not to mention his family background in performance art. This heady brew made his early-90s shows a wondrous thing to behold.

In the main, those in the audience wouldn't have had a clue about who Beck was (except perhaps for a few friends in the crowd), so nobody really cared who he was or what he was singing about. 'I'd only have two minutes,' he recalled, 'and everyone was drunk, so I'd sing my goofy stuff—that was my whole shot. I was like a side act in bars. I would come on and play to please the inebriated. That's why I have a lot of songs with the devil in them: it was the only way to get the attention of people who were drunk. That's how to get people's attention anytime, in fact—just bring the devil in.'

Sometimes even the goofy stuff didn't get the reaction he was hoping for, so he decided to start adding a little more to get the crowd involved. Originally, he recalled, he was simply playing his guitar and singing, 'but no one [in LA] really cares unless you are putting on some kind of show. So I started to get people from the audience and other bands to back me up, and the shows turned into these free-for-alls; I wouldn't have any idea what the show was going to be'.

It's especially sad that these shows weren't well documented, because every one of them was different. 'Sometimes I'd only play one or two songs. It would be all stories, or trying to orchestrate these audience participation events. It was fun.'

On one occasion, the 'audience participation' extended to Beck getting everyone to leave the venue and follow him across the street to a gas station, where he put on an 'al fresco' performance. 'Every show I would pull some kind of stunt like that. I was just trying to break down the whole structure of a stage and stretch it out a bit.' On another, he improvised his lyrics around prompts fed to him by a friend with a walkie-talkie headset at the back of the club. And his trusty 'Jazzercise' guitar was set on fire so many times (as documented in the 'Loser' video) that it eventually had to be retired.

These antics did not always go down well—not least when Beck played at Johnny Depp's Viper Room club. 'They obviously didn't like us,' he laughed, 'because in the middle of the set, they cut the electricity and dropped the curtain on us.'

* * *

The name Sunset Junction dates back to the early days of streetcars in Los Angeles, when the tracks spilt northeast to Sunset Boulevard and west to West Hollywood. The area, in the heart of Silver Lake, had a reputation for being gay friendly and was at the centre of civil rights protests in the 1960s. By the time local residents arranged their first street fair in 1980, the streetcars were long gone. A section of Sunset Boulevard was closed to traffic so that stages could be erected for a whole host of performances. A petting zoo was set up, food and retail vendors made pitches, and the whole event was very family friendly.

In August 1991, at the eleventh annual Sunset Junction Street Fair,

Beck jumped up onstage and set in train a number of events that would change his life. Visiting the fair that day was Rob Schnapf, co-owner of the tiny Bong Load Custom Records label. Schnapf happened upon Beck's performance under a little tent on the Hully Gully stage, and was reportedly stopped in his tracks and heard to mutter, 'What the hell is this?' Schnapf was at the show with his girlfriend, Margaret Mittleman, who worked for BMG. Mittleman sought Beck out for a brief chat after his set and gave him her card. Several months would pass before he got around to calling her.

About a week later, Bong Load's other co-owner, Tom Rothrock, was talked into attending a gig at the Jabberjaw coffeehouse in Arlington Heights by his friend Jon Neuman, at which members of the Actors Guild shared the bill with the quaintly named band Dicktit. At the start of the show, Beck jumped up onstage with his battered acoustic, harmonica, and two microphones. After hearing 'Cut 1/2 Blues', Rothrock was convinced that he should get Beck to record for his label. He immediately suggested they work together before reporting back to his partner, Schnapf, who remembered Beck from the street fair.[22]

'What hit me about Beck,' Rothrock later enthused, in the film *10 Years Of Mellow Gold*, 'was that here was this self-contained folk artist who it'd be great to make a record with. He was the only person I knew who'd listened to the same old folk records that I had.'

For Beck, the meeting was a one-in-a-million occurrence. 'It was a total fluke,' he recalled. 'I was playing at this place called Jabberjaw, this all-ages place in LA. This guy came up to me and said he liked the songs I'd played. We got talking and it turned out he was a record engineer, so he offered to record some stuff. We got together and we did some songs.'

It was around this time that Beck had started introducing rap to his repertoire, even covering Ice Cube at a few shows. When he met up with Rothrock again, a couple of months later, they 'got talking about rap music.' The conversation would prove to be a major turning point in his life. 'I was telling him about how I'd do a lot of rap sorta things, where I'd just stomp my foot and shout out all these lyrics,' Beck recalled. 'And he said, *Oh, I've worked with a guy does rap music*. After work one day he called me and said, *Do you want to come down tonight and I'll introduce you?*'

The producer in question was Carl Stephenson. He was born in Washington, DC, but soon moved with his family across the country to Olympia, Washington, which would duly become the spiritual home of the US underground. He later moved to Houston, where he worked with The Geto Boys, a gangsta-rap group so extreme that they had trouble getting stores to stock their X-rated albums, and at time even struggled to find a label willing to distribute them. Eventually, Stephenson became disillusioned with the group's attitude, and in 1990 relocated to Los Angeles to begin putting together a project of his own called Forest For The Trees. He had met the guys from Bong Load along the way.

On a hunch that something good might be in the offing, Tom Rothrock took Beck to Stephenson's house and waited to see what might transpire. '[Stephenson] had a drum sampler,' Beck recalled. 'I brought my acoustic guitar and started playing some folk songs.' Stephenson wasn't overly impressed with what he heard, however, and did little to disguise his irritation. 'He was really bored, like he couldn't care less. I think I remember him walking out of the room. It was a pretty awkward situation.'

Rothrock encouraged Beck to keep playing, and eventually he hit upon a slide-guitar riff that would go down in musical history. 'I went back to the guitar and started playing this slide riff, and [Stephenson] said, *Oh, that's cool*. He recorded it and stuck it over a drum beat.'

Stephenson added a sample from Dr John's 'I Walk On Gilded Splinters', and with that a generational anthem was born. To finish off the track, Beck added a bassline and several other instrumental parts using whatever Stephenson had lying around, which included a sitar. Rothrock and Stephenson then went out for pizza, but they left the tape playing on a loop. While the others were out, Beck attempted to rap over the track, but he thought it was the worst rap he had ever heard, so when he reached the chorus he sang, 'I'm a loser baby, so why don't you kill me?' repeating the title phrase in Spanish ('Soy un perdidor').

By the time Rothrock and Stephenson returned, Beck had written the entire lyric. They recorded the vocal, and that was it. 'When we recorded 'Loser', that was the first time I ever rapped,' Beck recalled. 'The chorus should have been, *I can't rap worth shit.*' They also did another song called 'Steal My Body Home'. 'The whole thing was said and done in a couple of hours. I went home, and we didn't see the guy for a year, and I totally forgot about it.'

* * *

More than a year passed before 'Loser' was actually released. In the meantime, Beck released his debut single, 'MTV Makes Me Want To Smoke Crack', on the independent Flipside Records label in 1992. The label had approached Beck some time after the session with Carl Stephenson, and he had agreed to let them release this live favourite, one of his humorous little ditties, about the poor state of the once-influential TV channel. 'Everything is perfect and everything's bright / everyone is perky and everyone's uptight,' he sings, before later referencing his job in the video store. The single also included 'To See That Woman Of Mine', on which he pays homage to the roots records that had influenced him so much, singing in a gravelly voice of how he needed to 'make it to Texas' to see his woman. It was quite a debut.

The flip side of the single comprised two tracks by Bean, an offshoot of the band Hill Of Beans, both of which featured Steve Moramarco, a Utah native who had come to Los Angeles via San Diego to study theatre.[23] Beck had given Moramarco one of his early tapes, and Moramarco liked what he heard enough to start helping Beck to get a few live bookings. Beck opened for the band a few times in Los Angeles, and as far north as San Francisco. Beck and Bean played together at Raji's as a kind of launch party for the single. The single is now one of the most collectable items in the Beck catalogue, with copies listed on auction sites for several thousand dollars. For someone who had, back then, been earning $4 an hour, this would likely have been mind-blowing. But things were about to get even crazier.

CHAPTER 7

'I was lost in my own little world.' (1993)

In January 1993, Beck compiled a tape of his songs for his mother's fortieth birthday. It was a tape that would be played constantly at Café Troy. 'I made it because she opened up a café and she wanted some of my music to play,' he explained. 'So I put together some of the different songs off the different tapes I'd made.'

He titled the twenty-two-song collection *Fresh Meat And Old Slabs*. It included a lot of the songs that he was playing live around LA at the time, and it was by far the strongest collection of songs he had compiled so far. More than half of them would be released officially over the next few years, including 'Go Where U Want', which he would later rework as 'Hollow Log'.

The breadth of styles showcased on the tape is impressive for someone so young and inexperienced. 'Grease' and 'Satan Gave Me A Taco' showcase Beck's wicked sense of humour, and are typical of the spoof songs he would perform to keep his friends amused and grab the attention of apathetic concertgoers waiting for the main band to come onstage. The former is a storming acoustic song with its tongue firmly planted in its cheek. Opening with Beck on the telephone, ordering pizza, it bursts into life with some of Beck's best lines, among them 'Life is short, can I have it to go / If it's not in the *TV Guide* then I don't know'.

'Tasergun', a humorous tale of Beck's experiences in a Hollywood boarding house, may or not have been based on true events. In the song, an old man in the next room takes offence at Beck's guitar playing and exclaims, 'Watch out son, I got a Taser gun.' Later, after an incident involving stolen toilet paper, Beck moves out of the house. 'Mexico' (or, 'The Ballad Of Mexico') is loosely based on Woody Guthrie's 'Buffalo Skinners'. It tells the (fictional) story of Beck working at McDonald's, getting sacked, going back and robbing the restaurant, and then running over the border to live in Mexico. And what does he do when he gets to Mexico? He gets a job at McDonald's, of course.

'Fume' is based on a true story about two kids who drove out in a pickup truck with a can of laughing gas and a plan to park up, close the windows, and get high. Tragically, they overdid it, and were later found dead by asphyxiation. 'Leave Me On The Moon' was one of the songs Beck had promised to Steve Hanft for his first feature film after Hanft agreed to shoot the 'Loser' video. The original *Fresh Meat* version is slower, and Beck's vocal is drawn out by comparison to the version that would later be used on the film soundtrack. The lyric is the same, but there are some sound effects in the background.

'Death Is Coming To Get Me' was inspired by Nimrod Workman, the old bluesman and coalminer, while 'Captain Brain' is a very stark song sung very slowly, in a deep voice similar to the one Beck uses on 'Trouble All My Days'. 'Captain Brain is coming down / Thinking about nothing at all,' he sings, and the whole thing is over in under a minute.

One song on the tape was later released as a standalone single. 'Steve Threw Up' is based on a story about Beck's friend Steve Moramarco, who threw up while on a Ferris wheel at a fairground. In the song, the incident comes after Steve takes some 'bad acid'. Beck then goes into a long and far too detailed list of everything Steve had eaten beforehand—and he'd eaten a lot. Moramarco later claimed that although the story was partly true, he had in fact vomited on himself, and not on a girl below him, as the song claims.

Several other songs on *Fresh Meat And Old Slabs* are about the plight of being in low-paid employment, and some of these bad-luck scenarios

75

would feature later on *Mellow Gold*. Beck loved working in such a high-speed, lo-fi way. 'That's why four-tracks are so great, 'cos you're writing it as you're recording, and it's all unknown territory.'

* * *

Around the same time as compiling *Fresh Meat And Old Slabs*, Beck released his first full-length album. *Golden Feelings* contained nineteen tracks that spanned the previous four years or so. It was a cassette-only release on the Sonic Enemy label and first saw the light of day in January 1993, housed in a sleeve depicting a kind of teddy bears' tea party. The Sonic Enemy catalogue that was given away with all of its releases had this to say about the tape:

> 'Like Neil Young on cough syrup' says his lawyer, and who am I to differ? Genuine and genuinely fucked-up, straight from the heart of spooky folky noisy unaffected tales of poverty & lucklessness, fast food & bad trips. Thirty-five or more minutes ... $3.00

Around 750 copies of *Golden Feelings* were produced and distributed, up until 1995 when Sonic Enemy was 'put on hold'. In the early days, Beck would sell the album before and after his shows. Original copies are virtually impossible to obtain today, but second-generation tapes and CD copies are fairly easy to get hold of, if you know where to look.

Golden Feelings includes early four-track versions of songs that would later get a wider release, including 'No Money, No Honey', 'Totally Confused', and 'Motherfucker'. Three more—'Trouble All My Days', 'Special People', and 'Supergolden Black Sunchild'—would later be issued in their original form on the 'Pay No Mind' single, with the latter's title changed to 'Supergolden (Sunchild)'. They were billed as having been 'evacuated to four track in 1998', which is interesting, as they were in fact recorded in 1992, while the 'Pay No Mind' single was released in 1995.

This first official release really captures the early Beck sound. It may be a little rough around the edges, but that is part of the appeal. Beck adds little bits of crude samples between songs, showing that his 'cut and paste' leanings were already in place. There aren't many straight-ahead country, folk, or blues songs on the album, but the influence of anti-folk is clear on songs like 'Trouble All My Days', which has a really distorted, bent-out-of-shape blues feel.

'I didn't take it all that seriously when I started,' he later admitted. 'It was a little bit of a stigma to being a songwriter or a folkie back then, so you had to hide that with a lot of humour. I did a lot of sendups of sensitive singer-songwriter stuff when I was starting out, which limited my development as a songwriter in a way. I wasn't really fully given license to explore that until the mid 90s. I'm still working on it—I'm a little bit of a late bloomer.'

On the tape, 'Magic Stationwagon' is a noisy, distorted guitar bash featuring some double- and maybe even triple-tracked vocals. Beck would record himself, then play along to the tape to double up his vocals, and then repeat. 'No Money, No Honey' was one of his earliest compositions, possibly inspired by his hard time in New York in the late 1980s. 'Bad Energy' is an oddity, opening with Beck's best Mick Jagger impression as he sings, 'I know who you are, but you don't know me'. 'Schmoozer' has a slowed-down Buddy Holly drumbeat, and is another of Beck's 'list' songs, with lyrics about how the subject has been 'a-talkin' now', 'a-rockin' now', 'a-guessing now', 'undressin' now', and so on.

'Heartland Feeling' opens with what sounds like an answerphone message, followed by Steve Hanft describing what the song is and name-checking Mellencamp, Springsteen, and Seeger. The actual song is a catchy, melodic tale of various characters going through their boring, everyday lives. 'Soul Sucked Dry' is a slightly bluesy number with stabs of blues guitar and a wailing harmonica in the far background. It could have been written during Beck's lowest moments of semi-poverty in LA. 'My soul's been sucked dry,' he sings. 'Emptiness surrounds me / Bitterness crowns me.'

After the fairly tuneless, dirge-like 'Feelings', comes the hidden gem of the tape: 'Gettin' Home'. This fingerpicked song could have been written by any of the blues giants of the pre-war period. Beck obviously liked it, too, as he would re-record it for his ten-inch mini-album for Fingerpaint Records.

The tape's second side is built around 'Will I Be Ignored By The Lord?', an a-cappella song with a religious tone sung by Beck in a deep voice. 'When I was born, lots of people sayin' I looked like a dead man,' he sings. It ends with 'People Gettin' Busy', which starts out as a jolly little acoustic strum—for the first thirty seconds—before turning abruptly into an electric monster. Beck supplies at least three different voices for the chorus, each layered on top of the others.

* * *

By March 1993, Bong Load had generated enough money to press up 500 promotional copies of 'Loser'. KXLU in Los Angeles soon picked up on the single, quickly followed by KCRW, while KNDD (aka '107.7 The End') in Seattle put the song straight into heavy rotation. Soon afterward, stations were calling Bong Load from all over the country wanting copies.

'Before the record even got pressed there was all this excitement,' Tom Rothrock recalled. 'There were bootlegs right away.' According to Beck, 'By the fall, all these heavy-duty commercial stations started playing it. They didn't even have copies! They were making cassette copies off of someone who had a copy of the vinyl.' By September, LA's influential KROQ station was on the bandwagon, too.

People were soon flocking to Beck's shows, and as such he wanted to beef things up a little. The first requirement on his list was to add a drummer, and he met one in the shape of Don Burnette, aka Dallas Don, at a Popdefect show at Toe's Tavern in Pasadena. Burnette also fronted the band Lutefisk, and was a member of 3D Picnic, Plain Wrap, and Thelonious Monster, but perhaps what most impressed Beck was Don's live performance of Rush's concept album *2112* in its entirety at a club in Silver Lake. As well as joining Beck's live band, Burnette would also accompany him for his first radio sessions.

Releasing a song called 'Loser'—with a chorus that asks, 'So why don't you kill me?'—at the time that he did meant Beck was thrust unwittingly into the spotlight as a generational spokesperson. A couple of years earlier, Richard Linklater had made a film called *Slacker*; Beavis & Butthead were showing the American youth of the day how to live their lives without ever getting up off the couch; Seattle's Sub Pop records sold T-shirts with the word 'loser' printed across the chest; and Sebadoh had a song called 'Losercore'. Now, with his hit song, Beck was cast at the centre of this 'movement', although in all likelihood this movement never actually existed outside the media's imagination.

Beck himself would always resist any attempts to place a generational slant on the song, however.

When we recorded 'Loser', I wasn't aware of the slacker thing. I saw the movie—it was before they invented 'Generation X'. I was lost in my own little world. I wasn't talking about apathy, or how cool it is not to care. I was just making fun of my rapping abilities. It was definitely a case of 'wrong place, right time'. People needed a designated candidate, and I was it. I mean, I didn't even know what a slacker was! But I was too naive to fight it—you do photo shoots and they say, 'Put this shirt on', 'Sit on this sofa', 'Look tired or something', and it's all perpetuated.

The few people who knew anything about the struggle Beck had been through to get to this point ignored it. 'Even in the 1980s, no one I knew was succeeding or slacking off,' he explained. 'They were just living normal lives and getting by. No one had time for that stuff. And I didn't grow up in a suburban environment, so I could never relate to that kind of suburban boredom. I've always been stimulated and interested in things.'

It was certainly a sign of Beck's relative naiveté that he allowed himself to be portrayed in this way, and before he knew it, the image had swollen to the point where he was being cast as a cartoon character. The way Beck was being portrayed in some corners of the music media caused him a lot of frustration.

'I was up in Olympia, Washington, and someone called me up and said they were going to premiere the video,' he recalled. 'The guy on the phone [was] talking about all this slacker stuff, saying that "Loser" was some slacker anthem or something. I was like, *What? Slacker my ass.* I mean, I never had any slack—I was working a $4-an-hour job, trying to stay alive. That slacker stuff is for people who have the time to be depressed about everything.'

His record speaks for itself. He is not someone who sits around waiting for something to happen—quite the opposite. 'I guess it all depends on how you define *slacker*. For me, it has a negative connotation; it seems to be: *young people are apathetic, they sit around making it their profession to be bored and uninspired.* That's insulting, because even when I didn't have the means to do much, I always tried to create some activity. So in that respect, I'm an anti-slacker.'

Whenever this kind of media overload occurs, there is inevitably someone standing to one side with a calculator, thinking of ways to make money from someone else's success. Brewing giant Budweiser was first on the scene. 'Budweiser said, *We'll give you $250,000 for the rights to the song.* I had a lot of opportunities to become a part of the whole business machine, or whatever you want to call it. I just stayed away and did everything I could to play that song down. Not that I'm ashamed of it or anything. I'm proud of the song, but I didn't want to let it be turned into what it wasn't meant to be. Basically, it was hijacked from its original place.'

It wasn't just the corporations that Beck wanted to stay away from. Many of those who championed the song were exactly the people Beck had spent his formative years feeling alienated from. 'The people who took that song to heart were the jock people, the popular people, the attractive, stronger ones. But it was really coming from someone—myself—feeling displaced from the 1980s, a time of materialism, where everybody was cashing in and making money. If you went to school and you were wearing the same shoes you had a year ago, and you'd grown out of them, and your toe was coming out of a hole, it was not your time.

You were not accepted. The people who embraced it represented the reason the song was written.'

To downplay the song a little, Beck went through a period of changing the chorus whenever he played it live. One night it might be 'I'm a schmoozer baby', or 'I'm a softie baby', or 'I'm a squeegee baby'; the next he might sing 'So why don't you hug me', or 'So why don't you squeeze me'. On another occasion he just stood onstage looking at a tape recorder playing back the song. What was clear is that he really didn't enjoy the baggage that came with having a hit, as he explained to Thurston Moore during their infamous MTV *120 Minutes* interview in 1994:

MOORE: How do you feel about 'Loser' being such a massive hit?

BECK: It feels like surfing through an oil spillage.

MOORE: I know exactly what you mean, man.

He also wanted to make it clear that he knew how fortunate he was to end up in the position he was now in, and that he hadn't forgotten where he'd been just a few months previously.

'A year ago I was living in a shed behind a house with a bunch of rats, next to an alley downtown,' he explained at the time. 'I had zero money and zero possibilities. I was working in a video shop, alphabetising the pornography section for minimum wage. Believe me, this has fallen in my lap. I was never any good at getting jobs or girls or anything. I never even made flyers for my shows. And until, like, six months ago, I didn't know that you could get paid for playing.'

Another downside—and one Beck felt strongly about—was the way his story would be simplified down to 'the lowest common denominator' in newspapers and magazines. 'How can you sum up my life, or any life, in a paragraph in *USA Today*? It takes all the dignity and all the expansiveness out of it.'

* * *

Beck made his live radio debut on July 23 1993, a few days after his twenty-third birthday. DJ Chris Douridas had heard some of Beck's early tapes after Geffen A&R man Tony Berg sent him a promo copy of 'Loser', and now invited the singer to drop in on his show, *Morning Becomes Eclectic*, on KCRW in Santa Monica.

The segment begins with Beck playing a Woody Guthrie spoken-word tape as an intro, then breaking into 'Loser', rapping live over a backing tape and ad-libbing a few new lines about 'Oakies running around in spandex' and 'A swimming pool full of Kool-Aid'. (Later, when tapes of the show started to circulate, people thought it was an alternate version of the song.)

As well as 'Loser', Beck plays five other songs: 'Mexico' (in a version later released on the KCRW compilation *Rare On Air*), 'Death Is Coming To Get You', 'Pay No Mind' (which he introduces by saying, 'I used to live in like this shed, this next song, it's about being bored and sitting in the shed'), 'Whimsical Actress', and 'MTV Makes Me Want To Smoke Crack'. Partway through this last song, Beck stops proceedings to declare, 'Hold the show, I'm gonna bum-rush this. Start the tape, we've got to do this another way.' The tape in question is a 'wine bar piano' version of the song, which Beck proceeds to perform in full cabaret crooner style.

Between songs, Beck talks to Douridas about his life in the early 90s, offering a few interesting nuggets of information. He says that he spent a brief period sleeping rough—'I lived out of my car, but not [for] more than a couple of days. I was homeless in New York'—and mentions his lack of work outside of music. 'I got laid off work last fall. I'm on unemployment.'

Throughout the show, Beck is accompanied by drummer Don Burnette, who is referred to on air as 'Dallas Don, the owner of the deepest voice this side of Calvin Johnson'.

That night, Beck and Don played a show at Café Troy, taking the stage at 10pm following a set by rap act Kill Whitney. By all accounts, people were hanging from the rafters to get in after hearing Beck that morning on the radio. 'You should have been here last week,' he quipped during the set. 'There were only six people!'

Beck continued to make sporadic live appearances through the summer. He was back on the airwaves in September, this time playing a session with Thurston Moore for KXLU. One track from it, 'Whiskey-Faced, Radioactive, Blowdryin' Lady', would later appear on a compilation album put out by the station.

* * *

During the early 1990s, Calvin Johnson's reputation was such that everything he was associated with reeked of indie-credibility. He'd started out as a DJ for the KAOS station at Evergreen State College in Olympia, Washington (and was one of the few students there to actually come from Olympia), and then in 1984 started his own record label, K Records, while also playing in the influential underground band Beat Happening. He also set up a basement recording studio, which he called Dub Narcotic.

Beck had met Johnson in Los Angeles, and would occasionally send him tapes of songs that he was working on. The two shared a common love of the DIY punk attitude; even if the music they produced didn't have a recognised 'punk sound', they both took a lo-fi, four-track approach, and it seemed inevitable that they would work together at some point. (Another northwest native, Kurt Cobain, was so fond of K Records that he had the label's logo tattooed on his arm.)

Beck had threatened on several occasions to travel up the coast to work with Johnson, and finally made it at the end of October 1993 for the first of two periods of furious recording. The sessions were recorded in Johnson's underground studio, which consisted of a small live room and a control room, its low ceiling and dark atmosphere adding to the mood of the songs Beck was performing.

This first batch of recordings comprise just Beck and his guitar on tunes like 'Whisky Can Can' and 'Hollow Log', as well as a version of Mississippi John Hurt's 'He's A Mighty Good Leader'. These sessions showed a different side of Beck to the one seen on the two tapes from earlier in 1993. This was a Beck who was acknowledging his own musical roots (such as Hurt) and delivering material in an intimate setting, devoid of the goofing around that characterised much of his early work. For the first time, he seemed to be taking his music seriously, and the results were highly impressive. It also showed that he could work with other musicians in a band setting, although he would shy away from doing so again until the sessions for *Mutations* five years later.

During the second half of 1993, record company interest in Beck intensified. After the release of 'Loser' in March and his KCRW appearance in July, the labels were circling ever closer. Exactly how many labels were in pursuit of his signature will never be known; estimates range from six to sixteen, but at least three major players were definitely in the race: Capitol, Warner Bros, and Geffen.

'The whole thing got a little crazy after a while,' Beck later recalled. 'I mean, David Geffen called me at home just to express his interest. I kept thinking the record companies would go away after a few months.' He certainly wasn't going to rush into anything. 'I'm happy that they like what I do, but picking a record company is kinda like choosing the best ATM machine.'

At one point, he decided he should put the various label reps through a little test:

All these record company honchos started coming to my shows in a local dive bar or hole-in-the-wall—the kind of place where there was a big pole in front of the stage. And all these limos would be pulling up with these industry people. People would be saying they love your song, they're coming down, they want you to blow them away! So I thought I would get a leaf-blower onstage and really blow them out of the room. The ones that survived the exhaust fumes from the landscaping machine, when the smoke settled down, that's how I found people I could work with, I guess. Put 'em to the test. Things like bringing a leaf-blower onstage—these things grew out of more of a performance-type thing. I wasn't trying to be a clown. It was a comment on keeping these red stucco fake-house communities clean, the breeze from the inner cities. It had something to do with that.

One major label—whom Beck declined to name—flew him out to New York for a meeting. He met two executives in an office tower in Manhattan, not that far from where he'd roamed the streets a few years earlier, during his anti-folk days. 'They sat me down across from this big desk and, out of these huge speakers, blasted my own song right at me [and] started bobbing their heads to the music.' When the song ended, they suggested that if he changed his image a bit, suggesting that if he made some changes they might be able to work together. Beck said goodbye, walked out, and flew back to Los Angeles.

The label-chase dragged on and on until the end of the year. 'It took a long time sifting through the possibilities, deciding whether to do it myself or let someone else do all the work for me, all the day-to-day business.' Eventually, in November, Beck put pen to paper with Geffen in their modest offices on Sunset Boulevard, having previously turned the label down earlier in the year. A&R man Mark Kates was instrumental in the signing, and was sure they weren't going to be stung by signing a one-hit-wonder. 'When we did sign him he made it clear that he wanted to be around for twenty or thirty years,' he recalled.

For his part, Beck was keen to keen to ensure that his artistic integrity would remain intact. 'I went for Geffen 'cos they offered me the most control—though the least money,' he said. 'I got some strawberries, some blueberries, a hackysack, a silver spacesuit … [but] I didn't get that much money. I got enough to pay my rent for a year and buy some equipment and stuff. But it wasn't a money deal. If I'd wanted to get a lot of money, I could've gotten three times as much.'

To his credit, Beck took a relaxed approach to the whole situation. He didn't expect—or really want—to be an instant rock star on a major label. To this day, he seems genuinely shocked that people pay so much attention to him. But despite this sense of wonderment, he would remain appreciative of the way the recording industry works. 'I was pretty aware of the music industry treadmill, the revolving door. I've been playing music for a lot of years, so I was always very reticent about having some business people dictate to me what I should be doing. It seemed way too foreign to me. I always did music for my own amusement, which is how anybody starts playing music.'[24]

He was also aware that his newfound standing would put him into the media glare—a glare that would include the target of his first single. 'I know it means I'll be on MTV, which is annoying. No one wants to be saturated and overexposed. That's, like, everything I'm against. Most people you meet in America are plugged into the whole entertainment thing—they have nothing to say.'

Beck's legal representative, Bill Berrol, negotiated a clause in the Geffen contract that would allow him to continue to release 'uncommercial' recordings on the independent labels of his choosing, so long as he delivered the required amount of albums for the major label—a wise move in Beck's case, not only because of how prolific he was, but also because David Geffen had once sued Neil Young for making 'uncommercial music'. He also signed up with John Silva's Gold Mountain management team, who handled the affairs of Nirvana and Sonic Youth, among others.

Beck was about to enter a new phase of his musical development—one that would see him record his major-label debut and go out on an almost year-long tour. It would all take some getting used to, as he explained to *Spin* in early 1994: 'All the shit that's happening now is just totally insane, because if you ask anybody that knows me, they'd tell you that I've had just the worst fucking luck. This is all an avalanche of confetti and balloons and kazoos. Before, the party was just an empty room with a bare light bulb on the ceiling. It was pretty bleak.'

It wouldn't be that way for much longer.

CHAPTER 8

'I nailed my earlobe to the speaker.' (1994)

During the period 1992–94, Beck was writing and recording at a furious rate. His major-label debut was one of the most anticipated releases scheduled for 1994, but he would in fact release an astounding four albums worth of original material before the year was out.

The first of these new releases arrived in January, when Fingerpaint put out *A Western Harvest Field By Moonlight* on ten-inch vinyl.[25] The album came together in the midst of the bidding war for Beck's signature:

> There had been all of these labels trying to sign me, and there was one, this girl Meredith, from Warner Bros, and she had her own label called Fingerpaint. She said, 'I really want to put out an EP.' And at the time, I had three different albums going, and I'd had so many years of trying to find someone who'd put something out—I had a lot of music stockpiled—so that record was just my project for two weeks. I recorded a bunch of it on the four-track and then did the rest of it at Poop Alley. That was a studio that a lot of bands were recording in at the time. It was in an auto mechanic garage—I had to wait for them to stop the auto-mechanic drills before takes.

The front cover artwork is a literal rendering of the title, while if you turn the back cover 90 degrees, you can see another harvest field by moonlight in strips that alternate with a floral pattern. The middle of each record has a series of doodles among the song titles, with the two sides of the record listed as the 'Bic' side and the 'Beek' side. If you hold the latter up to a mirror, a message appears: 'Happiness grows in your own backyard.'

The initial run of 2,000 copies each came with an original and unique finger-painting in a variety of shapes and sizes. Some were merely blurs of colour; others were mini-portraits. They would prove instantly collectable. '[The label] had the idea to put an original finger-painting in each one, so we had a huge party at my house,' Beck recalled. 'We covered all the floors with paper and we just let everybody at it. It was one of those Fellini-esque all-night painting melees.' (At least three more pressings—without the paintings—have subsequently been issued.)

The most experimental of the material on the album is a trio of songs entitled 'Feel Like A Piece Of Shit'. The first, subtitled '(Mind Control)', comprised a minute of keyboard-programmed beats and a distorted vocal repeating the title over and over. The '(Crossover Potential)' version is just a sped-up version of the first, while the '(Cheetoes Time!)' take is slower than the other two. Similarly, 'She Is All (Gimme Something To Eat)' is just over a minute long and is based around Beck repeating the title again and again. Anna Waronker and Petra Haden from That Dog make guest appearances once again, while 'Mango Vader Rocks' was recorded at Carl Stephenson's house. With its random noise, strange percussion, dog barks, and occasional spoken vocals—in, yes, a kind of Darth Vader voice—it's surprising to think that this track had been in consideration for inclusion on *Mellow Gold* until the last moment. Indeed, it's a good thing that Beck had that indie-release clause, because Geffen would have freaked out if he'd presented these songs for release on his debut album proper.

For Beck, though, *A Western Harvest* was simply 'a random collection' of songs he'd been working on during that period: 'Some four-track sounds, musical Polaroids, little pieces of music that I thought would be interesting to juxtapose. There's a couple of real songs on there, but I had this concept of this techno piece gone awry called "I Feel Like A Piece of Shit". Kind of my techno anthem for day three of the festival at the rave tent. You know, where you see people who are passed out at the fringes of the tent, face down. It's the other side of the rave that they don't talk about.'

One of the few 'real' songs on the album is 'Lampshade', a nice acoustic piece that actually manages to stretch past the one-minute mark. It was based around a New Year's Eve memory from the early 1990s, when Beck broke his collarbone at a party. There's also a version of 'Totally Confused' that's a minute and a half longer than the one on *Golden Feelings*. The final song, 'Styrofoam Chicken', is cut into the vinyl such that it continues to revolve and repeat over and over again, although 'song' is stretching it a bit, as it's no more than a short burst of garbled keyboard noise.

* * *

In January 1994, Beck returned to Olympia, Washington, to finish off some songs and record some new ones with a local crew of musicians, including James Bertram, Mario Prietto, Calvin Johnson, Sam Jayne, and Scott Plouf, who would later join Built To Spill. Chris Ballew was also present, and would become Beck's regular live guitarist for a while.

'My band, Lync, was born out of the eastside of the Seattle area,' Jayne explained. 'We played mostly in Olympia, and K Records put out a few singles and the LP *These Are Not Fall Colors*. So we moved there. I was there from around 1992 to 1995, bumming around, couch-surfing, and being a weird little menace.' Bertram was also a member of Lync and had moved to Olympia in 1991 to attend Evergreen State College.

The sessions would start at around eight or nine in the morning and were said to be pretty laid-back. 'It was all Calvin's handiwork,' Jayne recalled. 'Set to his standards of keeping the recording scenario simple with old salvaged gear and tape, it felt like someone had built an elaborate radio console from the nuclear era.' Beck gave minimal instructions to the extra musicians. 'We listened to recordings on our own,' Bertram added. 'For instance, on "See Water", I listened back to the recording a couple of times, then laid down the bass track with Calvin Johnson.'

According to Jayne, what Beck liked about the songs was the 'weird chords and energy':

> Later, he asked me what some of the chords were, and I told him I just made them up. Beck was a really chill guy to be around and had a good vibe in the studio. He could really take anything and really quickly put down lyrics and form a song around whatever people were playing. He also had songs ready to go which we did some overdubs on.
>
> I showed up, we played some extra guitars and I sang some extra lines on some stuff. When I look back it seems crazy to me that Beck didn't really give any direction, I guess if he didn't like anything he didn't have to use it.

Later in the year, Lync toured with Beck and That Dog. 'It was really awesome, except we hadn't really toured like that before,' Jayne recalled. 'We just did punk shows. So we said we'd go for like $75 a show, or something ludicrous. We went in one of James's vans. Beck was a great tour host—he knew we didn't have money, so he let us stay at his house.'

The product of the two Olympia sessions would subsequently see the light of day as *One Foot In The Grave*, but as Johnson revealed, much more had been recorded but not issued. 'He's already recorded another album for us, but it's not quite finished being mixed yet, and he's so fucking busy that it's hard to get it done,' he explained at the time. 'I guess I'm not aggressive enough about bugging him. I really need to, but since everyone else is pulling him every which way, I feel bad about going to him and saying, *Let's finish this fucking thing.*'

The material most likely came from the first session in October 1993. 'It's more acoustic stuff,' Johnson added. 'Half of *One Foot In The Grave*

90

was done with a rock band, which people seem to overlook. But this time it's mainly him, and it's great. The songs are just so incredible, and he's so fun to work with. I feel like I've got a pretty good job: I get to work with all these talented people that I really admire, like Beck and Doug Nartsch, and just stand back and watch them go. I'm really lucky.' The extra tracks would eventually see the light of day in 2008, when the album was given the deluxe reissue treatment.

Material from the sessions would also appear on Beck's three-track K Records seven-inch single 'It's All In Your Mind', which came out in 1994, and on the 1998 compilation CD *Selector Dub Narcotic*, which includes 'Close To God'. 'I don't know why that didn't get put on the record,' Beck explained of 'It's All In Your Mind'. 'I think [Johnson] just really liked it as a separate piece and just wanted it as a seven-inch. Very much of the seven-inch ethic, Calvin, you know—a real believer in that format—and I love that format, too.'

Rumours of a second K album continued to circulate for a while, with some suggesting that it would be called *A Tombstone Every Mile*. Beck, however, wasn't so sure that it would see an official release. 'I haven't had the chance to get back up there and work on it,' he said. 'I have a lot of stuff sitting around. I don't know if any of it's worthy to inflict on the world.' Eventually, though, he decided it was good enough. 'I made *One Foot In The Grave* for me,' he told *Q* in 1997. 'That's the one, when I'm sitting by myself, that I really get into.'

* * *

In April 1994, Beck was asked by *Rolling Stone* magazine to describe his debut Geffen album. His reply was typical of him, and would take some beating in the 'quote of the year' stakes:

> The whole concept of *Mellow Gold* is that it's like a satanic K-Tel record that's been found in a trash dumpster. A few people have molested it and slept with it and half-swallowed it before spitting it out. Someone played poker with it; someone tried to smoke it.

Then the record was taken to Morocco and covered with humus and tabouli. Then it was flown back to a convention of water-skiers, who skied on it and played Frisbee with it. Then the record was put on a turntable, and the original K-Tel album had reached a whole new level. I was just talking about that whole 'freedom rock' feeling, you understand.

Understand or not, the facts are that *Mellow Gold* was recorded between 1992 and the middle of 1993, first with the Bong Load gang at Rob Schnapf's house, and later at the home of Carl Stephenson, where the pair had originally recorded 'Loser', two years earlier. Mixed in with these sessions were a couple of trips to work with Tom Grimley at his Poop Alley Studio. Among the guests during these sessions were Beck's old keyboard-maestro pal Mike Bioto and Petra Haden from That Dog, while David Harte played drums on three tracks.

The sessions at Stephenson's were ad hoc, and would frequently take place in the kitchen. 'I'd be hurrying to finish a vocal before Carl's girlfriend came home from work,' Beck recalled with a laugh. This, of course, gave the recording a very lo-fi quality—one that Beck wasn't aiming for. 'If I'd had access to 24 tracks when I recorded "Loser", I would have used them. I was always trying to make it sound as good as I could. I was embarrassed by a lot of my songs, because of the way they sounded. This was before lo-fi became hip. I was ashamed of my music because it was so badly recorded.'

Beck would later describe the album as a collection of 'afternoon demo songs, very slow and not very energetic, not very conducive to playing a rock show in front of an audience that was excited and anticipated something'. He hadn't yet signed to a label when he started working on these songs, and in some respects, the fact that the album fell together in a haphazard way makes it all the more enduring, but Beck would have liked there to be a little more finesse. 'The whole album had been recorded in about two weeks overall,' he later told *Mojo*. 'Really it was like demos. I didn't get to take the songs as far as I wanted to.'

Beck re-recorded his breakthrough track for the album, but Carl Stephenson was unhappy with the outcome. 'I feel bad about it,' he later told David Quantick. 'It's not Beck the person; it's the words. I just wish I could have been more of a positive influence.'[26]

Having cut down the list of songs to twelve, Beck was ready to go ahead and release the album on Bong Load in August 1993, but those plans changed when bigger labels started circling. 'Geffen started talking to Bong Load about signing me in about April 1993, and I just thought, *yeah, right*. So I waited—I wanted to finish up all the artwork—and mastered it, and we were about to put it out in August [1993].' It was at this point that Geffen got serious, and the release date was put back to the following March.

The finished album is a self-contained, minor-league sonic work of art. The opening riff of 'Loser' immediately reminded people why they bought the album in the first place, and also put the song out of the way so Beck could introduce eleven new tracks. After getting his 'big hit' out of the way, Beck presents the listener with the gently acoustic—and by now ancient—'Pay No Mind', which conjures mental comparisons with early Bob Dylan (listen to lines like 'Give the finger to the rock and roll singer / as he's dancing upon your pay cheque' and 'and the drugs won't kill your day job').[27]

The third track, 'Fuckin' With My Head (Mountain Dew Rock)', takes Beck off in a different direction again, with heavy twanging guitars and Sonny Terry-like harmonica. If it's typical of Beck's songs about working for the 'man'—'Throw chicken in the bucket with the soda pop can, puke green uniform on my back, I had to set it on fire in a vat of chicken fat'—it shows progress from his earlier 'Mexico', in which he gets fed-up with his low-paid job and goes on the rampage. After burning his uniform, he's left cold but resolute: 'I ain't washing dishes in the ditch no more / I ain't going to work for no soul-sucking jerk.' Two tracks later, the funky bass line on 'Soul Suckin Jerk' itself highlights the fact that Beck is already a multi-dimensional artist—and that's only five songs into his major-label debut.

While Beck would later show off an eclectic mix of country, blues, hip-hop, and rock on his widely acclaimed second Geffen album, *Odelay*, the less heralded *Mellow Gold* draws on a different range of styles, its combination of folk, rap, punk, and hardcore hinting at the shape of things to come. 'Beercan' displays a swirling psychedelia-meets-hip-hop that assaults your senses in ways you wouldn't have known were possible, while 'Motherfucker' hits you equally hard, but this time with some death-throe feedback and screaming vocals. Courtney Love would later suggest that Beck and her late husband, Kurt Cobain, would have been great friends had they ever met, and this song shows a musical kinship, too, even if Beck couldn't be said to share Cobain's misanthropic worldview.

As if to make that point, sandwiched between 'Beercan' and 'Motherfucker' is the comedy acoustic number 'Nitemare Hippy Girl.' Again, the way Beck populates his songs with real-world characters and situations from his own blue-collar existence is reminiscent of Dylan: in this case, the title character, with her 'tofu the size of Texas', or the truck-drivin' neighbours fighting downstairs; elsewhere, the hotel dishwasher in 'Whiskeyclone, Hotel City 1997', or the fast-food worker who finally snaps and goes on the rampage in 'Soul Suckin Jerk'.

The album's mix of stream-of-consciousness lyrics versus narrative stories adds up to a genuinely fascinating collection that is sometimes hard to peg down, and the deliberate false starts and obscenities remind the listener of Beck's early home-made cassettes. With this album, Beck begins his leap into the mainstream without really getting his feet wet. Though yet to demonstrate his full genius, he was starting to show glimpses of it.

For the closing track, 'Blackhole', he put in a call to his old friend Rob Zabrecky.

[Beck] told me that he had signed a recording contract with Geffen Records and asked me to play stand-up bass on one of the tracks he was recording for his record. I was thrilled for him and gladly accepted the offer. I was happy for every bit of success that was coming his way. I showed up at a Spanish-style house in the hills of Silver Lake where he was recording. We set up in a bathroom to capture some natural acoustic sound, where wires ran to a nearby recording board. I had no idea what we were going to record, but after grabbing a nearby acoustic guitar, he played and walked me through a track he was calling 'Black Hole' with a drowning Appalachian feel. This creation of his had lots of deep and slow moving chords. I added a string of long and drowning notes by bowing the strings of the bass in a couple of takes. I hung out a bit and heard some of the other material they were working on, which was excellent, and bailed. It felt good to see him in an environment where he could record his whims and make the record he wished.

After Geffen agreed to release the album, Beck was keen to point out that it may not give a very good overall impression of him or his music. '*Mellow Gold* is probably not the best impression to give people of my music as a whole. The silly songs came from playing live at other people's shows where you only had about five minutes. In that situation, you often play something that'll make a few people laugh.'

Another mitigating factor was the way it had been recorded with no overall plan. 'It was such an anomaly in the way it fell together,' he said. 'It was just this concatenation of accidents that nobody could control, and it was beautiful that way.' On another occasion, he explained that his recording process had been anything but conventional. 'I nailed my earlobe to the speaker, and the sound was booming through my hollow skull. And my pen was on fire, so I had to write fast and not actually think about it.'

Although Beck claimed that he had a fair amount of artistic freedom—and this was pretty much true, to a large extent—he did have to go along with some of Geffen's demands. The first was that the label intended to rerelease 'Loser' in the USA, and issue it for the first time in Europe, too.

Steve Hanft's video for 'Loser' was, like much of Beck's early work, done on a tiny budget. Tom Rothrock had sampled some dialogue from Hanft's film *Kill The Moonlight* for the single, and one day Hanft asked if they could have a meeting, which Rothrock thought seemed very 'official'. In the meeting, Hanft pitched the idea of Rothrock letting him produce his first music video, to go with 'Loser.' He arrived well prepared with a storyboard presentation of what he would film. When Rothrock asked how much money he'd need to film it, he said $300. The clip was partly filmed in Humboldt, where Bong Load was based. 'Steve kept having problems with one of the cameras,' Rothrock recalled. 'It kept jamming and loading weirdly, [but] it created a great effect—a ghosting and stuttering in some of the shots. Once again, you try and do the best with nothing, but nothing could go wrong in that whole period.'

Hanft was also tasked with filming a follow-up video, for 'Beercan'. 'It was Beck's idea to have a bunch of homeless guys go in the front of a house and eat all the food,' he recalled.

Ross Harris was also involved. 'We just stocked this house with food and furniture from a thrift store and then just let them destroy it,' he recalled. 'The second time we went to get the homeless guys it didn't go as well. We went down in a van. The first time, we'd gone down to skid row and handpicked guys and slowly we filled up the van. The next time we went down, we went with a couple of guys who I won't name, and one of them just opens the van door and goes, *Who wants to make $100 and be in a music video?!* The van filled and we couldn't even shut the door.'

'Ross had this idea to re-create these 1960s *Playboy* ads, which were like, "The man who reads *Playboy*",' Hanft added. 'People chilling by a sports car with a chick. So we got my dad to come down, because we wanted the old guy with the young chick and then a homeless dude chilling in that position.'

These videos would get a lot of airtime on television screens around the world, and one of the effects of this was to reignite controversy over the 'slacker' tag—this time on a much larger scale. Again, Beck had to field questions about his background and outlook on life, and again he shied away from any connection to the so-called 'Generation X'. In fact, he denied that the 'slacker nation' existed at all:

That nation doesn't really exist, does it? I don't really know that nation. I don't believe it's there. It's just a created thing because I don't really know anybody like that. Maybe when you're a kid, and you're in high school and you don't have much to do and you're just sort of hanging out, but everyone I know is working hard, myself included. That song wasn't really a response to any sort of Generation X or slacker thing. It was more a reaction to the 80s, which seemed to involve this whole winning, materialistic thing. This whole *Top Gun* attitude, which for the have-nots was just kind of a drag. If anything, it was a reaction to that. But it was meant humorously.

Time and again, in interview after interview, in the USA and now in Europe, Beck had to explain that the chorus of his most famous song was addressing his lack of rapping ability, and not intended a serious generational statement.

Mellow Gold finally hit the shelves in early March 1994, its sleeve depicting the Armageddon figure of *Last Man After Nuclear War*, with several of the song titles missing a few letters to make them acceptable to retailers. An in-store promo CD was edited to remove 'Fuckin' With My Head', 'Truckdrivin' Neighbors Downstairs (Yellow Sweat)', and 'Motherfucker', with 'Corvette Bummer' added to beef up the playing time. While the CD came out on DGC, Bong Load put out the vinyl version of the album, which for some reason carried an alternate version of 'Pay No Mind'.

When reviewers got hold of *Mellow Gold*, all most of them had to go on was 'Loser', plus perhaps a few stories about Beck's wacky onstage antics. In the UK, at least, no one had yet seen Beck live—or heard him live, for that matter—so the album came as a blind introduction. Despite this, it stood up very well in the face of what could have turned into dismissals of him as a 'one-hit wonder.' The *New Musical Express* gave the album a respectable six out of ten, and commenting, 'At his best, he refuses to be what you assume he must be—an acid-fried LA novelty.' Ireland's *Hot Press* was more generous, awarding the record top marks while gushing that 'Beck is well on his way to rescuing rock and roll from the mundane'.

Q magazine gave *Mellow Gold* a glowing endorsement, with a four-out-of-five review and a sparkling overview: 'He's got everything going for him. He looks like a young Evan Dando; he shares management with Nirvana; Geffen are spending enough money on him to rescue Euro Disney; and, most important of all, he's very, very good.' The reviewer for *Vox*, on the other hand, liked what he heard, giving the album eight out of ten, but got Beck's background a little out of context, concluding, 'at last, grunge has a solo star to worship'. Grunge?! *Rolling Stone* meanwhile missed the boat somewhat but tried to cover its own tracks in its end-of-year issue by noting, 'Like all genius moves, only in retrospect does it seem obvious.'

Beck also received some direct feedback from people in the street: some was favourable, some less so. 'Every once in a while, somebody says, *Oh, I like your album,*' he told *Spin* that year. 'Mostly, people come up to me and say, *Hey, you faggot, you think you're really cool, huh?* I get most of that.'

It wasn't all abuse, though. Beastie Boy Mike D. was among those singing Beck's praises, noting how he 'fits into the nomadic folk tradition of Ramblin' Jack Elliott, the whole traditional coffee-house balladeer trip, but his hip-hop side legitimises Public Enemy as the real folk music of the 80s and 90s, because he draws on that aspect just as much as on anything else that he's picked up along the way'.

To coincide with the release of *Mellow Gold*, Geffen lined up a series of promotional appearances for Beck. The first of these was a transatlantic jaunt to take in the BBC's long-running show *Top Of The Pops*. Beck would be required to sing 'Loser' live over a pre-recorded backing tape. As he had no musicians with him on the trip, he decided to spice things up a bit, enlisting the services of a group of elderly gentlemen to act as his band.

'It was a group of eighty-year-old men,' he recalled with a smirk. 'Some were dapper, sprightly elderly gentlemen who still had hair. There was a portly guy with a Friar Tuck hairdo playing guitar. Then we had a hunched, slightly demonic old man, and he was playing drums. There's a genius part where the camera cuts to him like there's a break on drums, and he does the slowest drumstick spin ever executed in the history of rock drumming, it was really beautiful.'

The performance went down as one of the highlights of the show's long history. 'I knew they'd totally appreciate old men. We just asked around and a bunch showed up and we picked the best. We hung out with them for two days, just playing guitars and telling stories. One of them sold sunglasses and he tried to sell me an old police-issue pair. I wouldn't buy them, though.'

* * *

Back in the States, Beck was thrust into some radio appearances closer to home. On 1 March 1994, he returned to KCRW's *Morning Becomes Eclectic* with Chris Douridas. This time, accompanied by Chris Ballew, he opened his set with a version of 'Bogusflow'. After a discussion of how the two musicians met (Ballew went by the name Caspar, which made it difficult for Beck to find him, as he was asking for the wrong guy), it was announced that Beck would be playing the following day at Aron's Records, to coincide with *Mellow Gold*'s release.

The interview then moved on to the circumstances of Beck's signing to Geffen. 'I counted fourteen labels chasing you,' Douridas noted, before introducing another live track, 'Dead Man With No Heart', with Beck on banjo. Ballew joined in with his trademark two-string Bassitar on 'Hard To Compete'. Douridas then switched gears to ask Beck if he'd ever been in love. 'Once or twice,' he replied, 'couple of hundred times.' He also had to fend off the inevitable question about the 'slacker' tag. 'Slackers are for rich people or something,' he said. 'I don't know what's up with slackers.'

Asked if he felt the need to make up a 'Beck mythology', he gasped, 'Oh, no, I'm not that smart,' seemingly genuinely surprised that anyone might think that. This is most likely the truth. It's that he wasn't smart, but that most of the stories about him were true, even if they had been embellished a little by over-enthusiastic journalists.

'Howling Wolves' was introduced as 'a demo for our side band' and was described as 'sort of Bon Jovi in a vacuum cleaner' (a description that's surprisingly close to the truth). *Top Of The Pops* also came up. 'It was surreal,' Beck said. 'They made me sing it eleven times. Practice it eight times, then film it, but the cameras weren't working. I was kinda tricked into it, because I said yes before I knew what it was.' The segment closed with renditions of 'It's All In Your Mind' and 'It's All Gonna Come To Be'.

A week later, Beck teamed up with Thurston Moore for a session at KXLU. This madcap noise-fest was later sent out as an official Geffen promo cassette to college radio stations, to ensure that Beck retained his wacky image.

Around the same time, Beck put together a band—consisting of Joey Waronker on drums, Chris Ballew on guitar, and Dave Gomez on drums—in preparation for a tour due to start later in March. Big, burly Dave was a veteran of several Los Angeles hardcore bands, while Chris, aka Caspar, had participated in the second phase of the *One Foot In The Grave* sessions after being introduced to Beck in Olympia.

'I was putting together my first band, and a bunch of people had told me that there was this kid who was great and his name was Caspar,' Beck later explained. 'So he joined the band on guitar. He did the *Mellow Gold* tour with me, and during the tour we were making tons of four-track tapes, most of which I lost while we were on the road. I think he had a few things he was doing, and he recorded that and put it out as a seven-inch.'

That single came out under the name Twig. To go with Chris Ballew's pseudonym of Caspar, Beck took the name Mollusk. 'One thing about the Mollusk character that I didn't explain was that we had a tour magazine,' he recalled. 'I can't remember what the name of it was; *Serene*-something … I had written all these poems as this character, a German

100

punk who's name was Mollusk. Very broken English, just very crude kind of aggressive poems. [Twig] was his one appearance in musical form.'

After touring with Beck, Ballew would go on to form The Presidents Of The United States Of America and record two albums for Columbia.

Joey Waronker, meanwhile, is perhaps an unlikely rock-star in his own right. He's quiet, self-consciously polite, and has been described by *Drum* magazine as 'a wee bit spacey'—not unlike Beck in some ways. He comes from a strong musical background. His sister Anna was a member of That Dog, and his father Lenny was a producer who later worked as an executive at Warners. It was hanging out in the studios where his father was working that started the young Waronker on his way to being a drummer. Lenny worked with the likes of James Taylor and Randy Newman, giving Joey the chance to study drummers like Jeff Porcaro and Steve Gadd.

Most of Waronker's encounters with drummers of the day were positive, and they'd give little hints along the way. 'They were just friendly,' he recalled, 'and they'd hang out and play with me. I'd sit in the drum booth and watch them. I remember the main thing that I picked up on was the drum tuning. That was the big thing. I would obsess on listening to how the snare drum sounded in the room, as opposed to how it sounded in the headphones or in the playback. I'd try to imitate that at home. So I'd sit there and watch how Steve Gadd, after doing six takes, would just tweak one lug over here and one over here. It would be totally uneven, but he'd whack it, and it would have his sound. I'd listen to how his cymbals were really sort of dry and dead, yet he had a way of somehow bringing a lot of sound and character out of them.'

Waronker's interest in drumming waned as he approached his teens and opted to concentrate on his education. 'About the time I stopped playing, I had a weird realisation that I should use my mind and focus myself. I just got really into school for a while.' This lasted for a while, but by the age of fourteen he was not only back playing again but had joined his first band. The Radio Ranch Straight Shooters were a western-swing band with a guitarist by the name of Smokey Hormel (who would later join Waronker in Beck's band).

Although his favourite music was rock and punk, Joey put his all into the band and set about learning everything he could about jazz, blues, and country. He was aided by The Blasters' Bill Bateman—another drummer with a love of all musical styles. 'He was a real historian, and a real serious collector. He'd see me playing and he'd be like, *You can't use a Yamaha hi-hat pedal to play this music! You're not going to be able to get the right feel.* It was a little over the top, but for a fourteen-year-old, it was actually really cool. And I became obsessed with learning about the history of music.'

After graduating from high school, Waronker relocated to Minnesota and signed up to McAllister College, where he studied classical percussion. It was here that he joined the power trio Walt Mink. After completing his four years at McAllister, he hoped things might lead somewhere with the band, who by now had signed to Caroline Records. 'I definitely wasn't going to join a symphony. And there was a buzz going around about the band. We had gotten a write-up in *Rolling Stone,* and it seemed like things were happening. I just sort of bit the bullet and said, *If I really need the degree, I'll come back and get it, but right now, there's no time.* And there hasn't been time since.'

By 1993, Waronker was trying to add a little bit of experimentation to the band, but without much success. 'I was fascinated by the way The Beatles and Brian Wilson recorded,' he explained, 'so I was trying to integrate those kind of sounds: bells and tambourines and snare drums and timpanis and concert bass drums and vibraphones. We'd make demos and I'd break all this stuff out and then it would all get erased. Everyone in the band would kind of look at me funny, like, *Why are you wasting our time here?* But in the back of my mind I knew that the time would come when I'd figure it out.'

As a result, Joey quit the band and headed back to Los Angeles. Before he'd had a chance to settle in, however, he got a call from a friend for a session job with a singer named Beck.

I showed up and it was so funny. Beck was like, 'I'm going to play bass. Let me show you this song. It's really simple. It has two parts. The first part is going to go like this.' And it was, like, a I–V progression. 'So we do that four times, and then the next section goes like this.' And he plays the same I–V progression. So we played it, and I just sort of followed him, and he was like, 'That's great, but make the second sections a little heavier.' So I did that, and that was it.

Afterwards we hung out and were talking, and then we ended up just freaking out and recording sort of a noise jam. And then I split, and my friend dropped off a tape later that day. Beck put on some guitars and a tambourine and a bunch of crazy noisy things and some vocals and then tacked the noise jam that we did onto the end of it. I was blown away by how he visualised the song.

After a couple more sessions, Beck asked Waronker if he wanted to go on tour. As they prepared for the trip, he added, 'We need about two more weeks of practice, but we leave in two days. We'll work it out on the road.'

The band named themselves After School Special and played only their second-ever gig at Café Troy two days before they were to depart on tour, pulling out unreleased tracks like 'New Wave Cocksucker Blues' and 'Teenage Wastebasket' for the occasion. Seeing that some of his fans were wearing the infamous Sub-Pop T-shirts bearing the name of his most famous song, Beck asked, 'What's with all these *Loser* T-shirts? Don't you people have any self-respect?'

CHAPTER 9

'I wasn't prepared for any kind of success at all.' (1994-95)

Before going out on tour, Beck and his newly assembled band played their final warm-up show at Fuzzyland, a roving club that changed venue from night to night. On this particular night, it was stationed at a disused bowling alley with the stage set up at the end of the lanes. The show was intended to have doubled as a release party for Beck's compilation CD on Flipside Records, *Stereopathetic Soul Manure*, but the CDs weren't ready, so the plan was shelved.

The album itself was a real hotchpotch collection. Many of the tracks had been recorded with Tom Grimley, owner and operator of Poop Alley Studios, which had been called 'The best recording studio in Los Angeles' by *LA Weekly*. Grimley had filled the place with 1950s-era equipment and synthesizers that he'd picked up at second-hand fairs. A multi-instrumentalist himself, Grimley had fronted The Bennett Orchestra, and had also hosted The Rentals and That Dog at his studio. The latter also appear on *Stereopathetic Soul Manure*.

The few reviews the album received found critics struggling to get to grips with its eclectic selection. *Q* magazine gave the album just one star out of five and summed it up as music for 'those who find Pavement a touch easy'. But while it is true that some of the noisier tracks, like 'Pink Noise (Rock Me Amadeus)', 'Thunderpeel', and 'Rollins Power Sauce', take a few listens, there are also some lush country numbers—'Rowboat',

'The Spirit Moves Me', 'Modesto'—great acoustic songs—'Crystal Clear (Beer)', 'Puttin' It Down', 'Satan Gave Me A Taco'—and some plain old silliness—'8.6.82', 'Total Soul Future (Eat It)', 'Aphid Manure Heist'.

Dotted among the original songs on the album are little snippets of Beck messing around with a tape recorder in his teens and field-recordings he'd undertaken with hobos on the street.

> I had a microcassette recorder. I was fooling around one day and I started talking into it making up stories and then hit 'stop' by mistake and had to start again, but it sounded great the way it just cut off, the way the kid was talking, and then it had a high-speed mode, and I sort of just discovered this character and I just started telling stories into it like it was a diary. So I started using it in my shows. I'd talk about this kid and I'd found this tape and this was his diary, and I'd use little snippets between songs. A couple of them made it onto that record, I had a whole cassette full and I played it at a show in Seattle around that time and someone jumped up on stage after I'd left the stage and grabbed the tape recorder. All those stories are lost, but a couple of them survived on that record.
>
> Then there was a hobo by the side of the freeway exit, he had a big beard and I just went down there with a tape recorder one day and started talking to him and we liked a lot of the same musicians. I said, 'Do you know "Waiting For A Train?"' So he started singing that and a bunch of other songs.

Unconventional though it may be, if you give this collection some time, you'll find that it probably does reward you in the end. Indeed, it would go on to cement its place as a favourite among fans. 'I get a lot of people who say that,' Beck recalled. 'Probably more the record-collector types. I've always wanted to go into a studio for two weeks and do another record like that.'

In the meantime, Beck was still writing and recording at a furious rate. Following another set of sessions at Bong Load, Tom Rothrock claimed, 'We have about forty songs in the can, recorded during the year following the release of *Mellow Gold*. It's more an extension of the stuff on *Stereopathetic Soul Manure.*'

* * *

Beck's first real nationwide tour took in a number of major cities across the country before returning to Los Angeles in late April for a short break. 'Our first tour was in a van, it was insane, ridiculous,' tour manager Ben Cooley recalled. 'He had done a West Coast tour by himself, and that's when Chris Ballew joined the band. They all learned to play together over time, but there's no question that those early [band] shows were all over the place.'

'When it came time for him to tour, it was really hard for him because he'd never really had to focus,' Joey Waronker recalled. 'His shows in LA had been amazing but spontaneous, and we were trying to learn so many songs.'

Beck used the downtime to take a trip to the Beale Street Music Festival in Memphis in May before the tour restarted in June. For many of the shows, the crowds were surprised and even shocked by the Beck live experience, with the majority having probably only heard 'Loser'. In January 1999, Beck told *Guitar* magazine that the shows had become 'sort of confrontational'. At the time, he was 'still basically playing folk gigs', and 'Loser' was 'really a side project from my folk stuff'. Now it was time to figure out which way to go. 'Did I want to do something that was confrontational and explosive, or do something that was more country and folk-based, or did I want to create a whole different thing that I'd never really imagined before? I think I opted for the last one.'

As the tour moved into the West Coast and Midwestern states, some major media coverage ensued. The show at Minneapolis's First Avenue Club was reviewed in *Rolling Stone* and was the first of his shows to be bootlegged, resulting in the *Total Paranoia* CD. Opening with the non-album track 'Corvette Bummer', it includes unreleased material like 'Scavenger' and 'Color Coordinated', plus a healthy mix of acoustic numbers and B-sides to go with the better-known *Mellow Gold* songs. According to *Rolling Stone*'s review of the show, 'Beck seemed intent not only on shaking his erratic live reputation but on delivering a message: There's more to music than alternative rock, there's more to history than yesterday, and there's more to Beck than "Loser".'

'Erratic' was perhaps an understatement. Some nights it all clicked, and he was brilliant, but on others the performance was patchy to say the least. It should be remembered that for the previous six years, Beck had mostly played solo, and he sometimes struggled to put across a good show as part of a band. But while the overall performances were up and down, Beck did manage some consistency with the solo acoustic mini-sets that he played midway through the show each night.

The next part of the tour marked the start of a whole new ball game as Beck went down to Australia for ten shows in small venues and then on to New Zealand and Japan. While in Australia, he and the band stopped by at the Triple J studios in Sydney to record an eight-song radio session. After being introduced as 'the people's poet', Beck made clear that he was not just going through the motions of promoting his recent album, as only one of the eight songs ('Beercan') was from *Mellow Gold*.

Another bootleg, *Strawberry Communion*, was soon making the rounds, this time taken from his September 6 show in Tokyo. It contains an early romp through 'Minus', which would show up on *Odelay* two years later. Beck's reaction to Japan was one of love at first sight, and this feeling was reciprocated. So strong was the bond he formed with his Japanese audience, in fact, that four years later, when he decided to stage a mini-tour in support of his *Mutations* album, he played in Japan only. 'Japan is my very favourite place in the whole world,' he explained. 'I enjoy not knowing how anything around me is working. I just enjoy that constant derangement, and I'm really into that whole cleanliness thing, how you can go to the fruit store and the fruit comes out like it's from an antiseptic forest, it's so pristine and well.'

By November, *Melody Maker* was sending reporters stateside to review shows in anticipation of forthcoming British dates. In his report on a show in Boston, Everett True wrote, 'Before tonight, I'd never seen Slayer turn into Sebadoh. After tonight, I'm not sure I ever want to again.'

Despite this, Beck was still eagerly anticipated. Before reaching the UK, he undertook a whirlwind tour of fourteen dates in twenty nights across mainland Europe, finally debuting in the UK in Manchester on November 26. Two nights later, he put on a triumphant show at the Astoria Theatre in London, the setlist running from half a dozen *Mellow Gold* songs to some unreleased tracks ('Color Coordinated', 'Casio', 'Protein Summer') and a healthy dose of acoustic numbers ('Ziplock Bag', 'Puttin' It Down', 'It's All In Your Mind').

A few days earlier, Beck had stopped by Radio 1 in London for an interview. Asked about his plans for the next year, he replied, 'This is going to be the feedback year. The year of headphone solos. We got this helicopter thing happening. We're gonna drop musicians into depopulated areas and then get this big satellite and sorta hook 'em all up. It's kind of an unambitious year.'

For the show at the Astoria, Beck was joined onstage by pedal-steel player B.J. Cole, who would subsequently fill in with The Verve (replacing Nick McCabe) and play with Joey Waronker a few years later, when both were working with R.E.M. 'At first I thought he was just a space cadet off of Planet Zod,' Cole recalled of their initial meeting, 'but I soon realised the guy had something very interesting going on. He's got a strong vision of what he's doing and doesn't compromise for other people, but he has a thorough knowledge of all the base styles of popular music: Jimmie Rodgers, Sonny Terry, Brownie McGhee, and people like that. He's a dustbin of American popular music styles.'

Beck was obviously happy with Cole's contribution, because he contacted him again a couple of years later to play on another Radio 1 session recorded just before *Odelay* came out. 'I was the only other musician on it—he played all the other instruments, including drums, which he couldn't play! My favourite bit was when he completely detuned his guitar to overdub a solo. I realised he had this atonal effect in his head, and he knew exactly how to get it. That session just sold me.'

After a few more European dates, it was back to LA for another show just before Christmas, a well-earned rest, and a chance to reflect on a hectic first year of major label commitments. Looking back on the turbulence of 1994, he realised how unprepared he had been for success. 'I was just getting used to the idea of something as basic as putting an album out, so I don't think I went into this year ready for what happened,' he explained. 'It's been a year of intense learning and kinda struggling to figure out how it all works. The strangest thing is the way that people have come in and had an idea of what they think I am, and no matter what I've said or done, they've turned me into it. That kind of power is really disturbing.'

As the year drew to a close, *Spin* put *Mellow Gold* at #2 on its list of the best albums of 1994, with 'Loser' and 'Beercan' tied as the magazine's singles of the year. Around the same time, Beck wrote a piece entitled 'My Year Of All Dangers' for the French magazine *Les Inrockuptibles* in which he claimed, '1994 hasn't been very kind to me. People very quickly came to a false image of me.' Asked about the speed of his newfound fame he replied, 'I've no comparison. I don't know what speed it happens for others. For me, anyway, everything happens too quickly. The news goes round too quickly; records come out too quickly, trains go too quickly.'

The overall sense was that this had been a year of intense learning for Beck. He must have felt that he'd been dropped in at the deep end, but he'd just about managed to swim, even if he was occasionally slapped in the face with a big wave. The most important thing about making mistakes in public is that you learn from them and endeavour not to repeat them. Beck obviously took this on board, as he would change his band for the following year in an attempt to tighten up his concerts, and also began to grow a little more accustomed to dealing with all the media attention.

* * *

The new year started with Beck agreeing to release a four-track single on the British Domino Records label in January, with the title track selected as the original version of 'Static'. The label was all set to go, but the master tapes never showed up, and the project was scrapped.

At home, Beck played a high-profile support slot for Johnny Cash at Pantages Theatre in Hollywood. The aging country star was enjoying a critical and commercial rebirth, having released his *American Recordings* album the previous April. Beck took to the stage in front of the hard-core country fans and won them over with a performance on acoustic guitar and banjo that dispelled any doubts about his authenticity.

By now, Beck was living in Silver Lake with his girlfriend, Leigh Limon, whom he had met through her job at the clothing store run by his mother (his brother Channing had moved north to study art in San Francisco). He was also now composing songs on piano as well as guitar, but despite racking up almost twenty new tunes, he decided against using most of them, with only 'Ramshackle' making it onto his next album. 'I tried to record "Dead Melodies" and "Canceled Check" for *Odelay*,' he explained, 'but they just didn't fit. I approached *Odelay* as a sound project, not as a performative thing.'[28]

Beck continued to schedule random sessions whenever he could between touring commitments, most notably working for the first time with Beastie Boys collaborator Mario Caldato Jr. 'I first heard Beck's music when "Loser" was playing everywhere and caught my attention as being something really unique and funky, especially from a white guy with a leaf-blower onstage,' Caldato recalled. The pair had been introduced by Beck's manager, John Silva, who also managed The Beastie Boys, and enquired as to whether Mario would consider trying some sessions with Beck at his G Son studio. 'I said yes, of course,' Caldato continued. 'We did six or seven songs and one, "Minus", was used for the *Odelay* LP. The others were used on the deluxe edition [of *Odelay*] and the *Kill The Moonlight* soundtrack.'

Beck's next stop on his recording odyssey was to try something very different to the more traditional songs he'd been working on during the previous year. 'That stuff wasn't really turning me on,' he said. A change was required, and it came in the shape of two DJs with a home studio just minutes from Beck's house.

The Dust Brothers, Mike Simpson and John King, had met in 1985 and teamed up to DJ a college radio show in Claremont, California. They soon found themselves producing tracks for Tone-Loc, Def Jef, Young MC, and other rappers on the Delicious Vinyl label. The pair then set up their own studio, PCP Labs, in Silver Lake, and started work on an album of their own. After putting down a collection of instrumental tunes, they began discussions with The Beastie Boys about working on the follow-up to the rude-boy rappers' debut album, *Licensed To Ill*. The Beasties heard the tracks that King and Simpson had been working on for their own album and asked if they could rap over the top of them—and thus *Paul's Boutique* was born, and soon became one of the most influential hip-hop albums ever made.

One of the amazing things about *Paul's Boutique* is the vast amount of samples used on it. This isn't too surprising given the Dust Brothers' eclectic record collection, with Mike Simpson claiming to have once bought 15,000 records from a collector in one go. This would later help toward broadening the horizons of Beck's next album. They had a lot of time to listen to these records because they were using an early version of Pro Tools, the computer-based recording software, and it took an age to compile and save the data after every take.

John King (aka King Gizmo) was a classically trained musician into blues, rock, and punk, while Mike Simpson (aka E-Z Mike) was more into funk—a combination that dovetailed nicely with Beck's embrace-all-styles methodology. Their PCP Labs studio was basically their house, but with the addition of 'stacks of weird old gear', as Simpson put it. 'The living room is a live room, so when artists come here it's just a loose, laid back environment.'

This was just the kind of atmosphere that had characterised Beck's *Mellow Gold* sessions with Carl Stephenson—and was exactly how he wanted to make his new record.

'I prefer to record in houses,' he said. 'I can't go into those big studios. It's too much like a laboratory or something. Too scientific. I didn't have a place or anywhere to set up a studio, [but] I knew the Dust Brothers had one in their house, so ... we just hooked up. There was no agreement; we were just going to record a song for fun and see how it came out.'

With no formal plan to make an album, they just experimented:

We'd just go in the studio and we were all kind of doing stuff together production-wise. It wasn't one of those scenarios where the producer comes up with the track, and then the singer comes in and does their thing. That's kind of an old-school way of doing it. I started playing the music by working on a four-track, doing the music myself, and recording myself, so I still had particular ideas about how I wanted it to sound.

I played the instruments, Mike Simpson did a lot of the turntable scratching stuff, and Mike, John, and I picked out the samples together from whatever was lying around in the studio. I would write and record a song and one of us would grab a record and find a little something that fitted.

At times it was a descent into madness, as all good endeavours should be. I was so exhausted after touring with *Mellow Gold* and the whole overload of the 'Loser' thing that I probably should have taken six months off. But I had all this stuff I needed to get out and I wanted to push myself. I was afraid that otherwise I might just settle like a stone at the bottom of the ocean and just stay submerged forever.

If Beck had definite ideas about what he wanted to accomplish, so too did Simpson:

Modern records are very predictable. Usually if you listen to a song for thirty seconds, you get it; you know where it's going, you know what's gonna happen, you know what to expect. We wanted to try to keep the music exciting, so that you have to listen to the whole song, or else you're going to miss the best part. When I listen to old records, they have a certain sound you can feel—when you turn it up, you can feel it in your body. When I listen to stuff from the 80s and 90s, it's all very clean and precise, but I don't feel it. We use all this technology to get some amazing technical performances, yet we still want to create that sound that has some emotional impact.

This seemed to sit well with Beck, and he, Simpson, and King hit it off immediately. As Simpson put it, 'We could tell from the first day in the studio that we were going to have a lot of fun making this record. He was just amazingly talented and the ideas were just flowing from day one. We were basically just like kids in a sandbox, having fun with our toys.'

The positive dynamic allowed all three to bring their input into any part of the recording process. There were no defined roles—except, of course, that Beck had to do the singing—and for Simpson, it was important that they all started as equals in order to get the ideas flowing. 'It was like a free-for-all: he's a classic songwriter but also a big fan of weird sounds; we had a pop sensibility but at the same time we're into disparate off-sounding shit. Between us, we had an insanely eclectic record collection, so we got the vibe going by listening to everything from the obvious old funk and psychedelic rock records to crazy country and really cheesy religious records, not so much for a melodic line but more of an overall sound.'[29]

* * *

As well as his new collaboration was going, Beck had to break off the sessions midway through to meet touring commitments for the summer and beyond. European festivals and a Lollapalooza stint were looming, with headlining dates of his own to follow. He also had to juggle his touring line-up before the first shows, with only Joey Waronker retained from the previous year's band.

On keyboards, Beck brought in his old pal Mike Bioto, whom he would later call 'my best friend while I was growing up'. 'He was the archetypal thirteen-year-old jazz piano prodigy. I used to play with him all the time, but I veered off into more of a Professor Longhair thing. I can hang a little Booker T. if necessary, but I prefer to keep with the blues.'

Auditions were held to fill the roles of bassist and guitarist. Smokey Hormel was among the invitees, but with Beck unable to make an immediate decision, Smokey took up a more concrete offer elsewhere. As a result, the job of tour guitarist went to Sunny Reinhart, with Abby Travis coming in on bass. 'An A&R man from Geffen recommended me for the audition,' she recalled. 'We spent about a month rehearsing before the tour and he got through a lot of songs. Beck just has so many! He'd still want us to play songs we didn't really know anyways, once we got out on the road.'[30]

After five late-June warm-up dates in California, it was time to join up with the big boys on the Lollapalooza juggernaut, starting on the Fourth of July in Washington state. The touring festival was the brainchild of ex-Jane's Addiction front man Perry Farrell, whose self-imposed brief was to take a diverse selection of alternative acts on the road not only to a selection of major North American cities, but also to places that wouldn't normally see headline shows from major acts. The whole package included travelling sideshow circus acts and all the associated stalls and curiosities that you'd find at any stationary festival. He also ensured that at least $1 from every ticket sold went to AIDS research and environmental charities.

The first Lollapalooza took place in 1991, but by 1995 there was a feeling creeping in that Farrell was finding it difficult to keep the crowds happy, and that they always wanted something bigger and better than the previous year. Lollapalooza 1995 was, to some people, a great disappointment after the extravaganzas of previous years. None of the big four names of the past—Pearl Jam, Red Hot Chili Peppers, Smashing Pumpkins, and Nine Inch Nails—was available this time around, and ticket sales sank. Whether this was because of the absence of these bands, or just because the public had grown used to this kind of tour rolling in every summer, was unclear, but the opening show at the Gorge only sold out on the day of the event.

Vancouver was up next, and that didn't sell out at all. In Denver, where each of the previous years had been an 18,000 capacity sell-out, only 12,000 tickets were sold. Farrell tried to maintain the profile of the event by describing this year's line-up as 'a unifying thing, and what happens when you unify is that you dissolve slightly into anonymity. But it doesn't make it any less potent'. (It's unclear whether this was a weak cover-up of a poor line-up, or whether he really did believe in the acts that he was showcasing.)

The audience's apathy hit Beck hard. This was his first time playing in large-scale venues, and almost no one was paying him any attention. He would appear on the bill after The Mighty Mighty Bosstones and The Jesus Lizard, and right before Sinead O'Connor (before she pulled out) and Pavement. Hole and Sonic Youth topped the bill. He was generally on early in the afternoon and faced with what seemed like miles of empty seats, with the small scattering of fans seeming to be a long way away.

Asked what he remembered of the experience, it was the seats that continued to haunt him. 'What comes to mind? Blue plastic seats. Empty. Very empty. And it's 105 degrees, and there's a small cluster of youngsters who are displaying their energetic support, but they're about a mile and a half away, and there's ten security guys closing in on them. I think at that point there was a lot more happening at the falafel booth than where I was standing.'

Bassist Abby Travis agreed with this summation. 'I had fun,' she said. 'I liked that there were so many different people and bands around. Beck should have had a way better time slot, though. There were indeed a lot of empty seats.' Beck also enjoyed the company of all the other bands, and played a lot of table tennis along the way. He met up with Cypress Hill on the tour and discovered that they were almost neighbours, having grown up not far from each other. ('I said I was from Pico Hill and they were like, *Shit, that's right next door, we thought you were from Europe or something.*')

Beck and his bandmates had to do some re-jigging to get their material to work in the massive venues. 'When it came to songs from *Mellow Gold*, it was hard to recreate them live,' he recalled. 'They were kind of slow—even "Motherfucker", which seems rocking, but is really pretty slow. I had made most of them up on my own, so they didn't have a bigger audience in mind. We had to change the songs to play them live to a big audience, so they'd fit the atmosphere of that kind of show.'

A typical set would be based around 'Thunderpeel', 'Pay No Mind', 'Loser', and 'Fume', with new songs introduced as the tour unwound. He played 'Novacane' and 'Diskobox' in Chicago on July 15, and debuted 'Minus' and 'Where It's At' in Hartford on July 26. He was also inspired along the way to write a new song about that hot, faceless summer of empty seats. Originally called 'Electric Music And The Summer People' (a title he subsequently gave to a later B-side), it eventually became known as 'Devils Haircut'.

The title's from a poem, from a terrible record. I can't remember what it's called—some easy listening thing from the 60s. I spent that whole summer out in these incredibly, hideously, devil-adjective, tremendously hot, intolerably humid, outdoors facilities playing at two in the afternoon, watching the half-baked youth of the summer of '95, desperately trying to connect with them. It was futile. The original idea behind the song is a last gasp call to arms for everybody to come together—it was a somewhat cynical title. But it sounds good. 'Let's don't be like everyone else'—that seemed to be the current of that summer of '95. It was inverted homogeny: everyone's trying so hard to be different, but they're all the same.

Beck would generally perform with the band on the main stage early in the day and then pop up later in the evening to play a solo acoustic set on the second stage.[31] Each night, he would pull out a magical set of tunes from his back catalogue; 'Rowboat', 'Hollow Log', 'Asshole', and a cover of 'John Hardy' were among the favourites. Sometimes he'd finish up with an amazing medley that could include any number of songs like 'Mexico', 'Satan Gave Me A Taco', and even 'Ozzy'. While these performances lacked some of the spark from Beck's early-1992 shows, which he had also often played with just an acoustic guitar, he managed to strike up a better rapport with these low-key performances than he had managed on the main stage with his band. He clearly had the ability to put forward an onstage persona that could connect with all types of people when he could actually talk to them, as he had during his early LA shows, but he struggled to do so when they were half a football field away. It would take several years of refinement before he could achieve this same intimate feel with his full-band shows at larger venues and festivals.

The Lollapalooza tour ended on August 18 at the Shoreline Amphitheatre in San Francisco, with Beck putting on an energetic show that included 'Fuckin' With My Head', 'Thunderpeel', 'Novacane', 'Where It's At', 'Beercan', and two versions of 'Loser'. But the touring didn't end with Lollapalooza. After that he was off to Europe for more dates, starting with the prestigious Reading Festival—'one of the best shows we did', according to Abby Travis. The show was filmed, and parts of it have since been broadcast on MTV Europe. Further festival appearances followed in Belgium, France, the Netherlands, Switzerland, Austria, and Spain. Then, by mid October, Beck was back in California to play at Neil Young's annual Bridge School Benefit concert.

It was only after the tour ended that it was revealed that, as well as having to get through a second consecutive year of long, arduous touring (plus a soul-sapping stint at Lollapalooza), Beck had also had to deal with the deaths of several people close to him. 'In the past year I've had several people close to me die,' he explained. 'The shock mechanism that is stimulated when you hear about it was being pressed down all last year and at one point it didn't even pop back up.'

Al Hansen had died in Germany at the start of the summer, and Jac Zinder—the LA club promoter and music critic who'd been the first person to write about Beck (for *Spin*) in 1993—passed away a few months later. Beck had also seen two friends die of AIDS, while a friend of his mother's died after being hit by car. He also lost an occasional member of his band, pedal-steel player Leo LeBlanc. 'We opened for Johnny Cash,' he recalled, 'and it was Leo's last show. He died about two weeks later. I hadn't realised that he was battling cancer. I called him up to do the show and he said, *I can't play pedal steel, I'm getting this operation and I can't really play it, but I can play lap steel.* So he played that.'

So many losses in such a brief time must have taken their toll. As 1995 ended, Beck had a choice: he could either take a complete break to gather his thoughts, or he could decide to work his way through it. He opted for the latter, and in the aftermath of all this tragedy he had to pull his thoughts together as he began to think again about his follow-up to *Mellow Gold*.

Throwing himself into his work was, at least in part, a reaction to all that he'd been through. 'At the time I was thinking, *am I gonna write a bunch of songs about death?* But I wanted to get more into the celebratory aspect of these people being alive.' And that is exactly what he did. Soon, the fruits of this labour would be thrust upon an unsuspecting world to great acclaim, as Beck put the sadness behind him to produce one of the most stunning albums of the 1990s.

CHAPTER 10

'I thought it would be a disaster.' (1995-96)

As soon as he found time, Beck was back in the studio with The Dust Brothers to resume work on his new album. The two sets of sessions either side of the summer tour would give rise to two distinct sets of songs. Before he embarked on the Lollapalooza dates, he'd been working on a series of dense, abrasive sound collages. 'Hotwax' was the first, while others included 'Novacane', 'High Five (Rock The Catskills)', and 'Where It's At'. 'Most of the songs hadn't been written [in advance],' he recalled. 'I went into the studio and built those songs piece by piece.'

Work was slow initially, and some of the songs took up to two weeks to assemble. When he tried out some of the material on tour, he realised that to give the album the right balance, he'd have to change his writing style for the rest of the sessions.

'After doing those songs live, I decided I wanted to have more melodies,' he said. 'I wanted to have some kind of balance in there.' He had also been disappointed at the response the new tunes received during the Lollapalooza tour. 'Nobody cared what I was playing, and all the reviews were always awful, so I expected it to be a curiosity, expectations were low.'

On his return to the studio, Beck's songwriting and recording process changed drastically. Instead of working for weeks on one song, he and The Dust Brothers would sometimes do two in a day. This second phase of recording produced some of the most memorable songs on the album. 'Jack-ass', 'Sissyneck', 'Lord Only Knows', and 'Devils Haircut' were all quickly finished, while 'The New Pollution' was written and recorded in one afternoon. According to John King, Beck had 'a definite vision, but he seemed really comfortable masterminding his own songs and at the same time letting go of them to let us do our thing'. He was on a creative high, and he would try his hand at everything. 'You toss an idea his way, and instead of immediately rejecting it, he'll turn it into something fantastic. He looked in the *Recycler* [a free newspaper] one day and saw a guy in Santa Monica was selling Indian instruments. Two hours later, he came back with a sitar and tamboura. He said, *The guy tuned it up for me and taught me how. Let's record something.'*

Beck would describe 'Jack-Ass' as being about 'the midst of summer, when the only goal is movement'. The song has a country feel but is presented in Beck's own unique way. On its release as a single, several remixes were made available, as well as a Spanish version entitled 'Burro', complete with a damn fine impression of a donkey at the end. When asked about the line 'Tyin' a noose in the back of my mind', he explained, 'That's part of an interest in ropes in general. Could have been a lasso, too. Could have been a ship docking rope, but I don't know what the term for that is. I'm not too good with terminology. The attraction? With rope, you can hang something, if you need to.'

Beck revelled in the recording of the album. It was the first time he had been allowed to take his time and record songs with the idea of them forming part of an album, rather than merely collecting together disparate recordings spread back over a number of years, as he had done before. After months of work, the new songs were almost there, with only the final mix needing some work. 'Mixing it was where the real work was,' he recalled. 'Recording it was mayhem, but mixing it, we'd just sit there for hours and hours 'til we turned green.'

Although some of the new songs received a far from overwhelming response on tour, one that stood out was 'Where It's At'. Beck was not thinking ahead to how the songs would be performed onstage, however.

'I was never concerned as to how it would sound live. I was embracing the album as a totally different art form.'

Another tune that would become a live favourite is 'High Five (Rock The Catskills)', which includes Beck's first foray into classical music, with a sample from Schubert's *Unfinished Symphony*. 'We'd started talking about classical music,' he recalled. 'We grabbed that off the shelf. Nobody was sure if they liked it, but it ended up staying on there. A lot of things we'd just throw into the soup. A lot of times, we'd get rid of it later. I must have had twelve keyboard parts for "Where It's At", but only two of them are in the song. Each song was like that.'

The album was all but complete by the end of 1995. 'The whole time making it,' Beck said, 'I thought it would be a disaster. I thought it was going to be a beautiful way to go out—a beautiful disaster.' He would soon be proven wrong, although for now the album's release was still six months away.[32]

With the musical side of things finished, Beck had to give his new album a name and decide on the cover art. The song 'Lord Only Knows' was originally called 'Orale', but then fate stepped in. '*Odelay* comes from a Mexican slang word, just part of the LA language,' Beck explained. 'I had a song called "Orale", and the engineer misspelled it, so I thought I'd use the phonetic spelling to describe where I come from culturally. "Odelay" doesn't have an exact meaning, but it can be used in terms of "way to go!", "all right!", or "right on!"'

Acoustic versions of this pseudo-country song first emerged as early as 1994, when Beck played it on a Radio 1 session. It also made regular appearances during Beck's stint supporting Sonic Youth on tour in April 1996. 'It's a fare-thee-well tune, my closing-time song, a last salute, the last hurrah—another misspent evening,' said Beck of the song, which he played at his grandfather Al's memorial service.

'Lord Only Knows' was not the only song to get a late name change. 'Novacane' was originally called 'Novacane Express', 'Minus' was known as 'Minus (Karaoke Bloodperm)', and on early promo tapes, 'Devils Haircut' was still referred to as 'Electric Music And The Summer

People'. Beck had also teased a few journalists with the title of the album, referring to it as both *Mellow Tinfoil* and *The Sensuous Casio*.

The Hungarian sheepdog (or Komondor) pictured on the cover also came to be used almost by accident. Beck had been looking for a dog of his own at the time, and was flipping through the American Kennel Club's *Complete Dog Book* for inspiration. 'I just laughed so much at this ridiculous canine monstrosity being made to jump over this hurdle.'

Much of the rest of the album artwork is by Filipino artist Manuel Ocampo, a friend of Beck's whose work is full of religious imagery and strange views of animals and insects.[33] The back cover image of the egg-man is from his *Junior Masturbator* (1996), and if you look closely at the bottom right-hand corner, you can see the word 'Hansen'. 'I wanted to be Beck Hansen for this album,' Beck recalled. 'If you look on the back cover, in the lower right corner—they didn't want to put it on the front cover—it says, in really tiny print, *Hansen*. It's kind of too late to change, though.'

The CD booklet contains a collage of images by Al Hansen and Zarim Osborn, as well as more paintings by Ocampo, some of which were taken out and used for the singles drawn from the album. The vinyl edition features a large fold-out poster with extra line-drawings on the reverse that aren't in the CD booklet, while the back cover has a little more artwork at the top of the collage, with the words 'Tabula IV' visible at the top left, and a painting of a skinned turkey in the top right corner.

* * *

With his new album complete, Beck took up an invitation to tour Europe as an acoustic opening act for Sonic Youth. The tour took in several countries and received some major media coverage in the UK, resulting in some good and bad press. Beck would tend to play a set of ten-to-twelve songs that many in the crowd had never heard before. A couple would be from *Mellow Gold*, but most of the audience had only heard 'Loser', so they spent their time talking to each other or shouting for the hit. Undeterred, Beck resurrected old favourites like 'Heartland Feeling' and 'No Money, No Honey', and would commonly break up 'Mexico' into three parts and scatter them throughout the set ('It's too long to sing in one go').

In his *Melody Maker* review of Beck's show at La Riviera in Madrid, journalist Mark Luffman was of the view that 'Beck doesn't deserve to get away with this. Mediocre songs sung poorly, played worse. What makes Beck think we give a shit?' On the other hand, Kitty Empire sounded as though she could hardly wait for the new album in her report on the show at Le Zenith in Paris. Describing how 'the frenzied beat-box leaves the rest of us breathless', she was full of praise for Beck's new songs, although there was still a note of caution: 'It's impossible to gauge whether the finished product will pack the same punch.'

Once these dates were over, things went quiet for a couple of months in anticipation of the new album. Eventually released in June, the completed masterpiece that is *Odelay* was astounding. Like any new release, it would immediately get people searching for ways to define and pigeonhole it, to file it away neatly under a genre of their choosing. But unlike most other new releases, *Odelay* defies any attempts at characterisation, or even really to think up new categories for it to fit into. In the space of one album, Beck had managed to turn around the people that didn't care much for him after *Mellow Gold* and the Lollapalooza tour of '95. He had seen the future, but it was taken from the past.

Some of the influences are obvious and plentiful, but the way the songs were assembled (sometimes with many styles in one track) offered something truly new and exciting. Here, Beck is paying his musical dues, but in his own unique way. His early love of the Casio keyboard shows up at the end of 'Novacane'; his Mexican heritage surfaces again with a Spanish chorus on 'Hotwax'; 'Where It's At' acknowledges early-80s rap parties; 'Devils Haircut' contains a blues lyric in a rock setting; 'Sissyneck' and 'Jack-ass' update country music but still sound legitimate. Then, for the first time, there's a real pop song, 'The New Pollution', which with its 'Taxman' bassline tips its hat to The Beatles and other 60s bands. The song trots along at quite a piece, with its ambiguous chorus lyric ('She's alone in the new pollution') designed to get people thinking.

'I'm not trying to confuse people,' he told *Rolling Stone*. 'I want to communicate. A song like "The New Pollution"—I mean, pollution [is] a presence in our lives. And isn't it interesting to use a word like that, something with such horrible connotations, in the context of almost a love song? That's where you create friction. That's where you can start to get to someplace where you aren't dealing in the banalities of everyday, pedestrian rock lyrics. Not that I mean to be snobby about it, I can appreciate the good ol' song, and I still like to write that way sometimes.'[34]

While on first listen the album may sound messy at times, this only goes to prove that first listens can be deceptive. The danger when adding layer upon layer of sound is that you might overdo it and not know when to say enough is enough, but repeated listens to this album prove that Beck and The Dust Brothers got it right on just about every occasion. ('High Five', with its Schubert sample—a 'palate cleanser', according to Beck—was perhaps the only occasion they overdid it.)

The jubilation that Beck had mentioned as response to the numerous deaths that he'd recently had to contend with is evident in the overall feel of the record, even if it's not quite so apparent in songs such as 'Ramshackle' and 'Derelict'.

Beck's lyrical style had moved on enormously since *Mellow Gold*. Gone are the seemingly straight-ahead narratives and blue-collar situations— perhaps unsurprisingly, given that Beck quit his last day job over three years earlier—to be replaced by observations that are more oblique and sometimes downright confusing. If comparisons are to be made, they would again be to Bob Dylan (whose 'It's All Over Now, Baby Blue' is sampled on 'Jack-ass').

The mix of styles and the sometimes-odd lyrics combine to give songs that are fresh and inspiring while at the same time containing something that makes the listener think that they might just have heard it somewhere before—somewhere they can't quite put their finger on. This is 90s music at its best—something that no one else was doing, or had ever done before. Of course, it would soon spawn wannabes (Bran Van 3000, Cake, and 1000 Clowns, to name but three) but the fact is that they were just following a formula—Beck's formula. The copycats will always be trailing behind, because they don't have Beck's history and musical education to put into play.

As with *Mellow Gold*, Beck ends the album with an acoustic calm-down from the madness that had preceded it. 'Ramshackle' predates The Dust Brothers' involvement in the album, and features jazz legend Charlie Haden on upright bass. Beck would later describe it as 'southwestern, San Fernando Valley, San Gabriel ... the ranch houses, like cardboard cut-outs. Brown atmosphere'. With the lines about 'rubbish piles, fresh and plain / Empty boxes and a pawnshop brain', he could be singing about his grandfather's art studio.

The song provides an oddly restrained end to the album, after all the shenanigans that come before it. Was this a hint toward the direction of Beck's next album? He would later admit that he put 'Diamond Bollocks' at the end of 1998's *Mutations* to lead the way to the following year's *Midnite Vultures*; maybe he was doing the same here.

Beck's next move was to release a new single, 'Where It's At', in mid June. It would prove to be one the finest moments of his career to date. He had tried out the song during some of the Lollapalooza dates, but this new, recorded version is simply amazing. 'There's a lot of experimenting going on,' Beck recalled, 'but there's also grooves. Without them, this would be a pretty abrasive record. If you took out the keyboard, guitar, and bass, there's all this noise and shit—me breathing through these distortion boxes. I sound like some imploding cyber-donkey. That's kinda subversive.'

The main refrain—'Two turntables and a microphone'—would become a Beck trademark, and something that has been mentioned in just about every article written about him ever since. 'It's a tribute to the old house parties,' he explained. 'I'm not talking about house music— I'm talking about the old-school rap house parties. We're talking two turntables and a microphone.'

The weekend before the single was released, Beck was invited by The Beastie Boys' Adam Yauch to play the Tibetan Freedom Concert at San Francisco's Golden Gate Park. The Saturday show featured sets by Pavement, Foo Fighters, Smashing Pumpkins, and The Beastie Boys; Beck appeared on the Sunday, in front of 60,000 people, along with Björk, De La Soul, Sonic Youth, and the Red Hot Chili Peppers. The concert was filmed, and a triple-CD set was later released containing performances from both the 1996 and 1997 shows.

After completing his set, Beck popped into the studios of LIVE 105 for a special edition of *Modern Rock Live* with Adam Yauch. He played three songs and participated in some lively discussion about the festival and other Tibet-related issues.

To top off a busy weekend, Beck then flew back to Los Angeles for the *Odelay* release show and party on Monday, June 17 1996. The event took place at Tower Records on Sunset Strip and consisted of Beck playing a short set to a few hundred fans at midnight, the CD shelves having been pushed back to allow a regular stage and PA to be set up.

Beck was in fine form, taking the stage initially with just a drum machine and guitar. He messed around with the drum machine (as he had at the Tibet show), speeding it up to give the crowd some jungle beats and then slowing it right down to create a new style he said should be called 'tundra'. He improvised a song called 'John Tesh Blues' and then played 'Asshole' before introducing his two bandmates—Justin Meldal-Johnsen on bass and Sonic Youth's Steve Shelley on drums—for 'Fume' and 'Lord Only Knows'. The show ended with some freestyle rapping over a human beat-box volunteer from the crowd and a version of 'High Five'.

Finally, the waiting was over, and the album was in the hands of fans and reviewers alike. It started modestly, entering the US chart at #16 and the UK chart at #18, but would go on to sell in excess of three million copies worldwide. Reviewers were pretty much unanimous in their praise for the album—a fact that took Beck by surprise. 'I saw a few reviews and was completely floored,' he recalled. 'When the reviews came out, I got an incredulous call from my tour manager: *Have you seen the reviews?!* After *Mellow Gold*, I stopped reading them, and I said, *Are they awful?* He went, *No! They're saying it's a great record!* I was shocked.'

Beck's lack of confidence in the album was probably down to some of the less than overwhelming reviews for the new material he'd played at Lollapalooza the previous summer. 'Early on, we thought the record was going to bomb, but we just kept at it,' he revealed. 'I think, these days, being successful takes a lot more hard work than it used to.'

The hard work paid off. Two of the major US monthly magazines, *Spin* and *Rolling Stone*, gave the album top marks, with the latter declaring, '*Odelay* takes Beck's kitchen-sink approach to new extremes while also managing to remain a seamless whole; the songs flow together with intelligence and grace'. The review ended with a question: 'Could the future of rock'n'roll be a snot-nosed slacker with a bad haircut, an absurdly eclectic record collection, two turntables, and a microphone?' For *Details*, which gave the album nine out of ten, *Odelay* was 'Everything you could want from a subterranean blues-sick homey'.

In the UK, *Odelay* received one of its only negative reviews from *Melody Maker*'s David Stubbs, who may now look back on what he wrote as one of the most ill-advised reviews of any album ever. 'This album, for all its mess and energy, seems debilitated and shot through with all the wasted, lifeless mirthlessness that's afflicted American music for years,' he wrote. Continuing in the same vein of ill-chosen anti-hype, he decided that the album was 'goofing off its responsibilities to offer us something urgent and inspirational in our lives. I'm bored.' *Q* magazine, on the other hand, gave the album a four-star review, concluding that Beck is 'possibly the hippest person in the world'.

There was, however, one running theme that stuck in Beck's craw. 'In every review that I'd pick up, it would say *Man-child Beck*. What do I have to do? I've got hair on my chest. I'm twenty-six. I mean, granted, I look young. I always take it as a little disrespectful. It's like I'm not to be taken seriously.'

Beck also had to defend himself against criticism of the lack of intelligible lyrics on the album, although as far as he was concerned, it was irrelevant. 'They're meaningful to me,' he said. 'I'll get three or four subject ideas for a song and just mix them into this tapestry, it becomes a little more dense. I'm trying to invoke an atmosphere, as opposed to the specific events or specific story.' Pavement frontman Stephen Malkmus, who had recently become a good friend of Beck's, has a similar approach to lyric writing. Does the fact that he sings 'Focus on the quasar in the mist, the Kaiser has a cyst and I'm a blank want-list' make Pavement's 'Stereo' any less of a great song? Probably not, and the same should be said for Beck's 'Tyin' a noose in the back of my mind' or 'She's alone in the new pollution'.

As with *Mellow Gold*, the vinyl version of the album was issued by Bong Load, rather than DGC, and came with a fold-out poster of the CD artwork. It was released two months after the CD and cassette versions of the album. In the UK, the album's thirteen tracks were augmented by an extra track, 'Diskobox', while a limited-edition run of CDs added another, 'Clock', that was not listed on the packaging.

Advance review copies of the album also included a sample that had to be removed at the last moment: the voice of Cell Phone Barbie appearing on 'Sissyneck' to say, 'Oh right, great. You could get a pizza, with my sister, on Friday.' Until, that is, a certain toy manufacturer made a last-minute complaint. 'Mattel made us take it off the record,' Beck recalled. 'They said if we tried to approximate it in any form, we would be ruined. We thought we may be able to get away with it, but we played it for a three-year-old, and she immediately shrieked with recognition, screaming, *Cell Phone Barbie! Cell Phone Barbie!*' (The sample can still be heard, however, when the song is played live.)

Many listeners were fooled into thinking that there were hundreds of other samples on the album, à la *Paul's Boutique*. If he didn't know for sure, Beck might have been fooled, too: '*Odelay* sounds like samples, even to me, but there really isn't a whole lot of sampling on the record. The Them sample and a few others were obvious, but mostly it was me playing stuff on instruments. The sampling that's there is along the lines of frosting on a cake that I baked myself.'

One of the unsung guests on the album is the relative unknown Paulo Diaz, who plays tabla and sarangi on 'Derelict'. 'Those are all instruments with a craft that takes years to master,' Beck explained. 'But they're very interesting, just as raw sounds. I'm not trying to cop a Beatles thing; it just comes from a genuine love of the music.'

'Derelict' was one of the first songs completed for *Odelay*, with Beck describing it as being about 'coming into town on a ghost ship. The stowaways are finding themselves naked in the back of a police car, smelling like herring and bird shit'. He explained the line about giving his clothes to a policeman as being about how 'sometimes the authorities need to see everyone naked; the police would be better able to govern the citizens of their town if they could see them naked'.

Another memorable moment on the album is Charlie Haden's upright bass below Beck's acoustic strumming on 'Ramshackle', while on 'Hotwax' he breaks out the Spanish chorus again: 'Yo soy un disco cabrado, yo tengo chicle en mi cerebro', which roughly translates to 'I am a broken record, I have bubble-gum in my brain.' 'It's in my contract,' he explained with a laugh. 'Every album has to have a Spanish chorus. That's the formula—that bilingual shit drives 'em crazy. Spanish people don't even know I'm singing in Spanish—that's the sad thing.'

In interviews to accompany the album's release, Beck revealed how some of the now better-known songs were almost cut as part of the process of trying to make the record work as a whole. 'There are a few good songs on the album that weren't going to be included because I thought I didn't like them,' he said. One such example was 'The New Pollution', written and recorded in four hours. 'When we finished, I hated it. There was no way it was going to be on the album. Later, it grew on me as a kind of lightweight tune.'

'I wanted this album to be the kind of album they made in the 60s,' Beck told one journalist, 'when people experimented with whatever they felt like—folk, country, chamber music, Eastern sounds.' Sometimes he seemed to have too many ideas, but he would find ways to jam them into one song. 'It had been a couple of years,' he explained, 'so I had a lot of ideas fermenting. That's what "High Five (Rock The Catskills)" is all about—having too many ideas and throwing them together and watching them just kind of explode.' He would later attempt to sum up the song with the words, 'Waiting for a train. San Francisco Bay Blues, Jesse Fuller as an android in his own private sex militia.' What he didn't know yet was was that the song became a vital part of his live show, often as the last song of the night, for which he'd come out in his rhinestone suit, with the band in horse-head masks. 'How do you rock the Catskills? You play Lollapalooza there!'

One oft-mentioned instrument used in the recording the album was the Moog synthesiser. 'I tried to keep the Moog sound to a minimum on the album,' he said. 'It's such a trendy instrument now and can easily be overused. I used the Moog mostly for textures and kept it low in the mix rather than push it up front like, *Hey everyone, look at me, I'm playing a Moog!*'

One of the songs that received the most attention was 'Devils Haircut', which Beck wrote during the ill-fated Lollapalooza tour. He played all of the instruments on it, while also incorporating samples from James Brown's 'Out Of Sight' (as performed by Them) and 'Soul Drums' by Bernard Purdie (as performed by Pretty Purdie), and using the guitar riff from 'I Can Only Give You Everthing' by Terry & The Pirates. Much of the discussion about the song concerned just what Beck was talking about in it, with the man himself not very forthcoming about its meaning. Though he would describe it at times as a blues song, he would also make clear that it could be about anything you wanted it to be about, suggesting people make their own minds up:

I would like to say that everyone should have their own idea of what that song means, from the most obvious—'Oh, gee, I got a bad haircut'—to something incredibly involved and academic. For me, I had this idea to write a song based on the Stagger Lee myth.[35] The chorus is like a blues lyric. You can imagine it being sung to a country-blues guitar riff—'Got a devil's haircut—in my mind.' And all the images in the song—'Something's wrong / My mind's fadin' / Everywhere I look there's a devil waitin'—it's a blues song. So that's where I wrote it from. And that's why I get frustrated when people say, 'Oh, that's a bunch of gibberish.' It's the way you perceive it. Maybe people just aren't patient enough to get into it.

Elsewhere, he claimed, 'I've got five stories about "Devil's Haircut". It's a bogus poetic allusion to the evils of vanity. Or it could be just something that sounds good to sing to. Or it might be that I was putting my own lyrics to a Can song where I can't work out the real lyrics. And there's also a tradition of blues people talking about haircuts—gimme that wig back that I boughtcha.' In another interview, he described it as being about 'the summer of '99—electric music and the summer people. Stag-o-Lee has just got out of a penitentiary in Florida. He joins a school bus of camouflage artists tracking across the southern part of the United States. It's like an inverse freedom ride. Stag-o-Lee has lost his hat, he's hatless in this new environment.'

A number of remixes of 'Devils Haircut' were commissioned, with the most radical being Mickey P.'s 'American Wasteland' take on the song. Mixed to sound like it was recorded live in concert, it begins with the end of a hardcore thrash song; a bit of crowd noise is then heard before someone announces, 'This next song is called "American Wasteland".' A high-speed version of 'Devils Haircut' follows, with extra guitar and bass added for good measure. The song ends abruptly, with another track, 'Go To Hell', starting up as it fades out. Beck has actually played the 'American Wasteland' version of 'Devils Haircut' live on occasion.[36]

'Devils Haircut' was just one of a number of songs to receive the remix treatment, with the majority of them released as B-sides—a reflection, perhaps, of the fact that Beck felt that 'none of them were very good'. One, by Tricky, 'sounded like he just turned on this drum machine that was falling apart and left the room while my vocal track was playing somewhere in the background. I think it was meant to be a diss.'

Another more promising effort was held up by clearance issues. 'We're still trying to find Lloyd Price to get clearance for the samples The Dust Brothers used on the "Where It's At" remix. It sounds much better than the original version.'[37]

131

In the meantime, he found much more of a kinship with the world of hip-hop. 'The more hip-hop artists I meet,' he explained, 'the more I find they're down with me. I've never made any effort to put on anything that I'm not. You know, I don't come from suburbia, so I'm not some suburban kid puttin' it on. On some levels, I relate to it, but I definitely make it my own and I don't try to imitate it. But I'm always surprised. I've had people from South Central come up to me and say, *Oh, man, we're all down with your shit, all the brothers are rocking your album.* They're pretty open-minded, most of the hip-hop community, and they're much more aware than people give them credit for. They're tuned in.'

* * *

Following on from his spot on *Modern Rock Live,* Beck made three more radio appearances in June. He showed up on KOME in San Jose to play 'Jack-ass' and 'Curses', and then provided a commentary on a number of tracks from *Odelay* for KROQ alongside a DJ who seemed to find everything about the interview and the album immensely hilarious. Finally, he returned to his spiritual radio home: KCRW's *Morning Becomes Eclectic* with Chris Douridas. He played a few solo tunes—the highlight of which was a version of 'Jack-ass' for acoustic guitar and harmonica—and talked about the album's cover art and a bit about his family history. After that, it was time to put together a new band and hit the road.

The *Odelay* tour kicked off on June 27 at the Galaxy in Santa Ana, California. Beck was keen for the whole presentation to be more of a high-profile affair than the *Mellow Gold* shows, and arranged for some elaborate costume changes and choreographed dance moves. 'I get all my moves from Hong Kong movies, Mexican TV, and Arabic TV,' he told *Spin* for the magazine's January 1997 issue. 'They have really good moves on Arabic TV, especially on the pop-music variety shows.'

For the encore, he would return in a rhinestone-encrusted Nudie suit. 'I actually rented those Nudie suits,' he recalled. 'They cost anywhere from $6,000 to $20,000. I couldn't afford them at the time, so I found a place that rented them. They had two suits that fit me perfectly—they looked like they were made for me. The reference was really more of a country thing.' Explaining the thoughts behind his choice of costume, he added, 'The suit makes me feel kinda feminine, kinda weird. It's shining and silly, and I enjoy it. I always fantasised about having one when I was younger. I was very much enamoured of 1950s country & western, Hank Snow, Hank Williams—they had amazing suits.' More often than not, however, the point was missed, and another connection drawn instead. 'People started to take it as an Elvis thing, so I retired them.'

Beck also reshuffled his pack of touring musicians, adding Justin Meldal-Johnsen on bass, Greg 'Smokey' Hormel on guitar, and Theo Mondle on keyboards, while retaining Joey Waronker (fresh from honeymooning in the Caribbean) on drums. He gave them all stage names, with Meldal-Johnsen rechristened 'Shotgun', Hormel becoming 'Smokestack', Waronker taking on the name 'Showboat', and Mondle now known as 'Hound Dog'.

Asked about the various personnel changes, Beck described the new line-up as his most cohesive band to date. 'I've played with four different bands, because I started this whole thing on my own and a band was an afterthought. I finally hipped myself to what I needed from a band, and I hooked up with a great ensemble. And these cats are all riding the same wave. Before, it was like one person was on the beach, another was getting pulled out by a riptide, one was bodysurfing, and another one was being eaten by eels. I was the lifeguard trying to rescue myself at that point.'

He had also begun to tire of the revolving door policy that seemed to have characterised his previous bands. 'My last bass player joined Elastica, my last guitar player joined Porno For Pyros, the axe-man before him is in The Presidents Of The United States Of America. My band's like a quarantine farm team—we spay and neuter people to go on to other bands.'

Of the new recruits, very little is known about Theo Mondle except that he played keyboards, was in his forties, came from Bangladesh, and smoked a pipe. A little more is known about Justin Meldal-Johnsen. He had previously played with the LA band Medicine, appearing on the album *Her Highness* and co-writing one song, 'A Fractured Smile'. After leaving school, he had worked as a studio production co-ordinator, a position he went on to fill on several Beck recordings. He also played with Electric Company, Tori Amos, Amnesia, and Pet before joining Beck's band.

The other new member, Greg Hormel, had almost become Beck's guitarist in the early spring of 1995 before the Lollapalooza tour. Like Beck, he came from a musical background. 'My mother was a ballerina, and her grandfather was a classical pianist,' he explained. 'My dad played piano, as did his brother—who is the guy who invented Spam. My uncle was a jazz pianist/recording pioneer—one of the early multi-track experimenters. He owned a studio called Village Recorders. Steely Dan, The Band, and Fleetwood Mac worked there in the 70s. I fell into playing guitar and drums.'

Hormel moved from the West Coast to New York to study as an actor and work as a waiter in the early 1980s, but after that didn't work out he returned to Los Angeles, where a chance meeting would change the course of his performing career. 'In LA, in 1985, I met Paul Greenstein, who had a western swing band called the Radio Ranch Straight Shooters. He asked me to join. We opened for X and The Knitters. We had a fifteen-year-old drummer named Joey Waronker—it was his first band, and he was just incredible. He was a neighbour of my parents, and I became his friend. He was so young that we couldn't play clubs with him.'

The Radio Ranch Straight Shooters didn't have an explosive recording career. In fact it amounted to just one song, 'The Next Big Thing', on a country compilation called *The Hollywood Round-Up*. They also made a brief appearance on the MTV show *The Cutting Edge*.

The following year, Hormel was invited to join The Blasters following the death of guitarist Hollywood Fats. Smokey agreed, and frontman Bill Bateman set about teaching him to play the blues. He played with the band from 1988 until 1992, which proved to be a relatively successful period for the band. 'We toured Europe in 1991,' Hormel recalled, 'and had especially big followings in Italy and Scandinavia.'

After Hormel left The Blasters, he and Joey Waronker formed The Lotus Eaters, which proved to be an industrious undertaking:

We were going to do this ambitious thing of playing as an improvising ensemble. We would accompany spoken word artists. We did a few performances, and then Joey left with Beck. I auditioned for Beck in 1995, but I was booked for a Bruce Willis tour of Planet Hollywoods. Beck just couldn't make up his mind in time, so I just left with Bruce Willis. Beck's song 'Loser' was already a million-seller, but the Bruce Willis gig was in Jakarta, which was a really exciting exotic place that I wanted to see. I think Beck wasn't able to take his music seriously yet. I think he was intimidated by good musicians. He felt like I was a really good musician. At the time, I thought he just didn't think I was good enough. It worked out, because that tour was a disaster for Beck.

While 'disaster' might be a tad too strong a description of the 1995 tour, it had indeed prompted Beck to change his touring band for the third time in as many years, with Joey Waronker once again the only survivor. Before long, though, it became apparent that Beck and Hormel had very similar ideals about sound and the presentation of songs. 'I always loved the feedback thing,' Hormel explained, 'because I grew up on Hendrix. Beck is surprisingly traditional in his musical mind. He comes from a country/blues background. When he was a kid, he taught himself to play like Mississippi John Hurt. He listened to a lot of Jimmie Rogers, so we have that in common.'

When the two got together for the second time, Beck put Hormel through his paces. 'I wasn't very familiar with the experimental guitar players, like Sonic Youth, which Beck was into, but I learned what to play by copying it off the record. Beck likes things a little *off* and sloppy. On some songs, I'll even detune the guitar to get that vibe, approaching it like a non-player.'

These roles were reversed, however, when it came to some of the choreographed onstage routines. 'It's pretty collaborative,' said Hormel, who would bring in videos of old soul TV shows. 'I had Jackie Wilson and James Brown on *Shindig!* We would work on that. Beck's a good dancer.'

The results of these video lessons would soon be seen in the promo for 'The New Pollution', as well as onstage during songs like 'Devils Haircut'.

The enterprising Joey Waronker was the longest-serving member of the ensemble, and as such might well have felt disappointed that most of the drum work on *Odelay* had passed him by. This would sometimes spread over to the live shows, too: 'We had all of the things that we thought may need to be looped on separate tracks. We'd start with stuff that I could imitate, and erase it. Then we'd erase stuff that anyone else could imitate, and sometimes we were left with just a click track and a few weird things, so it's as organic as possible. Sometimes we would strip everything away, so we wouldn't have to use a click track at all.'

The overall show became so diverse that, as Waronker put it, any musicians playing this material would have to be able to change styles with little or no effort. 'Beck's whole thing is so diverse, so he needs musicians who can go from the hip-hop thing to more poppy stuff, to punk, to folk, to country. All of which he does pretty beautifully. There just aren't that many musicians who can do that. The challenge has just been to do it all and make it sound cool. That's taken a long time.'

He was forgiving, though, about being left out of the recording process. 'The records are really well conceived, and made in a certain way, for a reason. And right now, I'm intrigued by watching Beck work because I feel like there's something important going on. I'm not thinking, *I'm a drummer and I need to express myself.* Which I question from time to time, like, *Wait a minute. I AM a drummer! I should be in a rock band, playing everything.* I would like to be better represented on an album, but it's sort of a weird time.'

Beck's next album, *Mutations*, would be produced in a more traditional way, recorded live in the studio with the whole band and little or no studio trickery. Waronker was not totally excluded on *Odelay*, though, as he added drums to two tracks and percussion to three more. To fill in his free time, he worked as a session drummer for a number of other acts, including Smashing Pumpkins, R.E.M., Walt Mink, and Elliott Smith.

If you were to closely examine the difference between the recorded *Odelay* songs and their live counterparts, you'd see—or rather hear—

Waronker add new things to the song that a machine couldn't do, night after night. 'I feel that Beck and I have a really good rapport,' he told me. 'As a musician, what I want to achieve with this band is to be able to read minds. I think that's the best way to be. So I put all my energy into trying to figure out what Beck's going for, and just trust that I will interpret that and make it better.'

The initial part of the *Odelay* tour saw Beck playing European festivals, sometimes early in the evening, with a time slot that allowed only for a shortened set. One of these was the Phoenix Festival in Stratford, England, which was filmed for TV broadcast. 'It's a very medieval scene here,' Beck recalled with a laugh. 'Y'know, bodies passed out, and refuse and debris all about. Human specimens of all sizes and forms. I can't imagine after four days of this what the derangement of consciousness will be.'

One of the new band's first headlining shows was at Amsterdam's Club Paradiso on July 21, which gave a stronger idea of how the rest of the tour would shape up. The band started out with a triple whammy of 'Fuckin' With My Head', 'Devils Haircut', and 'Novacane' before settling into the rhythm of slow-quiet songs followed by loud-fast songs, followed by an acoustic interlude that included 'Truckdrivin' Neighbors Downstairs', 'No Money, No Honey', 'Puttin' It Down', and 'Rowboat'.

They would follow this basic framework throughout the tour, with a few refinements. Beck took the opportunity during the tour to use a lot of seafaring imagery and quotations. He would often wear an old-fashioned sailor's jacket and peaked cap onstage—sometimes smoking a pipe, too— and would give monologues about how 'the seafaring aspect is the theme of the tour we're embarking on now. With storm clouds on the rise we will sail headlong, and headstrong, and headless, if need be, toward that destination.' (On another occasion, talking about the genesis of *Odelay*, he said, 'The beats came forth, surged like a wave, and on that crest a rhythm was born.')

In August 1996, the band set sail across the USA and Canada. On August 20, *Mojo* magazine sent a reporter to write a two-page review of a show in Buffalo, New York. 'He displays the confidence in the power of *Odelay* to kill the curse of "Loser" by trotting out his signature song barely a third of the way into the set,' the review noted. 'It's an act of dismissal, and it catches the crowd off guard.' The reviewer did though go on to question the power of the live show compared to the album. 'The quartet assembled for this tour do a reasonable job of approximating the patchwork, but they aren't yet capable of providing the dimension that's always missing when studio wizardry hits the road.' This was a criticism that held some water—particularly early on in the tour—but one that fell away as the months passed, and especially following the addition of DJ Swamp to the line-up after Christmas.

A permanent record of the summer tour was made on August 22 in Toronto, when MuchMusic TV filmed its the *OdeBeck* special. Ten songs were taped, of which eight were from the new album.

On September 1, Beck played what started out as a solo acoustic performance at the tiny Maxwell's in Hoboken, New Jersey. In what would become known as a show for the ages, he worked his way through his back catalogue, taking numerous requests from the audience on the proviso that 'It's got to be something I can play on acoustic guitar. I've never heard of half of those songs!' The set included 'Girl Dreams', 'Painted Eyelids', and an early version of 'Cold Brains'. Then, after 'One Foot In The Grave', he invited 'The Three *S*s'—Showboat, Stagecoach, and Smokestage—out from the audience for a full-band rendition of 'Painted Eyelids'. Money Mark then joined the fray on keyboards.

'We've been on the road for about two months, three months, six months,' Beck declared. 'We've been on the road for about three decades, but now we're going back in time.' Sterling performances of 'Ramshackle' and 'Rowboat' were followed by a beautiful version of 'Totally Confused', which Beck aptly introduced by saying, 'We've been on the road for about three minutes.' He then rounded off the evening with an amazing solo medley of 'Pay No Mind', 'I Get Lonesome', 'Truckdrivin' Neighbors Downstairs', 'Alcohol', 'Cyanide Breath Mint', 'Painted Eyelids', and 'Fuckin' With My Head', jumping between songs and lyrics with consummate ease. 'Man!' he declared at the end of the seven-minute segment, to rapturous applause. 'That wasn't a medley, that was an orgy!'

After the New Jersey show, Back hung out in the Big Apple for a week before making his network TV debut on *Late Show With David Letterman*, performing 'Where It's At'. Two weeks later, he was back on the road, starting in the South and gradually working his way back to the West Coast by mid October. One new song now becoming a regular part of these shows was 'I Wanna Get With You (And Your Sister Debra)', the title of which would later be simplified to 'Debra'. This classic slow jam proved to some that Beck could be more of a 'white Prince' than just his size and work-rate indicated: this falsetto tale of his obsession with 'Jenny from J.C. Penny' and her sister Debra could easily have been written by The Artist Formerly Known As. He had apparently recorded the song for *Odelay* but left it off at the last minute. (It wouldn't fit the mood of *Mutations*, either, but eventually showed up on *Midnite Vultures*.)

The Prince comparisons continued after *Odelay*, and for good reason— and would of course intensify following the release of *Midnite Vultures*. Both artists are known for being prolific and extremely talented; each is a gifted multi-instrumentalist who can work in a variety of different musical environments. But while Prince is too often hemmed into the admittedly brilliant trademark sound of his keyboard-driven rock/pop/funk hybrid, Beck has been able to change his 'sound' easily from album to album, never staying in one musical place long enough for it to become stale. Another difference is Beck's ability to mix his often-eclectic influences into the body of a single song. Prince has managed this too, on occasion, but Beck has a far wider range of genres at his disposal—adding blues, country, mariachi, Latino, and folk music to Prince's grab bag of funk, rap, pop, and rock. (I don't recall hearing too many Prince harmonica solos that can match Beck's on 'One Foot In The Grave'.)

Back on tour, a two-week trip to Japan was followed by another visit to Europe. To hype up the British dates, *Melody Maker* sent a reporter to Tokyo, where Beck was in the midst of a four-night stand, to interview him and review the live show before it hit the UK in December. The hype

139

grew further in November with the release of 'Devils Haircut' as a single, complete with a UK-only remix by Oasis's Noel Gallagher, who gushed that 'Beck's a hero of mine—hopefully there'll be more collaborations in the future'.[38]

As the UK dates approached, the bootleggers of the world united to produce a litany of live CDs from his European shows. The show at the Cirkus in Stockholm gave rise to a bootleg of the same name that came with four CD-ROM video tracks, while Beck's performance at Le Bataclan in Paris produced the CD *Loser*, which includes a rare live rendition of 'Derelict'.

The *Odelay* tour made its UK indoor debut at the Academy in Manchester on December 9. In one of the more energetic shows of the tour so far, Beck dedicated 'Thunderpeel' to 'All the Spice Girls and Spice Boys'. *Q* magazine gave the show a two-page review, concluding that it was 'stunning'. 'Crowds in Germany or France, say, take a little more time to loosen up,' Beck told the magazine. 'Here, the audience go the full distance. It's very rewarding to have that connection when you're onstage.'

This near hysteria continued the following night at London's Brixton Academy. The show was broadcast live on BBC Radio 1 and reportedly attended by members of Oasis, Pulp, Blur, Elastica, and other figures from the Britpop community, all of whom were blown away (albeit only by the music, and not by a leaf-blower). Once again, the performance was captured by bootleggers, and issued on CD as *Swinging London*.

A hectic six months came to an end with a couple of Christmas radio performances, first for KROQ's *Almost Acoustic Christmas* in Los Angeles and then as part of LIVE 105's show at the Cow Palace just outside San Francisco, on a bill that also included The Beastie Boys. *Rolling Stone* decided in their year-end issue that 'Beck is rock'n'roll's man of the year—even if he only looks twelve.' It was only one of the many awards bestowed upon Beck at the end of 1996. Others included album of the year awards from *NME*, the *Village Voice*, *Spin*, and *Rolling Stone*, as well as artist of the year notices from the latter pair, and high commendations from *Alternative Press* and *Melody Maker*. Not such a loser, then, after all.

'You hear it and it instantly attacks your immune system.' (1997)

Ronald Keys Jr. was driving his street-sweeper along the roads of Cleveland, Ohio, for a living when he first heard 'Loser' on the radio. Right away, he could imagine how he might enhance parts of the song with some turntable scratching. 'I heard the song ["Loser"] and immediately had a vision of working with him,' he explained. 'I had never heard scratching on the rock station before and I was already a battle DJ that had won several DJ contests. I was a hip-hop head, but I looked like I belonged in a rock band, and maybe this was something I was going to fit in with.'

Keys had been working on his DJ act and entering local competitions, and then, in 1996, he won the US DMC Championships as DJ Swamp.[39] When he heard Beck was going to be in Cleveland, he hatched a plan to meet him. He compiled a cassette of himself scratching on various Beck tracks and blagged his way backstage under the premise of doing an interview. Three months later, he got a call and was invited to Los Angeles for five days of rehearsals.

'He had already seen me on MTV and knew who I was. He couldn't have found a DJ better than me at the time and I had the credentials to back it up. I ended up with Beck, Kid Rock, and Insane Clown Posse all wanting me to be their DJ at the same time, and I chose Beck. I was ready the first day, and I knew exactly what I was supposed to do. Beck said he had never had a new band member so prepared.'

Before Long, DJ Swamp was performing with the band at the 1997 Grammy Awards, with numerous other highlights to follow over a short space of time. 'Saturday Night Live, parties with famous people, staying in castles and crazy stuff like that, Japan, Australia, all those European festivals—there were so many highlights really. I really got to soak it up and have more fun than anybody else. I was the youngest, single and crazy as hell.' During Beck's shows, the rest of the band would exit the stage at the end of the main set and leave Swamp to entertain the crowd. 'It was a serious challenge to win over those crowds that had never seen turntablism before. I had to keep it very visual and rocking to demonstrate the turntable as an actual instrument in the band, but also it was so Beck and the other band members had time to change outfits and come back fully charged up for an encore.'

Joey Waronker in particular was pleased to have DJ Swamp in the band. 'It's a little like playing with a drum machine,' he explained. 'Because of the sounds and because he's coming from such a hip-hop background. He's used to turntables and drum machines. It's a whole different feel, so I find myself adjusting and playing more drum machine-type beats. But he also plays a lot of weird sounds, atmospheric stuff, a lot like a percussionist.'

The difference was felt in songs like 'Sissyneck', 'Jack-ass' and 'Where It's At', which all felt like they had had new life breathed into them. 'I think at first, Swamp really didn't consider himself a musician,' Waronker noted at the time, 'and now he's realising that he has this rhythmic gift and a sense of dynamics … in this band, he's being forced to be more of a percussionist.'

With this new line-up in place, Beck started the year by making his *Saturday Night Live* debut, playing 'Where It's At' and 'Devils Haircut' and taking part in a short comedy sketch with Kevin Spacey and Michael Palin. He stayed on in New York to play a show at the Roseland Ballroom before going home to play two songs at the Radio Free LA benefit on January 20: Woody Guthrie's 'I Ain't Got No Home In This World Anymore' and a rarity of his own, 'Don't You Mind People Grinnin' In Your Face'.

The *Odelay* tour got back into full flow in early February, with Beck mixing things up not just with the addition of DJ Swamp but also by bringing some old favourites and new songs into the set. In Vancouver, for instance, he added 'Alcohol', 'Canceled Check', a new version of 'Ozzy', and 'Don't You Mind People Grinnin' In Your Face'; in Oregon, he plucked 'Sleeping Bag' and 'Fume' from obscurity.

The tour took a temporary break after the show in Las Vegas on February 21 as Beck flew out to New York for the Grammy Awards. He had previously been nominated in the Best Male Rock Vocal Performance category for 'Loser'; this time around, he walked away with two awards, Best Alternative Music Performance for *Odelay* and Best Male Rock Vocal Performance for 'Where It's At'. For a while, though, he didn't even realise he'd been nominated. 'Nobody called, because everyone assumed I knew,' he told *Entertainment Weekly*. 'For about a day, I remember walking around not knowing. Someone in line at the supermarket congratulated me. I said, *Thanks. That's nice.* It was a little surreal but it feels good to be validated, to be acknowledged. For a while, I was one of the scapegoats for the whole slacker-Generation X thing. Somehow the perception changed, and I'm grateful.'

Of course, an event like the Grammys brings out millions of photographers from all manner of magazines, not just ones those dedicated to music. In the aftermath of the awards show, Beck's face was splashed across a myriad of publications. One shot that was used many times over showed him backstage with his father, David Campbell. Beck had rarely spoken about him in the press, and the fact that he had changed his name to Hansen hinted at some kind of falling out between the two. If this was the case, the two must have reconciled, as it transpired that Campbell was to add string arrangements to some of Beck's upcoming B-sides. Campbell also spoke publicly about his son for the first time, telling the *LA Times*, 'It's not surprising at all that he got to create all this brilliant work. The thing that is amazing to me is that he's managed to bring so much of the world into what he does. It's not your average stuff.'

'He always had an ear for the weirder harmonies,' Beck later said of his father. 'That's probably what he passed to me.' It was also apparent that Campbell was still working as hard as ever. 'I'm a monk,' he joked. 'You have these spurts where you go to do a session; you're active and social. But the rest of the time, you're there with a blank computer screen. Eight and twelve-hour days, just sitting there writing, just on my own with no interplay, feedback … anything.' The hard work was paying off, though. At one point during 1997, Campbell's arrangements featured on eleven albums of Billboard 200, including the soundtracks to *Armageddon* and *City of Angels*, and records by Hole and The Goo Goo Dolls.

As well as being photographed with his father, Beck was accompanied to the Grammys by his long-time girlfriend, Leigh Limon, and would open up about their relationship a little bit. 'I've been living with my girlfriend for about five years now,' he said. 'She comes along with me for the good tours, because you need a little stability to deal with all the chaos. There's a lot of patience required. Obviously, occasionally she pulls out her AK and puts a few caps in my ass, but mainly it's good— we're a team. It's not some kind of tug-of-war.'

Leigh looked almost like a female Beck, slightly shorter than him, slight of frame, and stylishly dressed. 'She knew me when I was a penniless nothing,' he revealed. 'She liked me long before anybody else did. And that's important. I mean, like any relationship, you have your work, and you talk about work, and if something's fucked up, your partner will comfort you.'

As usual Beck was surprised even to be considered for an award, let alone win one. 'I never had any expectations of winning a Grammy,' he said. 'It wasn't something I was set on, that I was hoping and praying and starving for. But it is incredible!' He also felt that recent acceptance by Grammy voters of more innovative artists had worked in his favour. 'I do think they're opening the umbrella a little bit to include stuff that isn't standard Grammy fare. On the other hand, I think in my case, I'm somewhat of a traditionalist to them. I'm working from a place that maybe someone who came up on folk rock or singer/songwriter stuff can relate to. Maybe that's it.'

On the back of these honours, Beck jetted over to London for an appearance on *TFI Friday*, where he played his new single 'The New Pollution' and was filmed dropping a rubber chicken into a giant cooking pot (don't ask why). He also picked up a BRIT Award, for Best International Male, beating Bryan Adams, Prince, Babyface, and Robert Miles. While in the UK, he took advantage of his schedule to play a couple of shows, at London's Kilburn National and Cardiff University, before flying back to Florida to continue the tour.

Beck continued on the road through March and April 1997, culminating in a show at the Universal Amphitheatre in Los Angeles on April 25. It had been a busy but exciting few months. 'So much air-travel can be like an endurance test,' he explained. 'Your fingernails disappear pretty quickly, and so do the fingernails of your soul. Tom Waits reckons that if you fly somewhere it takes a couple of days for your soul to catch up, and I know what he means. If there had been an evolutionary build-up to aeroplanes, it would be different. We could have done with at least another thousand years of hang-gliding. But I'm into refining the show as much as possible, so I guess it's cool.' He also noted 'an incredible cross-section of people' in attendance at his shows. 'Like, total dreadlocked, space rocker guys, White Zombie-lookin' dudes, Korean businessmen, little teenybopper kids, and old blues fans—it's pretty sick.'

If sickness were to be judged on this criterion, things would only get sicker, as Beck flew back across the Atlantic for his longest UK tour to date. Before he got down to business, he stopped by Jools Holland's *Later* TV show to perform three songs, 'Devils Haircut', 'Jack-ass', and 'Sissyneck'. The last of these was released as a single to tie in with live dates in Manchester, Birmingham, London, Nottingham, Glasgow, and Newcastle.

After a few more US dates, he then played a surprise acoustic set in Los Angeles on June 12, on the occasion of the premiere of his friend Steve Hanft's film *Kill The Moonlight*. Beck played 'Leave Me On The Moon', one of his contributions to the soundtrack, plus 'Rowboat' and covers of Jimmie Rodgers's 'Waitin' For A Train' and The Doors' 'Light My Fire'.

After a short break, his next show was a big one: the Glastonbury

Festival. As is typical for Glastonbury, the site was deep in mud when Beck arrived for his set on the opening Friday. On a main stage bill headlined by the Prodigy, he had to follow Phish, Echo & The Bunnymen, Terrorvision, and The Levellers. The last of these bands had received a severe pelting of mud bombs during their set, and Beck feared the worst. As it turned out, though, he needn't have worried, because after a few early shots, the crowd got into his set to such an extent that by the time he started 'One Foot In The Grave' the whole site was clapping along. The show was broadcast in part by the BBC, and reviewed by Andrew Male the next day in the *Glastonbury Daily*, which was distributed on site. 'Wild, filthy, and downright stupid, Beck's was the perfect Glastonbury performance,' Male concluded. 'And the rhinestone suit remained perfectly clean.' Rare praise indeed.

More festival appearances followed before Beck hooked up with the middle leg of the HORDE ('Horizons of Rock Developing Everywhere') tour alongside Neil Young, Kula Shaker, Blues Traveller, Ben Folds Five, Morphine, and several other B- and C-list indie bands. After several years through the 1990s as a poor man's Lollapalooza this touring festival finally bit the dust in 1999.

Another high-profile appearance ensued at the Bizarre Festival in Cologne, Germany. The show was broadcast on the *Rockpalast* TV show and turned up on the *Pulling Up Roots* bootleg. Beck then flew back to the UK—for about the hundredth time in twelve months, or so it seemed—to play at the V97 festivals in Leeds and Chelmsford.

The first week of September saw the release of the final single from *Odelay*, 'Jack-ass'. The CD featured several versions of the title song, plus 'Burro', a Mariachi version sung in Spanish. The same week also saw a trio of TV appearances, the first of which was a return to David Letterman's *Late Show* to perform 'Jack-ass'. He then stopped by the MTV Video Music Awards to perform 'The New Pollution' and pick up several awards for it and 'Devils Haircut'. The final stop was at the *Sessions At West 54th* studios for a live taping of fifteen songs. 'This'll be our last show until next year,' he declared, although there were in fact a few more still to go. A few weeks later, Beck and his band made an appearance at the Farm Aid benefit in Illinois, which included a duet with Willie Nelson on 'Peach Pickin' Time In Georgia'.

As 1997 drew to a close, Beck contributed 'Deadweight' to the soundtrack to *A Life Less Ordinary*, taking the opportunity to display another style he had mastered: the Brazilian bossa nova sound of early-70s South American acts like Os Mutantes. 'It's one of those things where you hear it and it instantly attacks your immune system until you're completely at its mercy,' he explained. 'It has all the elements: the groove, the beats, and an insane melodic flair.' (He would continue to experiment with the genre on 'Tropicalia', the first single from his next album, *Mutations*.)

In the fall, Beck's keen dress sense was honoured when he was named Most Fashionable Artist at the VH1 1997 Fashion Awards, where he gave one of the most entertaining acceptance speeches of all time:

Thank you VH1 people for embracing my appearance and bestowing this award, certifying the apparel and accoutrements which have clothed me this past season as measuring up to the stringent standards upheld in this arena of style. With gratitude, I claim this award and dedicate it to those who have aided me in breaking the fashion barrier: namely Leigh Limon for her impeccable guidance

Whether I am attired in uniform or civilian clothes,
buckskins or bloomers,
kimonos or cat socks,
lingerie or long johns;
cerements or tube socks,
espadrilles or chapeau,
loincloth or poncho,
skivvies or layette;
gabardine or crash helmet,
dashiki or camisole,
sombrero or tutu;

147

jackboots or skullcap,
codpiece or ascot,
Members Only jacket or Yashmac
whether naked or arrayed in the finest livery
I will strive to be worthy of this shimmering ideal
and scrape brute yet fondly on this zig-zag rampart.
Thank you.

Beck's last two live performances of the year—both of which took place at the El Rey Theater in Los Angeles—were totally out of character with the shows he'd been playing out for the past eighteen months. The first was a country show, featuring classics like 'Redball' and 'Peach Pickin' Time In Georgia' mixed in with Beck songs like 'Rowboat' and 'Sissyneck'. He also took the opportunity to play a selection of as-yet-unrecorded songs, some old, some new, including 'Cold Brains', 'Static', and 'Dead Melodies', all of which would be released within twelve months.

The final show was a surprise, as Beck turned up as the opening act for Bob Dylan—a somewhat ironic combination, considering the comparisons that had been made between the two over the years. Once again, he played a few songs that would soon crop up on *Mutations*, including 'Cold Brains', 'Sing It Again', 'Dead Melodies', and 'Nobody's Fault But My Own'.

It is perhaps not an exaggeration to say that, for Beck and his fellow musicians, producing and touring *Odelay* had grown into a mission in itself—a mission to open people's ears to a kind of music that didn't follow the usual rules and formulas. '*Odelay* was not an easy record to put over to people,' he later explained. 'It took two and a half years touring, and most of that time we were trying to convince people every night that they actually like this music. Not following a formula or jumping on a current sound is definitely a bit more work.'

Christmas 1997 saw Beck's star rise even higher. In the UK, *Melody Maker* named him as the Best Solo Artist of the year, an award he also won at the *NME* Brat Awards. In the USA, *Spin* readers voted Beck as both

Best Artist and Best Male Singer. The most outlandish award, however, came from *Select* magazine, the December 1997 issue of which put Beck at the top of a list of the 100 Most Important People In The World (the Dust Brothers made it in to #29). The magazine also included a three-track Beck CD containing 'Clock', 'The Little Drum Machine Boy', and 'Totally Confused'. Beck himself was unsure about being dubbed 'the coolest man in the world', however:

> I'm not really conscious of people saying that. If anything, I'd be the first to refute it. I'm willing to make a fool of myself, if that defines coolness. I really don't give much of a shit about how I'm perceived or about trying to fit into the matrix of a market place or tastes. I just go on a more instinctual level. Cool is something that's foreign to me. Maybe I should move to London, then I can soak up the glory. In LA, like in any hometown, you're rejected. I'll go to a club here and it's, 'Oh yeah, that guy.' I've been around forever. These are people who saw me playing coffee houses, smashing my phone machine onstage, doing some random act in a local club—they take me for granted.

At the turn of the year, it was reported that the Miller Brewing Company had offered to pay $10,000 to use fifteen seconds of 'Where It's At' in an ad, but Beck declined—and continued to do so even after the offer was allegedly raised to $100,000. Instead, he headed out to Sydney, Australia, to see in the New Year with some well-earned rest and relaxation. At least that's what everyone thought.

CHAPTER 12

'We had to run out in the rain and put him in a town car.' (1998)

Over the years, Beck had employed a series of backing musicians to help on tour and in the studio, the line-up shifting from song to song depending on the style he wanted to play. By 1998, however, he had hit upon a more settled line-up, and with plans to record his next album live in the studio, it made sense for him to use the group of musicians who he'd taken around the world and back for the *Odelay* dates.

The problem for the musicians, though, was that they had no job security. Beck might choose to take a long break, or decide not to tour at all—or, if he did, he might take a different direction, in which case they'd be out of work anyway. Drummer and percussionist Joey Waronker was one band member who kept his options open. He had already been approached by Smashing Pumpkins, and in fact played on a couple of tracks on their *Adore* album, but then the Beck *Odelay* shows kept coming, and he had to turn down a tour with them. Before Beck made firm plans to make a new record, Waronker had accepted the chance to tour with R.E.M. Fortunately, he was able to find time to do both. 'The R.E.M. guys were willing to work around Beck's schedule, which I couldn't believe,' he recalled.

Before work began on the new album, however, there were a few more shows to play. There were also a couple of changes to the previous touring line-up, with keyboard player Theo Mondle replaced by Roger

Manning Jr. (not to be confused with the other Roger Manning from the anti-folk scene of the late 80s).[40] After a few weeks of rehearsals, he was given the stage name Shotgun and bundled down under with the rest of the crew, which included two further additions: the horn-playing duo of David Brown and David Ralickie, aka The Brass Menagerie, who were invited to join the band fulltime after previously making several one-off guest appearances.[41]

Beck and his revamped band played a New Year's Eve show on the beach at the Bondi Pavilion in Sydney, followed by two days at the amusingly titled Mudslinger Festival in Perth on January 3–4 and then a 1,400-mile hop to Adelaide for a show on the January 6. Then, after playing two shows in Melbourne, on January 8 and 9, they spent the next four days travelling up the eastern coast of Australia for dates in Sydney and Brisbane, before flying down to New Zealand for two more shows. Finally, after playing the Wellington Town Hall on January 18, the *Odelay* tour was over, after twenty long months.

Beck was in no mood for resting, however. Having spent the previous two years touring the same songs, he was desperate to record some new material. 'It had been three years since I recorded *Odelay*,' he explained. 'I was restless and anxious to get back in the studio and do something creative. I had just gotten off my tour, and I knew I wanted to work with Nigel [Godrich], who happened to be in LA on somebody else's album.'

Godrich had in fact run into Beck's management at an Oasis gig in the city. 'The next day, I got a phone call,' he explained. 'Basically, Beck wanted to do a record with his band, because he'd never really recorded with them, and he was trying to figure out who to get as a producer. And they'd sort of mentioned my name, but they thought that it was a bit of a long shot to fly me out just to see if it would work. But then because I was in town, it was like it was all meant to happen. So basically I had a meeting with Beck, went round to his house and had a cup of tea and we sat and talked about stuff.'

Godrich had plans to return to the UK after a week, however, so there was no time to waste. He and Beck planned to spend a weekend together in the studio to see how they got along; if it worked out OK, Godrich would return a month later, for two weeks of album sessions. According to Beck, the sessions 'had to be very spontaneous and quick'. He had a good-sized collection of songs to choose from, many of which— like 'Dead Melodies' and 'Cold Brains'—predated *Odelay*. He decided to let Leigh Limon have a say in which tracks should be recorded for the album. 'In the weeks before the recording sessions, I played a number of older songs out of my notebook for my girlfriend, and let her decide which I should record. And she sort of said, *I like that one … and that one …* Other than that, I had no big plan.'

Godrich used the time before the session to get up to speed with Beck's previous work, and would admit to having previously developed a few misconceptions about him. 'He's very quiet and studied, and obviously very intelligent. For some reason, I actually thought he'd be a bit more aggressive and loud. All the kind of rap stuff on *Odelay* is pretty aggressive, but he's quite cerebral. I guess, as well, my exposure to him previously to that had only been the singles off *Odelay*. So I went away and listened to the whole of *Odelay* and thought, *Bloody hell, what does he want me to do?*'

For the trial studio sessions, Beck and Godrich booked the weekend of February 21–22 at Ocean Way (formerly the United Studio) on Sunset Boulevard. In its previous incarnation, the studio had been the scene of the recording of 1970s hits like 'Bridge Over Troubled Water', as well as numerous songs by The Beach Boys and The Mamas & The Papas.

Godrich was ecstatic about the choice of studio. 'Ocean Way is the best studio I've ever worked in,' he told *Melody Maker*. 'The desk was the forerunner to this American desk called an API—it was called a Delcon, and it was all gold. Basically it's a great studio, because the gear—as is the fashion—is fairly vintage, but everything works; it's maintained really well. It had quite a small control room and a very, very big live area with a separation booth, which we put the drums in.'

Beck's touring bandmates Smokey Hormel, Justin Meldal-Johnsen, Roger Manning, and Joey Waronker were all present, although DJ

Swamp's turntables were not required. The two songs attempted over the weekend were 'Cold Brains', which was pencilled in to be the album's opening track, and the old B-side 'Electric Music And The Summer People', which was due to be overhauled as a surf-style song. For Godrich, both tracks were complicated in their own way, and he thought that they would offer a good indication of how things might work out. '"Cold Brains" was the first thing we recorded, and we sort of finished that in a day,' he said. At the end if you listen carefully, you can hear Beck tell him, 'Yeah, I like that a lot.' The song is full of the references to death and decay that would litter the album, and would soon find its way to the head of Beck's setlist for the few gigs that he'd play in support of the album in early 1999.

Next up was the 'surfing version' of 'Electric Music And The Summer People'. According to Godrich, it was 'amazing, just completely over the top. It had this sitar solo and four keyboard solos, and huge timpani and stuff. It didn't make it onto the album, but it would be the kind of song that would be good for a film soundtrack. After that, we kind of looked at each other, and he said, *Hey, we could do an album in two weeks.*' (The song did in fact make it on to the Japanese version of the album, and would also feature on several of the CD EPs that came out the following year.)

The test run had been an unqualified success, and the scene was set. After returning briefly to England, Godrich flew back out to LA, with two weeks of sessions due to start on March 19. 'I like the challenge,' Beck said at the time. 'I like working with limitations.' In this case, however, he didn't have much choice in the matter. His band, too, had only a short time to prepare. A few nights of rehearsals at Beck's house and the songs they'd previously played live were all they had to go on. The song selection was still being refined right up until the last day of rehearsals, while Beck was still working on the lyrics in the early hours of March 19 in order to have them ready for when they all met at the studio.

In the time between the initial weekend trial session and the start of recording proper, Beck had decided to go for more of the traditional, singer-songwriter-type songs in the vein of 'Cold Brains', and less of the freaky

'Electric Music' material. 'Static' was the first song to be completed, and while Godrich was mixing it, Beck went back out into the studio to begin rehearsing the next song, 'O Maria', with the band. With Godrich taking only about an hour per mix, they soon fell into a rhythm of record, mix/rehearse, and repeat. To get the vaudeville feel for 'O Maria', they had to 'fuck up the piano sound', as Godrich put it, as they only had a grand piano. The song was recorded live, with the horns and Roger Manning Jr.'s Hammond organ dubbed afterward. 'Originally, the trombone solo—which is a particular favourite of mine—was at the end, and we did a bit of a hash edit that you can hear quite clearly to stick it in the middle.'

By the first Saturday, the band was playing so well that more and more of the material was simply recorded live. 'Sing It Again', for example, was recorded 'completely live, apart from one guitar overdub', according to Godrich. 'The vocal is live as well. We got a really good set-up going and he sang it really well. We did about four takes and I edited between three of them, I think. The drums were separated but the rest of them were literally in the same room, just all looking at each other. You get bits of sound bleeding between tracks, but it adds something … you get a sense that the people are in the same room. And he was singing so well. I could just sort of edit the track around his vocal. Even the guitar solo is live.'

The finished recording is a semi-waltz that features a great bit of guitar work by Smokey Hormel. Beck had originally written it for Johnny Cash, before putting it to one side until *Mutations* because, he felt, it was 'a piece of shit'. He couldn't have been more wrong.

One of the oldest songs the band attempted for the album was 'Canceled Check', and you can hear the lyrical progression from the early live versions to the final take that appears on the album. Beck had started writing the song in Japan, in August and September 1994, inspired by the motivational speaker Tony Robins. It was a story he told often onstage, before playing the song: late one night, he was trying to get to sleep in a hotel and channel-surfing Japanese TV when he stumbled on an English language channel that was showing an 'infomercial' by Robins, who, as usual, was expounding on the various 'easy' ways of making money and expanding real estate. 'The past is a cancelled check,' Robins claimed. 'Your maximum point of power is now.'

'The song just fit in with my life at the time,' Beck explained, 'and how certain things were at the time.' On returning to the USA in the autumn of 1994, he put it straight into his setlist for the rest of his tour. These early versions were musically identical to the final recording, but he would tweak the lyrics along the way.[42]

By the time the *Mutations* sessions were underway, producer Nigel Godrich had become more confident about putting his own ideas forward. He thought 'Canceled Check' was too smooth, and wanted a few imperfections to come to the surface, even if they were manufactured. 'We made everyone play with bags over their heads,' he recalled. 'The idea was to increase the chances of playing wrong notes, because the musicians were too proficient. We wanted to loosen up the feel, and it worked quite well, actually.' Once again, he altered the piano sound, this time to get a honky-tonk feel. 'We detuned the grand piano and stuck paper clips on the hammers to get that honky-tonk sound. Because most of the notes have three strings, if you detune one of them slightly flat, you get that kind of chorus-y sound. So that was a pretty straightforward backing track, and then everything was overdubbed on top.'

Beck had trouble finalising the song, so he and Godrich decided to get their money's worth from all the hired percussion instruments that were sitting unused in the back room of the studio. The lights were switched off, and everyone just let rip, throwing things around and generally making a heck of a racket—and after five years, the song was done.

Beck had fond memories of recording the song's car-crash ending:

We'd been recording very, very late into the night, and I couldn't figure out how to end the song—it needed some finality to it. We had this room full of percussion, piles and boxes of percussion, which we'd rented for the record and there was all kinds of crazy Brazilian stuff, stuff that looked like medical tools and handmade African stuff and timpani drums and all this stuff we hadn't got around to using. It was costing a lot of money, so I felt it was going to waste. So, in a moment of inspiration or idiocy—I don't know which—we all just descended into the room, we had the engineer turn on all the mics, and myself and the other musicians went crashing through the room. It was just a melee of 3am madness and it was a nice release—it was therapeutic, there were people flying through the air, and I think blood was drawn on at least one occasion.

The only single to come from the album, 'Tropicalia', recalls the Latin feel of 'Deadweight'. Beck would explain that it was the middle part of a Latin trilogy that he was working on. The band had trouble getting it right at first, but they eventually pulled it off memorably. It was the first time that Justin Meldal-Johnsen had played an upright bass, and Smokey Hormel struggled with the quica. According to Godrich, 'We got all the percussion going by getting everybody to do four sets of percussion with all the shakers and stuff lying around the studio. The vocal was difficult because it was so fast, and the breakdown was something that they figured out while rehearsing. So many things were happening so quickly.'

The lyrics reference the misery of waiting 'in big hotels' and living 'under an air conditioned sun'; according to Beck, the song 'covers the dichotomy and contrast between the fact that when these [immigrant] workers, who come from a culture which is very exotic and lively and exuberant, emigrate from Mexico or El Salvador to California, their life ends up being anything but exotic.'

The chaos that was building up in the studio—and the fast turnaround time required—was starting to cause problems. While the band were still working on 'Tropicalia', David Campbell arrived to arrange the strings for 'We Live Again', and with just an hour to go until the string players arrived, there was still no backing track for them to play to. Godrich had them bash one out in double time, saving everyone from even more confusion. 'In half an hour, we knocked out the backing track to that— harpsichord, upright bass, and acoustic and stuff,' he recalled. 'I had this

Scott Walker album that I was listening to, and I was just sort of thinking about the reverb they had on it, how amazingly over the top it is … that's why "We Live Again" has got so much reverb on it.'

With its lush string arrangement, 'We Live Again' is one of the most beautiful songs on an album full of beautiful songs. Manning's harpsichord and Meldal-Johnsen's upright bass are just perfect for the song, and Beck even managed to get in one of his favourite lines, 'Turns shit to gold'.

With the first week of recording almost over, there was still time to complete one more song. 'Dead Melodies' took just three hours from start to finish, with Joey Waronker playing on an improvised drum kit that included an ashtray and a petrol can. For Godrich, 'It was definitely that *children let loose in an expensive recording studio* vibe. It was slightly different for each song, but I ended up thinking, *Wow, this must be the way they used to make records.*'

Beck had previously played the song a few months back, in late 1997, when he supported Bob Dylan at the El Rey. Meldal-Johnsen's upright bass heightens the baroque feel of the recorded version, while the whole mood of the album is summed up in Beck's simple but atmospheric lyric. It became apparent as the sessions progressed that a theme was starting to appear: death, decay, failing relationships, misery.

'It's sort of a poetical crutch,' Beck explained. 'It's easier to write about things that are falling apart than things that are beautiful and perfect. That's the nature of creation; as soon as something is perfected and realised, it's immediately decaying and falling apart. That's part of the process, the first rule of the universe. But sure, a lot of these songs are blues songs, so I tend to look into that landscape. Maybe some of the lyrics are bleak, some of them are a comment on vacuousness—y'know, Disneyland is as much a wasteland as Death Valley is.'

He was keen to point out, though, that there was a sense of humour to the songs, too. 'Some of them are funny. There's a humour to "Cold Brains". I'm talking about a leg in the gravel and abandoned hearses and stuff like that. They're kind of silly, pseudo-romantic imagery. I guess they're more serious songs and I'd saved up enough of them to have an album's worth. Over time I think certain songs start grouping together, they pair off. It's like a party: you can invite a lot of different people, but certain people are just gonna stick to themselves.

The last weekend of recording saw some of the more pivotal songs put to tape—and it was tape they were using, in contrast to both Beck and Nigel Godrich's recent work. In this case, Godrich felt using tape would help with the overall scheme of getting the album done. 'I use computers and stuff as well,' he said, 'but with bands I prefer to cut the tape. With computers, you leave yourself with too many options, because you can undo everything. When you cut your tape, you're cutting it—you have to make a decision, and you can move forward. Being able to go back five steps is not necessarily a good thing for the creative process, y'know.'

'Nobody's Fault But My Own' is one of the album's most complex-sounding songs, but Godrich was once again unfazed by the processes involved. 'Beck had an idea for an Indian song, and he got in touch with these two guys who were Indian music freaks from some university. We cut that whole backing track pretty much live, which is why it's got that vibe. It's a big bass drum and Beck playing guitar and the Indian stuff … it all kind of went down together, and then we overdubbed more Indian stuff. I think that's probably the best song, because it's kind of got two choruses.'

The sitar comes and goes throughout the track—and, as Beck would point out shortly after the album's release, throughout his career to date. 'I've used a sitar on almost every record I've done,' he said. 'To me it's just a wonderful sound; it's evocative. A lot of times I try to get the guitar to get that sound of a sitar, that undulating drone. I tend to record a song with instruments playing all the way through, on every track, and then at the end of the day it's a matter of subtracting, taking things away, and opening up the space. That's why you only hear things in bits and pieces. It's tastier that way.'

The next song, 'Diamond Bollocks', is even tastier—and, even by Godrich's high standards, is a really accomplished piece of work. It's also totally out of keeping with the rest of the album, and its inclusion was in doubt right until the end, which perhaps explains why it appears as a bonus track on the US edition of the album but is listed as a regular track elsewhere. At one point, it was going to be the second song on the album. 'It would have been, like, get the listener all settled down and comfortable, then this would come along and get them in a headlock!' Beck recalled with a laugh.

'Diamond Bollocks' was also the only song on *Mutations* that was written in the studio. 'Beck had an idea that we wanted to do a bit of a rock opus,' Godrich explained. 'It was almost like, y'know, throw an idea into the machinery and see what comes out. We did four different sections of music with the intention of splicing them together. One of them turned out really cool, so we ended up making it longer and turning it into the verse. I spliced it and copied it and copied it again, so it's almost like a loop, but not quite. The beginning section is like a pastiche French thing with a harpsichord, and then the second section was like a spy thing, and then there was the acid rock section. Then he just wrote a melody over the top of it, but that one took nearly three days.'

The song's title came from a compliment that Beck received after a show in the UK, when someone came up to him and said something to the effect of, 'That was top bollocks, you diamond geezer.' Teasing the direction he would take on *Midnite Vultures*, Beck described the song in interviews around the times of *Mutations'* release as 'kind of a nice indicator of things to come'.

'Bottle Of Blues' is a straight-ahead bumping blues. It was completed in half a day, its straightforwardness summing up the overall approach to the album. 'There wasn't a lot of technology involved,' Beck explained. 'Just a simple tape machine. With these songs, I just didn't need to get bogged down in any technology. I'd written them on piano and guitar, they were more reflective. One of the reasons that I wanted to go back to this more traditional approach was that there are limitations with technology; there are so many possibilities, you get caught up in the possibilities, you can lose track of the moment.'

According to Godrich, 'Lazy Flies' started life the night before he had to head back to the UK. 'We worked until five in the morning, and that was just a double-tracked acoustic played to a percussion shaker thing that Joey was doing, and then he put the drums on afterward. We carried on working on it the next day, but we were so tired by the time he did the vocal.'

The last track to be completed was 'Runners Dial Zero', with Godrich subsequently explaining to the *NME* that the title was derived from a line they would often hear over the studio PA. 'You'd just hear "runners dial zero" all the time, and he didn't have a title for this last song, so that became it. It's a beautiful track, and basically we just got a flicked-up vocal sound and a flicked-up piano sound. I actually left before that was mixed—my cab turned up to take me to the airport.'

'I was doing vocals at the end,' Beck recalled, 'and we had to run out in the rain and put him in a town car and send him on his way.' Godrich left behind a hauntingly lonely song that features little more than drums and vocals, and bears comparison to Big Star's 'Kangaroo' or Dennis Wilson's 'Carry Me Home'.

The wonder-producer had run his body into the ground during the marathon two weeks of recording, but he enjoyed the approach taken with the album. 'We were trying to keep the momentum going,' he explained, 'because that was the thing that everyone was getting off on. I remember him saying that it was like having a party and not having to do the washing up, because you mix as you go and everything's finished. Usually, you have your freak-out recording bit, and then you have to tidy up at the end. We were digging the fact that it was all going very quickly, and we were having to make the decisions as we went along.'

The on-the-fly nature of the sessions did, however, mean that some things needed to be fixed later on. 'They had to slow the record down,' Beck told KROQ, 'because I made it so fast that it was at a frequency nobody could hear. This is a fruitful time in my younger life. I feel like I've got a lot of work to do.' Godrich, meanwhile, could leave the studio knowing that, by the end of the millennium, he had worked on some of the finest albums of recent years: Radiohead's *OK Computer*, R.E.M.'s *Up*, Pavement's *Terror Twilight*, and Beck's *Mutations*.

'*Mutations* is such a strong and interesting record,' said Joey Waronker.

'Beck is a genius. He might not know exactly what he wants to do when he shows up, but once he gets started, he knows exactly where everything is going to go.'

* * *

To get ready for some upcoming European dates Beck played a one-off show at the Galaxy Theater in Santa Ana. The set included 'Tropicalia', 'Cold Brains', 'Diamond Bollocks', 'Nobody's Fault But My Own', and 'Electric Music And The Summer People'—all from *Mutations*, which was surprising considering that Beck had said he wouldn't be touring the album.

After that, it was off to Europe for some outdoor festival shows. One of the first dates Beck was scheduled to play was at the largely dance-oriented Universe 98 festival, which was to be his only UK appearance of the year. A few weeks before the event, however, it was cancelled as a result of poor ticket sales, seemingly leaving Beck without a UK date at all. As it happened, though, The Verve—one of the biggest British bands of the past year—had a homecoming gig planned for the very same day, May 24, at Haigh Hall, a stately home on a hillside overlooking their home town of Wigan. The performance was to be recorded for (live) radio and (delayed) television transmission that night. The only problem was that, as of April, no support acts had been finalised. In the wake of the Universe 98 cancelation, Beck was drafted in to join John Martyn and DJ Shadow on the bill.

After playing in Denmark the previous day, Beck arrived in Lancashire to a grey overcast sky and the prospect of having to win over 35,000 mostly male fans who had probably heard little or none of his music apart from 'Loser', or maybe 'Where It's At'. He went down a storm, though, running through a selection of *Odelay* highlights and debuting 'Diamond Bollocks' and 'Nobody's Fault But My Own'. He then flew to Portugal for a show in Lisbon that was filmed and shown in part on MTV Europe.

Back in the USA, Beck played a run of ten large outdoor shows, drawing mostly on *Odelay* material plus 'Deadweight', 'Loser', and a sprinkling of *Mutations*. He would play all of the songs he'd debuted at

Santa Ana in May along the way, but no other new ones, and never all of them on the same night. Fans would have to wait until the following year for any full *Mutations* shows.

Originally, the idea had been that *Mutations* would be given a low-key release by Bong Load while Beck started work on a fully fledged follow-up to *Odelay*. As the summer progressed, however, reports emerged that those plans had changed. The album's release date pushed back from June to November, as Beck explained to the *NME*:

Bong Load were gonna put it out in June and it was all going ahead. We had it mastered, all the artwork was done, and then I was about to go over to Europe to do these shows in May when Geffen called and said, 'Y'know, we'd really like to put this out, we really like this record.'

I thought it would be too mellow for them: it wasn't even an album that I planned on performing live, [or] that contributed much to where I'm going in a bigger musical sense. It's nothing like the next record I was working on. So I was a little bit surprised. I thought people would gravitate toward it and discover on their own. Anyway, they really wanted it and they ended up buying it.

The situation would end up causing problems between Geffen, Bong Load, and Beck, and also meant, perhaps inevitably, that the album would have a much higher profile when it was finally released. Beck, however, was dismissive of the whole business. 'Bong Load could've put it out if they wanted to,' he told the *Guardian*. 'They got a shitload of money, so it worked out for everybody. It doesn't matter to me—I record my albums and mix them, and I send them to the record company. To me the whole debate is absurd, I mean, is the music good or is it bad? I don't get hung up on the personality who made the song. I don't care [about] the way somebody's dressed or who they slept with.'

In August, Beck travelled to Japan for an appearance in Japan at the Mt. Fuji Festival and the taping of a couple of interviews that would later be circulated as the electronic press kit for his forthcoming album. In the meantime, a deal was worked out that mirrored what had happened with *Mellow Gold* and *Odelay*: Geffen would release the CD and cassette editions of *Mutations*, while Bong Load would handle the vinyl, which included a seven-inch single of 'Diamond Bollocks' and 'Runners Dial Zero', as they didn't fit on the twelve-inch record.[43]

The album's front cover features a photograph by Charlie Gross of Beck wearing a hotel laundry bag, while the CD booklet contains various examples of the bizarre artwork of San Francisco artist Tim Hawkinson, including two shots of his model 'Finger' (1997) and several of his strange-looking 'balloon sculptures'. A detail of his 'Wall Chart Of World History From Earliest Times To The Present' (1997) appears alongside the lyrics—the first time Beck had included the words to all of the songs in one of his albums. When you hold the CD up to the light, meanwhile, you can see a photograph of Beck by Autumn de Wilde.

The most immediately striking thing about *Mutations* compared to Beck's previous output is the vocals. He had clearly put much more effort into recording them this time around, and the results are impressive. One of the few criticisms that could be made of *Odelay* is that the vocals are a little flat and unfeeling. The songs on *Mutations* needed an authentic delivery to match Nigel's Godrich's hauntingly understated production—and that's exactly what Beck gave them.

This delightful collection of songs has an agreeably low-key feel (as opposed to lo-fi, per previous efforts like *One Foot In The Grave*) that can be put down to the choice of producer and studio. The songs here are given a much more rounded production than those on *One Foot*, but they are also much stronger songs in their own right, with a greater emotional depth. While casual observers might have been surprised at the lack of samples and beats, pre-Geffen fans would have been less shocked by the content than by the polish and the delivery of the songs. Full of mournful yearning, Beck conjures up atmospheres reminiscent of 'White Album'-era Beatles in places.

Beck's lyrical scene-setting is also more accomplished here than on

163

any of his previous work, and the fact that the lyrics were printed and presented with the album backs up the theory that he was more confident with the words to these songs than any before. Of course, no Beck album would be complete without some silliness. Snipets of dialogue can he heard at the start and end of some of the tracks, while the ending of 'Canceled Check' is a glorious, masterful piece of noise.

That *Mutations* sounds like a band playing live in one room is quite an achievement, given that this was Beck's first attempt at really recording with his touring musicians. An even bigger achievement is that of actually pulling off such an album at this stage in his career. What other major artist would have tried to do an album like this at this juncture, especially after the success of *Odelay*? 'I was gonna put it out as this low-key affair,' he admitted, 'but it just grew into what it is now.'

What *Mutations* had grown into was an eagerly awaited album that was reviewed all over the place. Almost every UK newspaper carried a review of it, even though, at the time of *Odelay*, few of them would even have given Beck the time of day. In the USA, *Spin* gave *Mutations* eight out of ten, while for *Raygun* it was 'a delicious reminder that we can count on Beck to give us something worth listening to more than once'.

The UK music press was almost unanimous in its praise for the collection. *Uncut* gave it five stars and suggested that 'this could be Beck's masterpiece'. The *NME* gave the album eight out of ten, while in *Mojo*, Jim Irvin declared, 'If he can keep these parallel strands going he'll soon be pop's most important practitioner.' For *Melody Maker*, this was simply 'a quiet album of considerable scope and a pleasure from start to finish'. One of the few dissenting voices was John Harris, who gave the album three stars and was left with more questions than answers: 'Who is Beck? What does he do? Where does he go? What is he like?' Even on this more 'personal' album, these were not questions that could be answered directly by the music.

Similar enquiries were made by the *NME*, to whom Beck offered some typically oblique answers. 'Knowing about where I went, what time I went to bed, and who I did this with and that with,' he said, 'that style of confessional songwriting—you don't really know the person. You know the mannerisms and their habits. Who the person is, I think, is what inhabits their dreams. So the imagery in the songs is probably more me, or the essence of who I am.'

The journalist did his best to delve further, but Beck wasn't giving much away. 'I'm probably locked up in my thoughts a lot of the time,' he said. 'Although my friends and girlfriend are pretty good at occupying me with chores and barbecues and errands—lots of day-to-day things. Left to my own devices, I can get pretty lost.' Did he try to guard his privacy? 'No, I wouldn't say so. I don't live in a bank. I'm not locked away in a safe.'

* * *

As was becoming traditional, Beck played a session for KCRW shortly after the release of the album. It was his longest appearance on the station to date, lasting for almost an hour, with his full band also in attendance. Starting with 'Cold Brains', they ran through seven *Mutations* tracks, adding 'Debra' and a preview of 'Hollywood Freaks' at the end.

Although the original plan was to let the album slip out quietly, without any fuss or fanfare, Beck ended up taking part in a number of interviews around the time of its release, variously describing it as 'my take on the evolution of song craft' or 'more of a parenthetical addition to the equation [and] not the big bottom line'.

Despite its themes of social decay, death, and withered relationships, the album entered the *Billboard* charts at #13—Beck's highest chart entry to date. And as the New Year rolled around, numerous magazines put Beck on the cover, giving him space to explore the mood and creation of the album.

'Basically, I went into the studio with no preconceived ideas, and we recorded and mixed the whole album in fourteen days,' he told a journalist at the time. 'My goal was to make a timeless record, not a record for the 90s, not country music with a 90s electronic sauce all over it either, because that has already become something of a cliché.'

165

Elsewhere, he explained how this was the 'homogenous, coherent album' he had always wanted to make:

This time, I really wanted to make a subdued record with one beautiful mood. Also, that way, I've finally made a record that my girlfriend likes to listen to, because she didn't like my other records. And I like my girlfriend, so it's about time I made some music for her. She chose me when I was penniless and unknown, and that makes her about the most important person in my life. I just felt I should scale that down and let the music take centre stage again. Not that I'm going to be straight and super-serious; I'm perfectly willing to be the clown. I would get bored otherwise. And I do think it's important to weave a sense of humour through the music, while retaining some modicum of dignity.

Having been guarded about his private life in the past, he seemed more willing now to talk about Leigh in interviews. They had been living in Pasadena, he explained, but had moved back to Silver Lake in late 1998, having found that the house in Pasadena was 'too big' for the two of them. His songwriting style and methods also came under the microscope, as he revealed how he sometimes came up with his lyrics 'in a backward manner. I wrote a song recently about all these catalogues that come in the mail—I wrote this ridiculous song. Then, a few days later, I came back and wrote—with the same melody and all—I wrote about some born-again town that I was reading about. Then I wrote another one about a bunch of weightlifters, and then I just merged the three together, and they become all these elements just distilled into this tune.'

Beck would constantly be asked about his place in musical history; how he had taken elements of musical traditions, updated them, and turned them into something new. Discussion would often turn to how music might sound in the next century, as if in some way everything might suddenly be different in the new millennium.

I don't like to think in terms of decades of micro-era. I think this whole century is one continuous contemporary musical moment. It's all relevant. Son House is still relevant. Edith Piaf is still relevant. And The Damned are still relevant. It's all from the same banquet table. That said, there is a style of production from the 60s and 70s that really excites me. They were bringing in all kinds of instruments, a little fuzz guitar mixed in with some baroque music. I don't find that kitschy—I find it cool and contemporary. Maybe it's idealistic to think you can use all of music to get an idea across, but actually I think it's just compositional. All the sounds that have gone before out there are your orchestra, and you have to figure out the parts for them.

He also took part in some conversations that might best be described as 'deep and meaningful', including one with the *NME* in which he wondered 'if there's a word in English for what the nature of the universe is. There's a whole lot of words—I think there is an absurdity. The whole thing is a dance, y'know, it's silly and then it's dumb; it's the same circle. It's the same snake eating its tail to find out what its ass tastes like. Just when I think I've broken through to the next place in my life, I realise I'm doing the same things I was doing when I was twelve, or when I was nineteen. You think you're gonna evolve into something else, and in a way do, but on another level you never learn anything.'

In 1999, fans would start to see and hear what Beck had learnt. He would spend much of the year shrouded in secrecy working on his next album, with famous names like Smiths guitarist Johnny Marr, British electro-folk singer Beth Orton, and Ultramagnetic MCs founder Kool Keith (aka Dr Octagon) coming and going at his Silver Lake home. As anticipation surrounding his 'official' follow-up to *Odelay* mounted, he would also find himself the centre of numerous lawsuits between Bong Load and Geffen. Yes, the last year of the century would prove interesting, to say the least.

CHAPTER 13

'In the end it worked itself out.' (1999-2000)

At the century's end, Beck found himself in turbulent waters. Not only was he working on a new album, planning a mini-tour, and making TV appearances, but he would also soon find himself involved with a trio of lawsuits, lose two members of his band, and have *Golden Feelings* reissued on CD without his consent. On the plus side, he would also release a blockbuster of an album and set off on another world tour.

In January 1999, Beck opened what would be a busy and controversial six-month period in New York City. First he popped up on *Saturday Night Live*, for a quick nationwide showcase of 'Nobody's Fault But My Own' and 'Tropicalia'. The following night, January 10, he played a long-awaited show at Town Hall, an off-Broadway gem of a theatre, which was seen as such an event that reviewers from the *Hollywood Reporter*, the *New York Times*, and the British magazines *Mojo* and *Q* were all in attendance.

In contrast to the previous month's shows, this one was much more *Mutations*-based. After starting shakily with 'Cold Brains', 'Bottle Of Blues', and 'Sing It Again', the band shifted gears and set off for a memorable acoustic evening. 'We only had a day to rehearse,' Beck explained, and in fact it had been almost a year since the band recorded the album, so they were due a bit of slack. The show really took off with Beck's mid-set solo slot, which featured a rarely played cover of Mississippi John Hurt's 'He's A Mighty Good Leader' and the old blues standard 'Stagger Lee'.

He and his band then swerved through a phalanx of genres, including western swing, blues, and Latino, before ending the show with 'Jack-ass'.

The same week saw the release of the soundtrack to *The Hi Lo Country*, starring Woody Harrelson and Patricia Arquette, which featured Beck's duet with Willie Nelson on a version of Floyd Tillman's 'Drivin' Nails In My Coffin'. He and his band were due to play again a few nights later in Las Vegas, but it was cancelled after Joey Waronker suddenly fell ill with pneumonia. Rather than bring in another drummer, Beck rescheduled the show for May, just after a planned tour of Japan.

The band went their separate ways, and Beck headed back to Los Angeles for what was planned as a well-earned break. As ever, though, the man wouldn't lie down, and the next month proved equally busy. After playing a one-off show with British singer-songwriter Beth Orton and Til Tuesday guitarist-turned-producer Jon Brion, Beck was back in the studio, during which time he reportedly put down some tracks with Orton and rapper Kool Keith. He also recorded two new songs—'Diamond In The Sleaze' and 'One Of These Days'—for release over the coming months.

The end of the month was dominated by awards ceremonies. First, Beck showed up at the Grammys to present the Record Of The Year category, and then at the Rock The Vote event, where he presented an award to Neil Young. If that wasn't enough, he then picked up another award of his own: his second BRIT for Best International Male Solo Artist. Although he wasn't in London to collect the prize, he did send in a short film of him jogging through a finishing line and celebrating with the trophy.

Beck's next public outing was on March 21, when he played an Academy Awards after-show party at the House Of Blues in Los Angeles. His set included a cover of Eddy Grant's 'Electric Avenue' and a new song entitled 'Jockin' My Mercedes', with the entire show broadcast live over the internet for those not lucky enough to be among the 1,200-strong audience.

Mutations had been selling very well in Japan since its release in

November, and as a result Beck decided to play a short series of shows there. Japan was a country that Beck had always felt comfortable in. 'Walking the Philosophers Walk in Kyoto while the blossoms are going is one of my favourite things I've done in my life,' he told me. Japanese culture, while being very modern, also has a great respect for its history, which is something he definitely relates to.

The ten-day tour opened with two nights in Tokyo, with Beck tending to play a heavily *Mutations*-based set, with a few hits thrown in for good measure. Disposable cameras were given out to members of the audience, with the results then displayed at the official Beck website. After a few provincial dates, the band returned for two more shows in Tokyo. The whole thing was over in ten days. A new Japan-only single was released to coincide with the tour, with 'Nobody's Fault But My Own' backed by two of the new songs Beck had recorded in January, 'Diamond In The Sleaze' and 'One Of These Days'.

To break up the long journey home, Beck and his entourage stopped off for a show in Hawaii. Playing to a predominantly military crowd, they included more upbeat, *Odelay* material than they had during the Japanese shows. Mid-set, Beck left the stage while the rest of the band introduced themselves as Rainbow Warrior and did a version of 'Pass The Dutchie'.

On his return to California, Beck found himself in an unusual situation, as the man in the middle of a series of lawsuits and countersuits. The legal wranglings reached back over a year, to the recording of *Mutations*, which had originally been intended for Bong Load, until Geffen executives heard it and opted to pay the independent label a fee for the rights. Matters were further complicated as, in 1998, Geffen's parent company, Polygram, was purchased by Universal. Beck had been in the midst of negotiating a new royalty rate on his contract when the Geffen representatives he dealt with lost their jobs as part of the takeover, leaving him with a new team with whom he was reportedly unhappy. As a result, he decided he wanted out of the whole mess.

On April 23, it was reported that Beck had informed Geffen and Bong Load that he was no longer required to fulfil the obligations of his contract. He cited the so-called 'California Seven Year Rule' (California Labor Code Section 2855), which states that personal-service contracts can only run for seven years. Under that ruling, his contract would cease at the end of 1999. This law has been invoked before, by Metallica and others, but it had never been challenged in court by a record company.

The following Monday, April 26, the two labels filed lawsuits against Beck in the California Superior Court, asking the court to enforce the contracts and to determine damages against Beck. Geffen's suit alleged that Beck had approached the label in order to renegotiate his contract in May 1998, even though it still had over eighteen months to run. The label also claimed that he owed a further four albums as part of his existing deal.

A few weeks later, on May 10, Beck filed counter-suits. His lawsuit against Geffen alleged copyright infringement by the label for releasing *Mutations*, and also claimed that Beck was owed an advance and royalties for the album, which at the time of the suit had sold well over 400,000 copies. The suit further stated that Beck found himself working with a different set of record company employees 'who apparently decided to place improper exploitation of Beck's work above contractual and copyright obligations'. The lawsuit against Bong Load sought $500,000 in damages, as well as a release from his contract.

In the midst of all this, Beck still managed to get out and play some shows, beginning with the rescheduled Las Vegas show, which was now to take place on May 6. That night, the tiny Tiffany Theater inside the Tropicana Hotel and Casino played host to Beck and band in a sit-down dinner setting. The assembled 'Beck freaks' were arranged in cabaret style booths, which the band clearly found amusing. 'Well, we feel real safe,' Justin Meldal-Johnsen smirked. 'We normally get Visigoths gnawing on each other's thighs,' Beck laughed. 'This cafeteria thing is … nice.'

A largely *Odelay*-based set was interspersed with 'Tropicalia', 'Girl Dreams' and another run through Musical Youth's 'Pass The Dutchie'. DJ Swamp was in full effect, and after his solo stint at the end of the main set, the band returned in wild costumes—Beck in a cape, Meldal-Johnsen in a pink vest and tight pink trousers, and Joey Waronker in a heavy-metal wig—for an even wilder charge through 'Electric Avenue' and 'Devils Haircut'. It was quite a sight to behold.

Two days later, the whole crew had ventured back across the Mojave Desert for a weekend stint in Los Angeles. Two years had passed since Beck last played in his hometown, and anticipation was at fever pitch. The venue was the Wiltern, an art deco beauty of a theatre, the interior of which could pass for an inside-out version of the Chrysler. The first night was filmed for future broadcast by HBO, and was heavy on *Mutations* material.

After being greeted by shrieking reminiscent of The Beatles' arrival in the States in 1964, Beck and his band put on about as good an acoustic-rock show as you could hope to see anywhere. Nine *Mutations* songs were included in the set, and were impeccably played by all, with the usual band augmented by two extra string players, a sitar player, and Jay Dee Maness on lap-steel. The recent 'One Of These Days' sounded better here than on the recorded version, while Beck dipped into his back catalogue at one point to come up with an unexpected rendition of 'Lampshade', prefacing it with a hilarious ten-minute story about how he had once broken his collarbone at a New Year's Eve party, and then later re-broke it falling out of a bunk bed when he was awoken by a screaming cat at his bedside. He finally brought the house down with a funked-up 'Debra' and a chaotic 'Devils Haircut', with the latter song featuring widespread instrument destruction, Roger Manning Jr. standing on the piano with a keyboard between his legs while flapping his cape in a vain attempt to fly, while Beck was eventually piggy-backed offstage by Justin Meldal-Johnsen.

After the show, Beck looked back at the gig in a kind of a haze. 'I took some caffeine tablets just before the show because I was so tired,' he explained, 'but now I don't remember too much about it—the first half, anyway. It seemed like everything was going at eighty miles an hour, but in slow motion.'

The following night offered more of the same, with 'Canceled Check', 'Sleeping Bag', and 'Diamond Bollocks' also finding their way into the set. And that, as Beck announced, was 'the beginning and the end of the *Mutations* tour'. A week later, he played at a Sony PlayStation launch party, for which he put on a show similar to the Vegas extravaganza of earlier in the month, again mainly consisting of *Odelay* material.

The recent shows highlighted Beck's distinct two-pronged attack on modern music. In Vegas, he was the flamboyant showman, with all the beats, good-time tomfoolery, and manic sound assaults; two days later, in LA, he was the serious, traditional musician playing a laid-back set and chatting with the audience. The fact that he could simultaneously carry these two halves of his personality forward is pretty amazing in itself, and is something he would continue to do as his career progressed.

As the last summer of the millennium reached its midpoint, Beck's website gave his fans the chance to peek into the process of the recording of his next album via weekly video updates. The five-minute clips were directed by Bart Lipton, and would invariably concentrate on the comings and goings at The Dust Brothers' Silver Lake studio. The album was tentatively pencilled in for release in November 1999—lawsuits permitting. That would be the earliest that Beck fans could expect to see or hear anything new from him, live or on record, as Joey Waronker would be out on tour with R.E.M. until October.

In the meantime, Beck had given plenty of hints as to the mood of his 'official' follow-up to *Odelay*, but there were also some red herrings, too. 'It will be positively artificial,' he told one journalist. 'It's going to be like one of those *Best Of The 90s* party discs. The 90s ain't over yet. Give me another year, because I'm getting ready to drop some party jams. The first part of the decade you weren't allowed to party; it was the introspective half of the 90s. Now we've got to make up for lost time.'

He would also wax lyrical about the future of his work, and the copycat acts that he was 'inspiring', even if he didn't mention any of them by name. 'I was a little disappointed no one followed Marilyn Manson's lead,' he said. 'I guess they will soon. There's always this two-year gap before the copycats come out.' For Beck, though, the point was *not* to follow Manson's lead. 'It's more about raising the stakes. It seems like the great bands were always upping the ante a little bit and doing their own thing. Every time a band raises the ceiling a little bit, there's a little more air for all of us. More room to go up.'

During the first week of July, Beck made a couple of guest appearances with other performers. First, he joined Brazilian legend Caetano Veloso in Los Angeles for a few songs before Veloso played an instrumental version of 'Tropicalia'. Four nights later, he borrowed Beth Orton's guitar at the El Rey Theater to play a last-minute guest support role under the pseudonym Silver Lake Menza, strumming his way through four *Mutations* tracks—'Cold Brains', 'Lazy Flies', 'Tropicalia', and 'Nobody's Fault But My Own'.

Behind the scenes, July marked the end of the recording of *Midnite Vultures*, and the beginning of the mixing process. He had managed to keep it pretty quiet until now, but now it was revealed that he had been planning the album for a long time. He'd actually started work on it back in January 1998 but shelved the project after a computer error intervened. 'I tried to start the record before *Mutations*,' he revealed, 'but the computer destroyed one of the songs, so I took that as a sign.' This hard-drive crash left him looking at 'the huge mountain I had to climb', so he meandered off to record *Mutations* instead. He then spent the first seven months of 1999 recording a large number of songs, from which he would select twelve for inclusion on his new record.

Most of the album was recorded at Beck's Silver Lake home and co-produced by Mickey Petralia, a DJ, engineer, and LA club promoter, with help from occasional Beck guitarist Tony Hoffer. Some sessions had taken place at The Dust Brothers' PCP Labs studio, although only two of the finished tracks actually made it onto the album. After more than a year in the studio, the mixing gradually gathered pace, and by late August, Beck had completed over thirty tracks, with the final six weeks of the process taken up by eighteen-hour working days.

'This record is a two-year project that we crammed into one year,' Beck explained. 'It easily could have taken another year, if we'd done it in a civilised manner, if we hadn't completely surrendered our lives. It was an awful lot to bite off. I knew how much work it took to make *Odelay*, and I knew that the level of production and programming I wanted on the new album would be immensely time-consuming. It turned out to be that, and then some.'

Indeed, those who thought the production and layering on *Odelay* was intensive clearly hadn't heard nothin' yet. 'Sometimes we'd spend sixteen hours on four seconds of music,' Beck revealed to *New Music Monthly*. 'I figured this was a chance to get that deep.' The co-producing duo of Petralia and Hoffer spent time creating and editing the beats using a computer and a 'techno map', which allowed them to give Beck multi-layered grooves to work with.

The music wasn't all computer-created, however. The entire touring band appeared at some point or other, and Beck got them to play with the same free spirit with which they had imbued *Mutations* tracks like 'Diamond Bollocks'. 'It was really exuberant, and we all got wild,' Justin Meldal-Johnsen told *Elle* magazine. 'Everything was rendered in a really passionate way, and often the tracks were built from the mistakes we made.'

While Beck was applying the finishing touches to the record, however, a whole new set of spanners was thrown into the works. First came the unauthorised reissue of Beck's first ever tape, *Golden Feelings*, on CD, and then the announcement that the longest surviving member of Beck's band, Joey Waronker, was leaving the fold. It then emerged that Smokey Hormel would also be saying adios.

Sonic Enemy, home to the original *Golden Feelings* tape, had apparently gone under in 1995, but by the autumn of 1999, rumours had emerged of the label's resurrection—confirmed in September with the release of the album on CD in a pressing of 1,000 copies. The problem was that Beck had not been consulted about the rerelease, and it was made more complicated by the fact that album fell somewhere between a bootleg and a legitimate release without actually being either. In the end, it seemed like nothing could be done about it, and Sonic Enemy continued to press and sell the album.

The second dilemma, though more serious, was perhaps more predictable. Joey Waronker spent much of 1999 playing with R.E.M., and although he was still available to play on five songs on *Midnite Vultures*, it was apparent that his heart now lay elsewhere. He wanted to do some production work of his own, too, and the idea of playing in two bands— both of whom would require his services throughout 2000—was simply too much to take on.

'It's not about leaving one band to join another,' he explained. 'I've been asked to participate with R.E.M. for events scheduled for next year. Plans for their next album are already on the blackboard. I have this sense I'll still be involved with Beck, even if it's just to help break in the next musician. I'm really lucky to have worked with him for six years. I know that in fifteen years, Beck will be right where R.E.M. is now. He has that in his heart.'

As far as R.E.M.'s manager, Bertis Downs, was concerned, Waronker wasn't 'joining' the band, but he was 'the right drummer' for now. The other members of R.E.M. had always maintained that Bill Berry, who quit the original line-up in 1995, would never be replaced.

Things stepped up a gear in October, as news about the new album began to leak out. First came the news that the album would indeed be called *Midnite Vultures*, then came the track listing, and then advance copies of a new single, 'Sexx Laws', began to circulate. Beck himself was busy shooting a video for the single and warming up for his appearance at the Coachella Festival in Indio, California. After making an appearance at the food court of the UCSB Student Center in Santa Barbara on October 6, he rushed up to Fresno for a show at the Satellite Student Union the following night. Then, at the weekend, he formally unveiled the new songs 'Debra', 'Mixed Bizness', 'Sexx Laws', and 'Pressure Zone' at Coachella.

In mid October, Beck made his way to New York to discuss the album with the world's media. 'I've had the luxury of being underestimated,' he told *New Music Monthly*. 'In a way, I think this is the first time that people will be expecting more than I'll probably be able to give. *Odelay* surprised a lot of people who had written me off. And *Mutations* surprised some other people, because they assumed it was all cut-and-paste, a very artificial smoke-and-mirrors type of sound. I don't know what this album will mean to people.'

It's true that expectations were high, and in a sense he would always be fighting a losing battle in terms of meeting them, but *Midnite Vultures* came pretty close in terms of overall quality. The content, however, would throw some listeners off a little. The album came with something of a reinvention of Beck's public image, and, simply put, he'd never been quite so rude before.

The Prince comparisons seemed inevitable, once the album was out, but in fact Beck had already given an indirect hint as to the direction of his music earlier in the year. 'I'm sure the next record I do will annoy a lot of people,' he told the *NME* in October 1998. 'It's not finished yet, but I'm sure it's not for everybody. It's like *The White Album* and *The Black Album* arm-wrestling. I think it'll eventually become *The Beige Album*, but I hope it doesn't become too beige, because I think of beige as the colour of complete resignation and conformity. Maybe it'll be *The Fuchsia Album*.' Asked to sum up the record at the time of its release, he called it 'sexcapades in the biosphere. A lot of music was inspired by the R&B world. People like Silk'. For many fans, the question remained: what the heck was this going to sound like? The answer was quite simple: it sounded stunning.

The album opens with a sound Beck hadn't used to begin an album before: horns, courtesy of The Brass Menagerie, who play on four of the eleven tracks. 'Sexx Laws' sets the lyrical mood for the album, if not the musical tone. 'Can't you hear those cavalry drums / Hijacking your equilibrium?' Beck sings, as if to tell the listener what is going on. 'Brief encounters in Mercedes Benz / Wearing Hepatitis contact lens / Bed and breakfast and away weekends.' This is Beck at his most lustful. The chorus line, meanwhile, would be familiar to fans who'd attended his concerts over the past couple of years, which would often see him falling to one knee, like a preacher, to scream, 'I wanna defy the logic of all sex laws.'

After that, the album proceeds to explain just how he'd like to achieve that goal. 'Nicotine & Gravy' continues the theme—raising the stakes, too—as he promises to 'feed you fruit that don't exist' and 'leave graffiti where you've never been kissed'. It might have sounded like Prince-by-numbers to some, but listen to it again and you discover all manner of mood changes within a single song. Admittedly, the opening section isn't a thousand miles from Prince circa *Controversy* or *Purple Rain*, but the many twists and turns take in an operatic bridge section, some aggressive strings (featuring David Campbell on viola), and—for the first time on a Beck album—some scratching from DJ Swamp. As the song comes to an end, a distinctly Eastern rhythm rises to the fore and carries the song to its conclusion. Here in particular, you can easily understand why it took hours and hours to come up with just a few seconds of this music. The depth of sound and attention to detail are amazing.

DJ Swamp's cameo on 'Nicotine & Gravy' marks his only appearance on the album, although he actually played on many tracks during the sessions that were cut from the final release, including 'Sweet and Low', 'Arabian Nights', and 'California Rodeo'. 'There's probably dozens floating around on a hard drive somewhere,' he recalled. 'The heavier, harder-rocking ones I liked the most never got to see the light of day.'

Beck would later confirm that a large number of tracks—twenty-five or so, many of them finished—were left on the cutting-room floor. 'A lot of them were on hard drives from the late 90s, and it took me several years to find a specialist who could get them to work with a modern computer, because some of them were made in old operating systems with programs that nobody knows how to use anymore. A lot of [the outtakes] are probably better off not having seen the light of day. But it was an experiment, and all the things that were recorded during that time were of a piece. There was a specific sound and idea behind it.'

'Mixed Bizness' is one of the album's highlights, and sounds as though it came straight from a mid-70s Blaxploitation soundtrack. The call-and-response chorus again recalls Prince, with Tony Hoffer adding the wah-wah guitar over playing by the full Beck live band. For 'Get Real Paid',

Beck mixed in some weird synthesiser trickery with what sounds almost like an unreleased Kraftwerk demo and a robotic, arcade-machine vocal about how, 'We like the boys in the bullet-proof vests / We like the girls with the cellophane chests'. (With lyrics like these, fans could rest assured that some things never change.)

Beck had been saying for the best part of a year that he was being influenced by R. Kelly and the music he heard on LA's R&B radio stations. 'Hollywood Freaks' is the most obvious product of this. 'I love listening to the beat stations, Power 106 and all that,' he said. 'It's always been over the top, the super R&B shit, which is so slick, but I'm addicted to it. It's so evil, but so unbelievable, the production, the slickness and the commerciality. You can plug right into that culture by hearing those songs, the sexuality. Last year, when Montell Jordan came out, it was like, *What the hell is this?* He's singing gangbanger lyrics, but it's sort of lightweight R&B singing. It's kind of twisted that way.'

Beck's take on all of this was originally known as 'Jockin' My Mercedes' when he played it at a show in February, and it almost came out as 'Hlwd. Freaks' until he opted to avoid pronunciation problems by spelling the whole thing out. The song has some bizarre lyrics, with even Norman Schwarzkopf getting a mention.

'Peaches & Cream' returns to the twin recurring themes of sex and food. 'We're on the good ship ménage à trois,' he crows. 'You make a garbage man scream.' This sly melodic seduction bumps and grinds its way to another mid-song reinvention, as the Arroyo Tabernacle Men's Chorale request that the object of Beck's desire 'keep your lamplight trimmed and burning'.

'Milk & Honey' is the hardest-rocking song on the album, and recalls Lynyrd Skynyrd by way of The Black Crowes, with Johnny Marr popping up on guitar. 'It was fairly surreal, watching Johnny Marr play Skynyrd riffs,' Beck recalled. 'I don't think he was too enthused. He said he would do it, but only for me.' Of course, Beck being Beck, he couldn't just let this be a straightforward arena-rock song. The middle section morphs into a kind of disco strut with horrible 80s-sounding drums and laser-beam sound effects, before Beck turns husky and whispers, 'I can smell the VD in the club tonight.' At that, a woman bizarrely asks, 'Excuse me please, can you tell me how to get to the Soviet Embassy?'

'Broken Train' was almost released as 'Out Of Kontrol', until the title was changed at the last moment. Beck sings of a strange place where 'snipers are passed out in the bushes again', and notes that he's 'glad I got my suit dry-cleaned before the riots started', to the accompaniment of a jazzy little instrumental track with some even jazzier percussion. 'Did you ever let a cowboy sit on your lap?' he asks. Oblique lyrics aside, it's one of the most straightforward tracks on a very un-straightforward album.

The most out-of-place track on the album, meanwhile, is also one of the best. A duet with Beth Orton, 'Beautiful Way' is a beautifully tender, country-tinged ballad that would have fitted well on *Mutations* (and bears a strong musical resemblance to The Velvet Underground's 'Countess From Hong Kong'). The lust of the earlier tracks is nowhere to be heard as some gorgeous pedal steel swirls around the chorus.

The album ends with a song that would already have been well known to many Beck fans: 'Debra'. A live staple since 1996, it was the one song he just had to include on the album. The recorded version is a little more refined than the live incarnation, but it brings the album to a neat close, the gentle horns evoking a late-night atmosphere as the album is put to bed. Sleep, though, is the last thing on Beck's mind. 'You got a thing that I just got to get with,' he coos, in his best falsetto, 'And you know what we're gonna do.'

* * *

All in all, with *Midnite Vultures*, Beck achieved what he set out to do, and managed not to let anyone down despite the high expectations that were set for him (and that he had set himself). He had succeeded in adding new styles to his repertoire, reaching back to early-80s electro-funk and forward to his newfound love of R&B. On the tour that followed, he would be spreading that love all over the world.

Of course, none of this would have been possible, had the legal situation between Geffen, Bong Load, and Beck not been resolved. The terms of the resolution were kept quiet, although Beck did reveal that 'any musician on a record label believes they're not getting what they deserve. In my case, it was brought to my attention that it was grossly unfair. It was below what any musician off the street would be getting as far as a deal goes.' He went on to dismiss the various lawsuits as 'perfunctory legal manoeuvring, and in the end it worked itself out'. Although it remains unconfirmed, it seems likely that he had managed to negotiate a higher royalty rate than before, but the trade off was that he would now face more difficulty if he wanted to release 'low-key' projects on independent labels—one of the things that had drawn him to Geffen in the first place.

Whatever had gone on behind closed doors, the main thing was that he had a new album out on Geffen in November 1999, with only minimal delays caused by the legal shenanigans. *Midnite Vultures* reached #34 on the *Billboard* 200 and #19 on the UK charts, and was met with generally very enthusiastic reviews. 'Far be it from us to look a gift Hansen in the mouth when he's given us the year's most relentless gas—laughing or otherwise—of a party album,' *Entertainment Weekly* concluded, giving the album a score of A-. *Rolling Stone* gave the album four stars and noted that, 'Hansen, born in 1970, knows we're too self-conscious now to party like it's 1978. But on *Midnite Vultures* … he takes a twisted time trip back to a decadent era that he was too young to enjoy fully.' For the *NME*, the album was 'bound to entrench opinions on both sides of the Beck divide … [but] just because this isn't a conventional dose of "reality" doesn't mean Beck can't be sincere, and the force of character laid bare here is quite an awesome thing to behold. Narrower in scope than *Odelay* but more immediate in impact, it's clearly been conceived as an accompaniment to our hedonistic habit of choice, the last great party album of the millennium.'

Unfortunately, considering it was such a great album, *Midnite Vultures* has a terrible cover. While Beck had been careful to match *Odelay* with artwork that had no connection to the music, and illustrated *Mutations* with a simple portrait, for this new album, he attempted to capture his mood circa 1999. The DayGlo-green background is a bad enough start, but the waist-down shot of Beck wearing some too-tight pink plastic trousers is simply too much to take. Maybe the image—and the graffiti-style lettering—did somehow fit the mood of the album, but it certainly wasn't everyone's cup of tea. On the back cover, meanwhile, are some surreal swirls of colour reminiscent of the 'New Pollution' singles, plus an airbrushed figure in black that recalls the 'Sexx Laws' sleeve. All in all, it's a mess, and an eye-straining one at that. But maybe that was the point.

For the first time in his career, Beck seemed to be reacting to what was going on elsewhere in music, rather than just ploughing on regardless.

Music was taking a really severe turn around that time. On the one hand, you had all the nu-metal and dude-rock, and on the other side you had all the teen-pop boy bands and Britney Spears coming in.

For someone like me, there was this narrow margin of space that was quickly evaporating, and it just felt like a good time to do something that was antithetical to the time. The music was so un-tough, but also complex and weird. It wasn't pop music. Maybe certain aspects of what I was doing were reacting against what was happening or what people said, too. That's something that happens when you're starting out. After some time goes by and you get a little perspective, you realize that you don't need to react. You can just carry on with what you're doing.

Beck would spend much of the next two years touring in support of *Midnite Vultures*, including a busy summer of 2001, where he appeared right across the European festival circuit, playing large dates in eleven countries. He also took the tour to numerous radio stations and TV events, including the American Music Awards, in January 2000, for which he and his band gave a memorable 'performance' of 'Mixed Bizness'.

'The producers told me that we wouldn't be allowed to play live—we would have to mime to tape,' Beck recalled in a 2014 interview with the *Daily Telegraph*. It was something he'd never been asked to do before, and it 'seemed stupid'. So, inspired in part by William Klein's *Mr Freedom* and 'dystopian pop art in general', he decided to have some fun. 'I dressed my band up in radiation fallout suits and DayGlo gym clothes. My keyboard player was wearing a pink cape and shorts, and my drummer was wearing a ski mask and hitting his cymbals with his hands.'

Thirty seconds into the song, the musicians stopped playing and began to run amok, doing star-jumps and wrestling with each other. Unsure what else to do, the show's producers instructed the cameras to zoom in tight on Beck, who continued to sing his (live) vocal while chaos ensued around him. Every now and again, they would cut to 'the befuddled faces of people such as Garth Brooks' in the audience. 'We caused complete mayhem on mainstream primetime TV,' Beck continued, 'and the funny thing was that it was just before the internet, so nobody really knew about it. But apparently Dick Clark was pretty upset, and we were never asked to [perform at] an awards show ever again.'

CHAPTER 14

'It was a reunion
of sorts.' (2001-03)

In the midst of the madness surrounding the *Midnite Vultures* tour, Beck and Leigh Limon quietly broke up. There was no official announcement; the news merely slipped out later, through the occasional gossip-column mention. Her absence was especially noted when Beck arrived at his thirtieth birthday party alone during the summer of 2000.

The breakup—which came after nine years of being together—hit Beck hard, and unsurprisingly would inform a lot of the songs he wrote during the period. When he eventually came to record and release the songs, he drew a lot of questions about the end of the relationship— questions he didn't really want to answer. 'I don't want to be in a situation like some of these musicians who might as well not have a front door—anybody can walk in and see anything,' he told *Rolling Stone*. 'I'm about making art and music and performing. I'm not a big believer in the everything's-on-the-table-all-the-time philosophy. I don't understand these people who overexpose themselves all the time. What kind of life is that?'

He would also find himself having to fend off enquiries about possible new romances. In one instance, he was photographed with the actress Winona Ryder, and people quickly jumped to conclusions. He'd known Ryder for a number of years, though, and when he was asked directly, he replied, 'If you're seen standing next to somebody, [people assume that you are] together with them. I've been keeping to myself mostly.'

As the New Year dawned, Beck headed south for shows in Argentina and Brazil, but he was otherwise fairly quiet until June, when the European Festival circuit opened for business. With a touring band comprising long-time bassist Justin Meldal-Johnsen and keyboardist Roger Manning, drummer Victor Indrizzo and guitarist Lyle Workman, and the now ever-present Brass Menagerie, Beck began in Ireland and made his way across twelve countries, playing at large festivals and slipping in a few smaller indoor shows of his own. Then he was off to Japan, arriving home just before 9/11. The rest of the year passed quietly. There was one final bit of business to play out in December, in the form of an appearance at a benefit show for the Hollywood Sunset Free Clinic (a cause he had supported in the past), on a bill that also featured Aimee Mann, Jurassic 5, and the Red Hot Chili Peppers.

In the spring of 2002, Beck played a few small shows in the Los Angeles area to warm up for an appearance at Coachella on April 27, but otherwise he was away from the public eye for almost a year, until August. He used the time to record a new album of very personal songs, while also working with Marianne Faithfull, among others. Faithfull had been impressed by *Mutations*, and asked Beck to contribute to her 2002 album *Kissin Time*, which also contains collaborations with Dave Stewart, Billy Corgan, Pulp, and Blur.

'She was so natural,' Beck recalled. 'She just speaks and her personality is so completely married to her art that it was so effortless to work with her. She just handed me some lyrics and we wrote the song in ten minutes, and I just assembled some musicians I thought she would like, and she would just stroll in and read a book and tell some great stories, and then two, maybe, three vocal takes and—I don't know, she has a grandness. I like her because in a way she reminds me of some of the people I grew up around, my mother's friends—she's of that generation. The same reference points.'

'I wrote the lyrics beforehand,' Faithfull added. 'I thought, *Oh fuck,*

I've got a genius coming in here and I'd better have something done.' Beck appears on the opening track, 'Sex With Strangers', an eclectic slice of electronica awash with sound effects, and on 'Like Being Born', an almost baroque lullaby, both of which he co-wrote with her. Faithfull also sings a version of his 'Nobody's Fault', which, at a plodding six and a half minutes, is probably about two minutes too long.

Sessions for Beck's own new album began during the first week of March at Ocean Way in Los Angeles, with production once again handled by Nigel Godrich. The usual trio of Justin Meldal-Johnsen, Roger Manning, and Joey Waronker formed the backbone of the band, with Beck's own guitar work augmented by the playing of Jason Falkner. Waronker had to leave partway through the sessions to resume his R.E.M. duties, at which point James Gadson replaced him.

They had only around three weeks to complete the recordings, as Joni Mitchell had pre-booked the studio for the period immediately after that, but as she didn't work weekends, Beck would sneak back in to record some more while the studio was empty. The plan had been to follow the *Mutations* model by recording each basic track in a day or two, with minimal takes, before adding strings and other overdubs later on, but it ended up taking a little longer than that.

It turned into a song every two days. *Mutations* we recorded and mixed in two weeks, but we got a little more ambitious I think because we had orchestral arrangements and different musicians coming and going ... Joey Waronker had to go off half way through, [so] half of the [drums on the] record is James Gadson, who played on a lot of the great soul and funk records. He played on Bill Withers records. So he added a new dimension. We recorded in the same studios—it was a reunion of sorts. It was something we'd been planning for four years, talking about, but it took a while for people to line up.

One aspect of the new songs that would quickly stand out to listeners was Beck's vocal delivery. 'We listened to *Mutations*, and his voice sounded like Mickey Mouse,' Godrich recalled. 'His range dropped. Now when he opens his mouth, a canyon-esque vibration comes out. It's quite remarkable. He has amazing tone.'

Before recording started, Beck made a trip into the desert. Looking out across the vast openness was in many ways like peering across an ocean, when the horizon is hard to make out. That ambience would infiltrate the album right from the off. 'Everything with him is that simple,' Godrich added. 'Unlike most people, he always seems to know exactly what he wants to do.'

Once the basic tracks had been completed, a new phase of recording began with addition of string parts, for which Beck collaborated on the arrangements with his father. 'I went over there and he'd have a rough sketch out,' he explained. 'Some chords and some melodies. I think the idea with the orchestra was that we really wanted to feature the orchestra and not just use it to augment a pop song. Just bass, drums, and then let the orchestra fill the rest of the space—really use it dramatically, not just as padding, use it for all it's worth.'

The album really does use the strings to their fullest effect. The dreamy opening of 'The Golden Age' gently lulls the listener into the mood of the album, with its 'desert winds' and the weight of the world 'drifting away'. The stark 'Paper Tiger' showcases Beck's new vocal approach, before the real emotional core of the album is ripped open on 'Guess I'm Doing Fine', 'Lonesome Tears', and 'Lost Cause'. Using gentle acoustic guitar and sympathetic percussion by Joey Waronker, and sometimes veering toward country before swerving back to more indie ground, these three songs are the broken heartbeat of the record. On the last of the three, he says of his hometown, 'This town is cruel / Nobody cares.' 'It's an LA line,' he later explained. 'I wanted to take that line out, but I was too lazy. It is, though. People are very—I don't know—blasé.'

Among the new, post-breakup songs is an oldie, 'It's All In Your Mind', which dates back almost a decade, having been first issued as a stand-alone single from the *One Foot In The Grave* sessions. 'I just started playing it,' he recalled. 'Before we would start a new song, I would sit in front of a microphone and play different things ... I started playing it and Nigel was like, *What's that?!* He said, *We have to do that.* He really took to it, and I thought, *Well it's just languishing on that single ...*'

The version that ended up on *Sea Change* is quite a radical reworking of the original.

Some of the songs, especially from that period, I was still writing the songs or had just written the song on the spot. So the lyrics weren't even finished. 'Feather In Your Cap' was re-recorded. In the original version, I'm singing about phone machines and whatever came off the top of my head. A lot of those songs from that time, I've developed over the years and they're evolved songs. Songs sit in my head for a while.

I have dozens in there, songs from eight years ago that I've written but never recorded. After a while, I just sort of decide to record them. I wrote a lot of those songs in a certain moment, but some of them were hanging around. I think it was a relief. It was something that I felt like I had held back. It took a long time for me to see the value in putting something like that out.

One of the songs left off the album at the last moment was 'Ship In A Bottle'—the record's 'super-pop' cut. 'I think it was a little too corny,' he said. 'I mean, it was heart-felt, but since then people have been telling me they really liked it. At the time I thought it was kind of an Elton John type song, older Elton John. I don't know what the fate of that will be. I like the recording—it was very cool. I think we felt that the album was so long already. [It was] intended to be even more bare, mostly just acoustic guitar. It was getting to speak in a new way.'

While touring *Midnite Vultures*, Beck would listen to Leonard Cohen albums for a much-needed change of mood. Hints of Cohen and other classic songwriters can be glimpsed right across the new album: Nick

Drake, Syd Barrett, even Big Star's *Third*. 'Round The Bend' could be the theme for a traditional James Bond villain, living on a Pacific Island as the waves slowly break on the shore. In an interview with *Rolling Stone*, Beck noted that his approach to making the album was similar to those employed in the early 70s, and that if this collection had been issued in 1972, it would have fitted right in:

> I get cast as an ironist, but I'm not really like that. I think it's important to have a sense of humour. The Beatles, The Rolling Stones—all the great bands had that quality. But to me, irony is not meaning what you say. And I really mean pretty much everything I say.
>
> That's what came out [on *Sea Change*]. What else could I do but say it? I wanted things to be direct. Some of my other songs get lyrically obtuse, because I like that style: impressions rather than literal directives. But I wanted these to be at that point where everything is stripped away. I think every songwriter can appreciate the discipline of Hank Williams. He says exactly what he needs to and nothing else. I needed to do something like that.

The directness of the lyrics would obviously open up a lot of questions when it came to promoting the album—not that Beck would necessarily feel like answering them. In one such conversation, with Dorian Lynskey for *Blender*, he was clearly not in the mood to talk about his personal life. 'It's a thing that everybody goes through,' he said. 'Those breakup moments.' Asked whether he wrote the songs before or after the breakup, he replied sarcastically, 'I'll send you the dates. I have them written down on my calendar at home.' And on whether he and Limon were still in touch: 'That's none of your business.' *Mojo* magazine received similar treatment, with Beck responding to questions about Leigh by simply saying, 'I'm not gonna talk about that.'

He was happier to talk about the perceived change in direction he had undertaken on the album, even though he had made changes from record to record before, and explored many styles and approaches. But with a title like *Sea Change*, he was making a very obvious statement, and the confessional singer-songwriter approach was something new to him, as he told *Blender* in October of that year:

> I respect musicians who put out the same record over and over again and develop some thing. My grandfather started doing images of the *Venus* figure. He spent thirty-five years doing that figure over and over and over. He explored every aspect of what that figure could do, and every material you could apply to it, and there's something beautiful about that. But I just decided to cast my net a bit wider. Maybe I won't catch as much. I think I gave indications early on that mine wasn't just going to be a commercial, err, career. If that were the case, then the first record would have been ten versions of 'Loser.' I always thought it would be interesting if there was no such thing as gold and platinum records or record deals, and people were just making music. What would the music sound like?

The overall feeling was that, as well as sounding more personal and emotional, *Sea Change* was also much more straight-faced. Certainly, there was none of the humour that had appeared on his previous efforts. 'I just wanted the record to be simple and clean,' he told *Time*. 'I wanted economy in the lyrics, and I wanted the songwriting to be very, very straightforward.'

When it came to the critics, *Uncut*'s Andy Gill was one of the few dissenting voices. Awarding the record just two stars under a downbeat heading of 'Sullen Impact', he described how Beck 'blubs' and 'employs the classic country-weepie denial', adding, 'This is gloomy going, not rendered much easier by the lugubrious baritone in which Beck delivers his emotional autopsies, or the vague, amorphous melodies.' (All this while Badly Drawn Boy's *Have You Fed The Fish?* got the five-star 'album of the month' treatment.)

Elsewhere, the feedback was much more favourable. In *Mojo*—which did grant *Sea Change* 'album of the month' status—Chris Nelson pointed out the record 'aches too thoroughly to be [a] mere career shift.' *Q* devoted two full pages to its four-star review, with Stuart Maconie concluding, 'No one's going to be dancing to it, that's for sure. But you'd be making a mistake to sit this one out.'

In the USA, the album received possibly the best press reaction of Beck's career date. It also became his first top ten album, reaching #8. In *Rolling Stone*, David Fricke awarded the album the full five stars—making it one of only records to achieve that mark in 2003—before declaring *Sea Change* to be 'the best album Beck has ever made, and it sounds like he's paid dearly for the achievement. This kind of candour does not come easily, even to great record-makers, and Beck, one of our sharpest, has never had much cause for such direct reflection.' Fricke closed his piece by putting Beck right up with the greats. 'Beck set out to be his own Dylan. With *Sea Change*, he has made it the hard way, creating an impeccable album of truth and light from the end of love. This is his *Blood On The Tracks*.'[44]

Beck wasn't having any of the comparison, however. 'There's only one *Blood On The Tracks*, you know? I can't have my own,' he said. 'There're a lot of dimensions to a record like that. It's got all these stories and mystery and intrigue. I get a different feeling from *Sea Change*. I see the songs as being more simplistic.'

The *Village Voice* offered a more sober appraisal of the album: 'If you haven't already noticed from those song titles, the most disappointing aspect of this record is that Beck has fallen into the trap of confusing earnestly repeated clichés for personal lyrics. On some tracks, he even pushes his voice toward the deep muscular wail that Seattle made famous, while aping the chromatic choruses of the early 90s. Maybe it just feels tired because These Troubled Times call so loudly for something less indulgent … Listen too closely to this siren song, and those sea nymphs will pull you down full fathom five.'

* * *

In the weeks leading up to the release of *Sea Change*, Beck and Smokey Hormel undertook a small tour. Chatting with the audience, playing some new songs plus a couple of covers and few oldies, the pair rambled their way across the country and back again, clocking up twenty-one shows in just twenty-eight days. The focus was on Beck and his acoustic guitar, fooling around and telling stories. 'The songs have been pretty emotional,' he revealed at the time, 'but the bits in between have been pretty silly. I wanted to do different songs at every show and keep each show different, so it doesn't get into a routine.'

Shortly after *Sea Change* was released in September, Beck announced a major tour to promote the record, with a whole new band—The Flaming Lips. Singer/guitarist Wayne Coyne, drummer Steven Drozd, and bassist Michael Ivins would play as Beck's backing band for a full autumn tour. This unusual approach came after Beck had seen The Flaming Lips play earlier in the year and liked what he saw. The Oklahoma trio had just released their tenth album, *Yoshimi Battles The Pink Robots*, a melting pot of indie-rock and electronic psychedelia. The idea of a joint tour seemed to suit everyone, and would breathe new life into both acts' live shows.

Before meeting, Beck asked the Lips to listen back to his albums and select the songs that felt they had some connection with. Although they tended to veer toward 'the classics', as Wayne Coyne put it, they also requested songs like 'Get Real Paid', which Beck had never played live before. 'I thought I'd try something different,' he told KCRW. 'After you do the same thing for a number of years, I like putting myself in a tenuous situation sometimes.'

'It was just a radical, different idea,' Coyne added. 'I thought, *Oh-oh, I'm going out to California, to see this weirdo. I don't know what's going to happen …* and [he] probably thought even worse of us.'

Rehearsals began in mid September at a practice facility in Los Angeles, with the musicians working from noon until midnight for twelve days in a row. It wasn't always easy to work out arrangements for the delicate *Sea Change* material—especially with a background thrum of noise generated by heavy rockers Mudvayne, who were practising in the room next door.

'Some of those rehearsals went well and some of them were very lazy,' Coyne recalled. 'Some of those days we got a lot of work done, and other days we just walked out and talked about sunsets and things like that.' After a week off they reconvened for 'production rehearsals', which meant setting up in a theatre and working with a PA and a light system, as though it were an actual show. 'We ran through that for a week as well,' Coyne continued. 'So, you know, a lot of preparation for these shows. A lot of money, a lot of time, a lot of people hassling with it.'

It was all very different to what the Lips had done before. 'We just rehearse at my house,' Coyne explained. 'I set up the gear, and we just get together and figure all of these things out because, you know, we don't have to set up the big thing; we just go to the show and set it up and we're good to go.' This new approach would cause a little friction between Beck and the Lips as the tour wound on.

What everyone wanted to hear was the new spin that the Lips would provide to well-known Beck songs. 'I think Beck likes the idea of turning a song that was once a hip-hop song into a country song,' Coyne said. 'I've never seen that work that well. I think, occasionally, an artist can get lucky and take a song that's really great in one genre and put it into another. But I really don't agree with that.'

Beck was pleased with the Lips' input, though. 'I love what they've done with the songs,' he enthused. 'You play the same songs for years and years, but then you get them through someone else's eyes and ears.' The musicians agreed on a settled list of songs to start the tour, but continued to attempt others at soundchecks as the tour progressed.

Once the tour started, both sides felt a little nervous, but as far as Coyne was concerned, the pressure was more on him and his band. 'A lot of people don't know who we are,' he told the *NME*, 'but they know Beck. They don't care if it's Beck and The Flaming Lips or Beck and The Rolling Stones—they just come to see him. I didn't want people who'd been seeing you for years say, *You know, when we saw him with The Flaming*

Lips, it really sucked. So we wanted to make sure it was not only up to par, but something special and unique.'

The tour was to run from mid October until just before Christmas, encompassing thirty-two shows across the USA and Canada. Each night, The Flaming Lips would play a forty-five-minute set, and then Beck would take to the stage alone, before the lights came on to show that the Lips were onstage behind him, partly hidden behind a mesh curtain. Older songs such as 'Lord Only Knows', 'Loser, 'The New Pollution' and 'Where It's At' were revamped, while at least half of the set was dedicated to the new material—and that, too, received the Flaming Lips treatment. A Beatles-esque crescendo at the end of 'Lonesome Tears' threatened to break into 'A Day In The Life'; a much faster, almost jaunty take of 'Lost Cause' fairly bounced along; and as Coyne put it, that they gave 'Cold Brains' the 'Butthole Surfers guitar treatment', which basically meant searing noise at the appropriate points.

In, Chicago, Beck and Coyne foxtrotted down the aisle, while the Lips brought the house down with a cheeky rendition of the Sonny & Cher classic here renamed as 'I Got You Beck.' The combination seemed to confuse reviewers, however, with Beck sometimes called out for playing too much new *Sea Change* material, and the presence of the Lips onstage often viewed as a detraction. In her *NME* review of the tour's Halloween show in New York, April Long described the pleasure of seeing Beck 'stripped of pretension', wishing that he'd 'play it this straight more often'. Then, later in the same piece, she praised him for coming out dressed in a suit covered in fairy lights for the encore, adding, 'If only he'd slipped in a few tricks like this sooner.' It seems he couldn't win.

All seemed well after the final show in December. New friendships had been made, and the tour was deemed to have been a success. It came as something of a shock, then, when in an *NME* report the following month about how Beck had declined to bring the tour to Europe because of slow ticket sales, Wayne Coyne described Beck as 'a little bit of a diva'.

'He's kind of high maintenance,' Coyne continued, 'especially when you compare him to the way I work. I don't really need people to drive me around town, when I check into a hotel I don't check out because I don't like the way the pillows smell or something like that. It'd be 2am and we'd arrive in some city and I'd just simply just get in to the hotel and go to sleep. He would have, sometimes, these irrational rules, like you're not supposed to be able to see the highway from his window.'

In hindsight, none of this seems particularly outrageous, and Coyne himself seemed to play it down when he added, 'He knows I'd call him a diva because he would go onstage and make fun of it himself.' He would delve further into the dynamic between them—this time taking a more conciliatory tone—in an interview with the *Lipservice* newsletter. 'Being around Beck, I did get the feeling that he's just removed from everyday existence. Beck didn't treat people badly; he was just so oblivious to other people's lives. None of it's horrible. He's not a Nazi or anything. He's just a little inconsiderate. To be considerate you have to have some idea of what's going on. I mean, we'd be set to rehearse from noon till midnight every day. And there'd be days when he wouldn't show up at all, and he doesn't call. I mean, we have cell phones.'

Part of that 'obliviousness' might have been down to the fact that Beck had been ill for some of the tour, and rather than party each night after the show, he'd often just go back to the hotel and get some sleep. In any case, while he admitted to being 'totally surprised' by Coyne's comments, he seemed to take them with a pinch of salt. 'The last time I saw him, he was like, *I love you like a brother, you've helped us so much and I'll always be your friend.* He's a showman, and he picks on people sometimes. He does it to everybody—his band, his friends, anybody who walks in the room. I think, in the press, it comes off as an attack, but he's just on permanent truth serum.'

* * *

As usual, Beck had other projects in the works, and it was later revealed that during his run of summer 2002 solo shows, he had lost a bag containing the tapes of a whole other batch of new songs. He'd also been working with the electronica producer William Orbit.

'I think we probably will work [together] again,' Beck explained. 'He sent over a bunch of ideas he had, I picked one I liked, he came over, and I wrote some lyrics, put some guitar on it. We had a couple of nice chats, and his process is fairly similar to the way we recorded *Odelay*, using computers. I was able to improvise for an hour or two, and then from that we took from that what the song was. So he's a builder, an arranger, a composer.'

He also gave some clues as to the direction of his next record. 'It's maybe more of a marriage between some of the experimentation on [*Odelay* and *Midnite Vultures*] and some of the songwriting on the new record. I'm probably due to do something more in the *Odelay* vein—that's my sound. The last three albums, anytime anything gets a little too close to that, I just start going in another direction.'

None of this was in evidence in the spring of 2003, however, as Beck headed across the Atlantic for some European solo shows. They were similar to the 2002 summer shows, but this time he put on a true one-man show with a whole host of instruments. Programming his Roland drum machine onstage, playing his way through a selection of guitars, and sitting down at a '$200 piano that cost $4,000 to ship over', he told stories, interacted with the crowd, and pulled out a mesmerizing selection of cover versions, from a 'haunted house' version of Justin Timberlake's 'Cry Me A River', through The Velvet Underground and The Flaming Lips. 'When the undisputed King of Mutant Pop is in this sort of mood,' the *NME* concluded, 'the only thing to do is stare in wonder.' And they were spot on.

CHAPTER 15

'I think it meant something at some point.' (2003-05)

In June 2003, Beck unexpectedly made the headlines for an onstage mishap that occurred when he wasn't even playing, after he was scheduled to appear at the Field Day Festival—an ill-fated venture that became known as the Field Day Fiasco.

Originally planned to take place in rural Long Island, the event was moved to Giants Stadium in New Jersey due to poor ticket sales and issues over policing. An initial list of more than thirty bands was cut in half, but Beck was still due to perform alongside the likes of The Beastie Boys, Underworld, Radiohead, and Blur.

While standing at the side of the stage, watching Blur play in a rainstorm, Beck took a stray bass guitar to the ribs. Fearing he had punctured a lung, the attending paramedics whisked him off to hospital, and by the time that worry had been discounted, it was too late to go back and take a later slot. By the following Wednesday, Beck was back onstage in Chicago. He would continue to play shows through to the end of August.

In the autumn, Beck was ready to return to the studio, with a batch of lively new songs that were far removed from the quiet introspection of *Sea Change*. He was just starting to get some momentum when he was rocked by the news in late October that the thirty-four-year-old singer-songwriter Elliott Smith had died as a result of two knife wounds to the chest. Theories abounded as to whether it was suicide or murder.[45] Few were truly surprised when news broke of Smith's death—he had often spoken of taking his own life—but it hit Beck had. In 2002, Smith had been arrested at a show on the Beck/Flaming Lips tour after a disagreement with local police, and had spent a night in jail. He had lived near Beck in Silver Lake, and they had discussed working together. Beck subsequently played at a Smith tribute concert, and helped out when his photographer friend Autumn de Wilde published a book about him.

Beck's personal life took a turn for the better when he started dating the twenty-eight-year-old actress and writer Marissa Ribisi, best known for her roles in *Dazed & Confused* (1993) and *Pleasantville* (1998). Then, late in 2003, he again began to concentrate on working toward his next album. He had worked on a number of demos while travelling during the short solo tour that followed *Sea Change*, recording almost forty new songs with just an acoustic guitar. All of that work was lost, however, when he left the tape containing the demos backstage at a show in Washington.

'I was never able to retrieve those songs, which I thought were so much better than *Sea Change*,' he told *American Songwriter* in 2011. 'Anyone could have those songs. Somebody has them. I don't want to name any names, but I thought I recognised a few of those songs over the years!'

Losing so much new material in one go was a huge blow. 'Those were songs I worked particularly hard on, and I felt like I really had something with them,' he explained to Pitchfork.com around the same time. 'I could remember the music to about three or four of them, and a couple lines here or there, but most of them were just on those tapes. They were fairly complex songs, and much more involved, technically, on the guitar, than anything I'd done. So, for a year after that, I didn't write any songs.'

It wasn't until Beck decided to go back and work with John King and Mike Simpson—aka The Dust Brothers—that he started writing again. He also had a batch of much earlier songs that he had put to one side back before making *Midnite Vultures*.

Writing new material and revisiting the older songs would prove to be a long process. As ever, Beck was seeking out new music from which to take inspiration. The Dust Brothers had their legendary vinyl collection to work with, when a sample or two was needed, but Beck also spent time searching out obscure or forgotten tunes.

I buy a lot of CDs now, just out of ease. When I collect vinyl, it's just at different record stores when I'm travelling. The best was when I was touring with Sonic Youth because they knew where all the great vinyl stores were. Thurston [Moore] would take me out to some amazing store in the middle of nowhere, he'd flip to the racks so fast it was like lightning and he'd rip out one and say, 'Here, you need to get this.' Usually, with me, I've read a fair bit about music, so I know what I'm looking for. A few years ago, I was collecting a lot of rare Brazilian vinyl—Caetano Veloso, Os Mutantes. I would go to the Record Swap Meet—that was my favourite place—and get there at six in the morning, because literally there's these hip-hop kids and Japanese there at four in the morning helping them unload their trucks, and they're going through the records while they're still in the trucks, and they just skim the best stuff.

The sessions for what would become *Guero* began in September 2003 and continued all the way through to the following August. Beck went through a series of life-changing events during this period. At the end of 2003, Marissa became pregnant, and the couple married on April 3 2004. The following August, she gave birth to a son, Cosimo Henri Hansen.

Of fatherhood, Beck noted, 'It brings a certain happiness and fullness to your life, there is no denying that. You're handed this huge responsibility, but it does make you look at the relative importance of things. It makes things a little less serious. You're sort of going back to your childhood, [and] you start rediscovering certain aspects of yourself.' When it came to choosing a name for his son, meanwhile, he was keen to avoid the obvious. 'I heard that, in America at least, 70 percent of all men have the same ten names. It's quite homogeneous in the boy name department, but then again you don't necessarily want to give them something unwieldy. His middle name's Henri, so he always has an out.'

Marissa, like her twin brother (and fellow actor) Giovanni, was a member of the Church of Scientology, which no doubt led Beck to become more involved with the church than he had been since his late teens. On Marissa's official website—which, at the time of writing, doesn't seem to have been updated in several years—she talks about her relationship with the church, and how it has helped her find success.

Around this time, Beck began to open up a little more in interviews when he was asked about his involvement with Scientology—and he seemed to get asked about it in every interview he gave. While he sometimes declined to comment—not wishing to have his life spread open for all to comment on and pick over—he did give some insight into his thoughts. His overall view seemed to be that he concentrated on the good the church does, and that the criticisms others had made of it were at odds with what he had experienced first-hand. There was a strong sense that he didn't necessarily follow every aspect of the religion closely, but that he took guidance from parts of it, just as he did from other areas of his life and culture.

In Beck's view, as he explained to *The Age* in 2006, the church could be a positive model for 'education, helping people with illiteracy, second language students, all that stuff. The drug rehabilitation programmes have the highest success rate of any in the world. If you actually look at what's been done and the things that have come out of it, it kind of blows away this kind of criticism.'

'There's whole aspects that you probably don't see,' he told *Mojo* in 2005. 'I think it's really something that has helped [my father] a lot. And there's aspects of it that have helped me. ... If it's something that helps you in your life, it's a positive thing, so all I have to say is that you can't really make a judgement on something unless you know something about it first-hand. That's always kind of being my policy on life, to learn about something before [criticising it]. So many problems in the world stem from that kind of intolerance.'

* * *

The recording sessions for *Guero* took place at the Boat, The Dust Brothers' studio in Silver Lake, with Beck and the Brothers sharing production duties, and spending much of their time in postproduction trying to make the songs sound less polished. One of the methods they employed was to run the high-tech recordings through a transistor radio to rough them up a little bit. The songs were noisier, poppier, and more hook-laden than Beck's recent material.

'It's like musical crop rotation or something,' he told *Billboard*, 'to keep the soil from being depleted. Otherwise you'd just have to step away from music for a while. We had some unfinished songs from years ago, so the original plan was to go in and finish those. We've been talking about doing something for years and years—it was just finding the right time, when we all had a good five or six months to do something proper. Once we got in there, we instantly had about fifteen songs that just flowed out.'

Though eight years had passed since they made *Odelay* together, Beck found that he and The Dust Brothers easily fell back into the groove. 'There's this intangible thing that happens when we work together,' he explained to *American Songwriter*. 'We speak the same tongue. Most of the time, I know what I want to do, or when I'm going in the right direction. But it's nice to bounce something off of somebody and see whether it's a stupid idea or not. There're certain things I would do and I'd say, *Oh this is stupid. It's simple. It's too cute. It's trite.* And they'd say, *No, it's great.* And so I'd leave it there. It takes two to have a conversation sometimes. Also, they're just great with beats.'

The main difference between the two sets of sessions was the studio. Previously The Dust Brothers had worked from PCP Studios, in what was basically a converted spare bedroom in their house. Then, in 1997, they bought an unusual Silver Lake property built for the purpose of radio broadcasting in 1941. It became known as the Boat because, well, it looked like one, stranded on dry land. Simpson and King then set about converting it, filling it with a mixture of vintage and state-of-the-art equipment.

'Combining old and new has been our goal as musicians and producers and now as studio owners,' Simpson told *Sound On Sound* magazine. 'We've made our name staying abreast of the latest technology, but at the same time we've used that technology to sample all those brilliantly recorded recordings from the 1970s. As it got more and more painful to use samples, we realised that we were better off creating those sounds ourselves, and the way to do that is to get all the equipment it was originally created on.'

Beck was concerned that if he recorded an album in his 'own style', he'd be accused of simply repeating what he'd done in the mid 90s, and that the new songs would end up sounding like the songs he heard in commercials that were clearly 'influenced' by his *Odelay* material. But while there are some vague comparisons to be drawn between *Odelay* and *Guero*, it's safe to say that the latter explores a wider range of musical territory.

The album bursts into life with 'E-Pro'—which, it must be said, is not a million miles from 'Devils Haircut'. Beck played all the instruments on it, apart from the drum programming and a sample of The Beastie Boys' 'So What'cha Want'. The genesis of the title is elusive, though. 'I think it meant something at some point,' Beck told *American Songwriter*, 'but no one remembers. When we're working on songs, usually we're just working on stabs of ideas first, and [songs] get called things for clerical purposes. Occasionally, there's a fake name that stays.'

'E-Pro' segues right into 'Que Onda Guero', the album's centrepiece, which takes listeners on a virtual walking tour of one of Beck's old neighbourhoods. The sound snippets of voices, street sounds, and effects that pop in and out of the mix give the impression of field recordings from an East LA ghetto. Beck tells us of the characters and stores that he passes by, all the while being heckled in English and Spanish. 'If you go to that neighbourhood,' he explained, 'you'll see the song: the popsicle guys, the vendedoras, the ladies with the shopping carts, the peeled mangos.' The title translates either to 'Hey white boy' or 'Where you going, Blondie?' 'Guero' was a word Beck heard a lot while growing up. The song ends with a laughing voice that claims the Guero is 'going to Captain Cork's to get the new Yanni cassette.'

The mood changes again on 'Girl', and already, in the space of three songs, we've gone from the album-opening guitar blasts to a Latino stroll and now to a summer-pop anthem that could just as easily be about a boy catching sight of a girl at the beach as it could be a serial killer planning his next murder. It's followed by the hypnotic trance of 'Missing', complete with a sample from 'Você E Eu' by Claus Ogerman & His Orchestra, plus strings newly arranged by David Campbell.

'Earthquake Weather' shuffles and scratches along, marking the first appearance on the album of old hands Joey Waronker, Justin Meldal-Johnsen, Smokey Hormel, and Roger Manning Jr., while the organ adornments come courtesy of Money Mark. 'Hell Yes'—co-written by The Dust Brothers, and with a cameo vocal appearance by the actress Christina Ricci—sees Beck return to the kind of stop-start rap territory that he hadn't attempted since the late 1990s, and would later inspire a whole host of remixes.

'Broken Drum'—dedicated to Elliott Smith—slows things right down and shifts the mood to that of a funeral procession. Beck is all over this track, singing and playing guitar, bass, drums, celeste, and piano. 'Scarecrow' speeds things up again, and, if anything, comes close to being the quintessential Beck track, with its sound effects, incessant beat, guitars coming in and out of the mix, and a lyric that delves into the deepest Delta blues. As he sings of how the 'Devil's trying to take my mind' and his soul is 'just a silhouette', he could literally be sitting at Robert Johnson's crossroads. 'I was into this idea of including more human sounds,' he explained. 'There's a haunting, high-pitched sound that goes through the whole thing, [and] that's me singing through the echo effect. All the percussive type stuff on there is just me yelling through the delay pedal.'

Jack White co-wrote and plays bass on 'Go It Alone', having dropped by the studio and offered to play on the song in return for Beck writing him a speech for the Grammy Awards show. White's playing is right at the front of the mix during the verses, with Beck's crunching guitar taking over on the choruses.

'Farewell Ride' sounds like an outtake from the *One Foot In The Grave* sessions, before one of the oldest songs on the album, 'Rental Car', comes in sounding like a long-lost cousin of 'Novacane' mixed with 'Diamond Bollocks' via 'The New Pollution', although the original concept was to merge the nu-metal sound of the late 90s with 'Austrian yodelling'—like 'Julie Andrews goes to Fred Durst's house', as Beck put it in his *American Songwriter* interview. 'Then it eventually morphed into this hand-clappin', summertime-on-the-road song,' he continued. 'There is that little bit when it just goes full metal, and then [it] ends up lederhosen.'

Few other than Beck would have come up with such a description—or indeed, with such a song. After that, the standard version of the album— which would be issued in several different forms and formats—chugs to a close with the work song-like rhythm of 'Emergency Exit'.[46]

On the whole, *Guero* is something of a departure from *Odelay*, but you could certainly trace the lineage of some of the songs back to the 1990s. The overriding feeling was that, once again, Beck had successfully pulled off bringing together a whole range of styles and approaches on one album—just. Trimming a couple of songs here and there might have made the whole sound that much stronger.

In January 2005, with the album having been pretty much finished for several months, a version of *Guero* was leaked onto the internet. The sound quality wasn't up to commercial standards, but otherwise it was almost the final album, aside from some differences to the track listing and titles.[47]

The leak had no effect on the scheduled release date of March 29. Two weeks before the album hit the shelves, 'E-Pro' was released as a single, with a press release claiming, 'Beck's back. And the world's a better place for it.' The energetic video and prominent guitars garnered considerable airplay in the USA, which no doubt contributed to *Guero* entering the *Billboard* 200 at #2—Beck's highest album-chart placing to date.[48] It didn't do too badly in the UK, either, reaching #15.

Various versions of the album were released, with a deluxe edition housed in a hardcover book featuring fifty-two glossy pages of lyrics, photographs, and artwork, plus a DVD. Around the time of its release, Beck revealed his excitement about the possibilities of music formats in the nascent twenty-first century:

> There are so many dimensions to what a record can be these days. Artists can, and should, approach making an album as an opportunity to do a series of releases: one that's visual, one that has alternate versions, and one that's something the listener can participate in or arrange and change. It's time for the album to embrace the technology. I'd love to put out an album that you could edit and mix and layer directly in iTunes. In an ideal world, I'd find a way to let people truly interact with the records I put out—not just remix the songs, but maybe play them like a videogame.

When they heard that Beck had gone back to work with The Dust Brothers, many reviewers immediately decided—often without having heard the whole record—that *Guero* must be *Odelay II*. But they seemed to miss the fact that the album is more varied in scope and depth. From the rock of 'E-Pro' to the Latino influence of 'Que Onda Guero' and the pure pop of 'Girl', Beck was mixing genres in a way that he had never attempted on a single album before. And that's just the first three songs on the album.

'Who's saying that?' Beck asked, when told of how many of the reviews of *Guero* were calling it a return to the 'sonic playground' feel of his mid-90s breakthrough. 'I think they just see that I'm working with

The Dust Brothers and assume that. But you can never really re-create the past. It's probably a bit of old and new, but there's plenty of new stuff.' He also questioned the accusations that his music revealed little, and that he avoided expressing any emotional depth. 'Have you listened to my records?' he asked. 'What are you looking for?'

Discussing the album with *American Songwriter* magazine, Beck explained that he was more concerned with providing impressionistic images for a song than spelling out his point in explicit detail:

> I started to realise that some people thought I was being obtuse, or I wasn't saying anything. That's happened on a few occasions. But I do like that approach where you can take someone to a space, rather than just give them a laundry list of events. Make a bunch of colours and images and pictures and try to transmit an experience that couldn't really be explained in a situation where it's a direct, basic line. To convey loneliness, or contentment, you can't always use traditional storytelling methods. You want words that cut through the basic experience and take you right to where that place is, mentally. That's what words are for—they're there to be used. There aren't any rules.

Giving the album a grade of A-, *Entertainment Weekly* described *Guero* as 'the first record on which the many moods and sides of Beck coexist, and it's about time'. But if that seemed like a positive (and accurate) start, the magazine spoiled it by ending the review with the outdated cliché: 'When *Guero* ends, we don't know this elusive man-child any better than we once did. But we have a lot more fun than we've had in a while trying to figure him out.'

Rolling Stone also dipped back into the mid 90s in its review of Beck's 'liveliest and jumpiest music in years. Suggested ad slogan: "The slack is back!"'. The *NME* gave *Guero* eight out of ten, reckoning that '75 percent of *Guero* is … very good indeed'. The review ended with some advice: 'In pop, there's nothing big and clever about being clever, but *Guero* represents a very clever man being clever enough to recognise what he's good at. Keep on, brother, keep on.'

* * *

Something that Beck has always been interested in—and would take to more logical extremes before long—is the concept of re-interpreting work, be it his own or anyone else's. Having started out essentially as a cover-singer, he knew what it was like to try to give your own slant on a song. His attention had also been drawn to *Fresh Meat On Old Slabs*, one of several fan-made CDs that broke down and brought new insight to areas of his back catalogue.

'I found it touching and kind of sweet,' he said, 'because it was just fans doing versions, some interesting versions, [and] I was kind of amazed. We [also] did a remix and got hundreds of versions of one song. Each one had about twenty seconds that were amazing at the time. I annotated in each version where the great part was, and I was going to produce this master version—[a] twenty-minute mega-mix that would have been created by a thousand different people—[but] I lost those notes. It would have been a free-for-all, but a great thing to listen to.'

The marketing campaign for *Guero* included the sending out of numerous promotional and remix CDs. Various versions of 'Hell Yes' were circulated, followed by *Gameboy Variations* and a *Hell Yes EP*, while Interscope also sent out a collection titled *Beck: A Brief Overview*, an unusual thirteen-track CD comprised mostly of songs from his last five albums, plus a couple from *One Foot In The Grave*, which had originally been released by K Records.

Then, in 2005, Beck decided to rerelease *Guero* in completely remixed form. *Guerolito* ('Little Guero') was released in December 2005 and pulled together remixes by Homelife, Air, The Beastie Boys' Ad-Rock, Mario Caldato Jr., Boards Of Canada, and Dizzee Rascal that breathed new life into the songs and ranged from slight diversions to radical reworks.

Mario C. provided one of the highlights with his 'Terremoto Tempo' take on 'Earthquake Weather'. He had worked with Beck before, recording half a dozen tracks with him in the mid 90s, one of which ('Minus') ended up on *Odelay*. He'd also remixed Beck songs before at his home studio in the Glassell Park neighbourhood of north LA, but 'Terremoto Tempo' was his favourite of all. 'I only had the vocal,' he explained, 'so everything else had to be new—no recycling. I found some cool elements that worked together really well, then added some hand-played drum programming on an [Akai] MPC by Domenico from Rio, then it really came to life. It's really one of my best remixes, musically and sonically. Beck is a great artist to work with, very open-minded and creative, and he allows others the same space to express within, much respect.'

As with *Guero*, *Guerolito* was accompanied by various promo CDs—including *Beck Remix EP #2* and a four-track album sampler—as he continued to test the boundaries of what an album should be in these changing times. Gone were the days of sides A and B on a record or tape. The CD had allowed albums to grow longer than in days of old, and now the age of downloading single songs was putting the very concept of the album in danger. Beck wanted to challenge that view, and on his next album he'd show that he had ways of making the album concept more appealing than ever.

CHAPTER 16

'It's something else.' (2006-07)

In the mid 2000s, Beck was writing new material at a furious rate—probably more so than at any time since 1992–93, when he produced more than four album's worth of songs. From 2002–03 onward, he had recorded more than two dozen songs for *Sea Change* and *Guero*, and that was on top of the three-dozen or so songs he'd recorded as demos and then lost on tour. Now, in 2006, he had another expansive project ready for release. *The Information* would be his ninth studio album, and following on from the extra efforts he had put into the art and videos for *Guero*, this was going to be his most ambitious release to date. Many of the new songs had been held over from the *Guero* sessions, but this time he brought back Nigel Godrich as co-producer.

Unlike the more introspective mood of the material they had recorded together for *Mutations* and *Sea Change*, the songs on *The Information* would be more wide-ranging, and assembling them proved to be a long, painstaking process. Even naming the record proved difficult. The album's title track was originally called 'Colourforms', but that had to be changed because the term is a registered trademark. For a while, the album itself was known as *International Dreambag*, until Beck decided—quite rightly—that it sounded too hippie-ish. He eventually settled on *The Information*, which he felt fitted with what he was trying to get across in a number of the songs.

'Information is what keeps the world turning,' he said. 'Things travel so quickly these days, and it's difficult to know what the effect of that is, because it's all so new. I'm addicted to all these things as much as anyone.' Having a running theme throughout was unusual for him and the way he tended to put albums together. 'I look at each song as if it's a completely separate song,' he explained, 'so it's all unrelated and a bit random. It's just kind of putting yourself into an uncomfortable zone, and seeing what you find.'

The sessions began in a specially constructed studio in Beck's garden before being completed at his and Godrich's studio of choice, Ocean Way on Sunset Boulevard. There were significant changes to the musicians employed for the sessions this time around, with drumming duties split between James Gadson, Joey Waronker, and Harvey Mason. Occasional live guitarist Jason Faulkner was used throughout, as was newcomer Justin Stanley, while new touring instrumentalists Brian LeBarton and Greg Kurstin played everything from berimbau and piano to a child's Speak & Spell toy. (Old stalwarts Smokey Hormel, Justin Meldal-Johnsen, and Roger Manning Jr. are credited only for 'intro sounds'.)

In the liner notes to the album, Beck is listed as having played seventeen different instruments and noise-makers, as well as singing, while Nigel Godrich, who co-wrote five of the songs, played percussion, whistle, kalimba, drums, and various other gadgets. 'We work well together because most of the time we're on the same channel and thinking the same things,' Beck explained, in an interview with the BBC. 'I like working with him because he encourages me to do things that are less obvious, or no one's going to get.'

The length of time taken to get the songs down and to their mutual satisfaction proved difficult, however. 'We started the record in 2003, and we got together annually,' he continued. 'We combed over everything, and got rid of the things we were tired of, the things that seemed trite. It started out painless and ended up being painful. It's as if we made the album once, and we made it again, and we made it a third time.'

As a result, the final album does feel like something that has been dissected and put back together again. It also sounds like the co-producers couldn't decide what to cut, and so left everything in, making *The Information* a very long album.

Things start well enough, with 'Elevator Music'. It was the first song completed for the album, and was reported to have once had more of a sing-along chorus, but in the first example of his going back and changing a song, Beck decided he wanted to give it a more reflective feel, rapping over a bump'n'grind shuffle constructed from strummed guitars, shakers, and a host of percussion.

The relentless drive of 'I Think I'm In Love' is a song Beck has described as fitting 'somewhere between Bridget Bardot and Krautrock', its lyrics addressing the confusion of modern life. 'Cellphone's Dead' was the first single to be drawn from the album, and its stop-start feel, robotic beeps and clangs, and high-speed rap—plus the voice of Beck's young niece, Lycia, telling us, 'One by one I'll knock you out'—would perhaps have given the average listener the wrong impression of what the record was all about. Much more representative of the overall feel of the album is the fourth track, 'Strange Apparition', which with its shakers, piano, and soaring vocals led many to draw comparisons with early-1970s era Rolling Stones.

'Soldier Jane' is another track with slight Krautrock leanings, but is one of the album's weaker efforts. Next up, 'Nausea' is one of the record's most raucous tracks, and would become a centrepiece of the live show. 'I wanted it to sound like The Stooges in South America,' Beck explained to whiskeyclone.net. 'We'd jam and then take three or four minutes from it—the beginning or the end—and turn it into a song.'[49]

'New Round' comes from the same dark stable as many of Beck's album closers—think 'Ramshackle', 'Runners Dial Zero', or 'Emergency Exit'—but when it appears, the album is only halfway through. (In the old days, it would probably have closed side one of the record.) We go deeper still on 'Dark Star', which Beck has described as having a feeling of imminent disaster—'It was in the air when we wrote it'—while his gently rapped verses lull listeners in to the gloom.

The mood livens up with the sprightly rap of 'We Dance Alone' and the dense acoustic strumming of 'No Complaints', but the rest of the collection is patchy, to say the least, not least the schizophrenic rap of '1000 BPM', which should probably have been left as a B-side. 'Motorcade' is one of the album's more lyrically interesting tracks, while 'The Information' is a pulsating tale of drowning in data, with Beck giving the title concept a female slant: 'She's the sister of avarice / The wife of a poisonous tide.' 'Movie Theme' is based around a series of organ chords that Nigel Godrich came up with, and marks perhaps the first time that Beck has written about Scientology in song, as he sings of 'looking for a ladder in the stratosphere' so that he can 'be happy' and 'let my bones melt away'.

Beck had recorded numerous extended experimental pieces in the past, but aside from on *A Western Harvest Field By Moonlight*, they had never made it on to one of his albums. As such, the ten and a half minutes of 'The Horrible Fanfare / Landslide / Exoskeleton' came as something of a surprise. The opening section is built around a drum'n'bass rhythm, with Beck rapping almost incomprehensibly over it, before an abrupt shift a couple of minutes in: things get louder, beats from 'Cellphone's Dead' drift in and out of the mix, we hear Dave Eggers and Spike Jonze in conversation, the shipping forecast is read out by actress Rachel Shelley, and the feeling of incoming doom first hinted at on 'Dark Star' seems to flow from the speakers.

Expanding on the ideas he'd had for *Guero*, Beck purchased some video recording equipment to make short films for each track on the album. 'We're going to put out a version of the record that people will be able to watch on sites like YouTube,' he told *Wired*. 'We filmed a series of very low-budget, homemade videos for all the songs on the record. We got a bunch of cameras and a $100 video mixer off eBay and shot fifteen silly, impromptu videos against a green screen. We even invited our friends and family into the studio to be a part of the action—my mother-in-law did the lighting, and my son and nieces and nephews are running around acting crazy. It was just a complete free-for-all, done on the fly.'

'We were thinking it would be fun,' Godrich added, 'because there are outlets for this kind of stuff now. You're happy just to put it up on YouTube to get people to see it.' As if any further evidence were needed, it demonstrated how musicians were now beginning to bypass MTV, which itself was finding visitors to its online streaming service usurped by the likes of YouTube, Yahoo, and AOL Music. The *Information* videos, meanwhile, were also made available to buy from iTunes for $1.99 each.

Another visual medium that Beck played about with on *The Information* was the album sleeve. The front cover was essentially a folded piece of plain graph paper, with one of four different sheets of stickers of pictures of Beck, song titles, and other random images included inside the package— the idea being that buyers could create their own unique artwork.

Beck hoped that the stickers would take on a life of their own, and be stuck to things other than the CD sleeve, thereby infiltrating people's homes rather than being left on a shelf. 'I'm excited about being able to take totally different approaches to creating and distributing different types of projects,' he told *Wired*. 'I like the idea that I can quickly record a few acoustic songs that I've been working on and immediately put them online for people to download. And then I can record songs with a producer in a big studio for a big label and put them out as a CD, a DVD, and a remix project and let people experience that music in very different ways.'

While most observers would consider the concept of the stickers to be innovative and fun, in the UK, the Official Chart Company disqualified *The Information* from the listings because their inclusion gave the album an 'unfair advantage'. Nobody else took this view, however, and in the USA it reached #7 on the *Billboard* 200, and #3 on the Rock Albums chart.

In the UK, the press reaction to the album was somewhat mixed, ranging from very good to warm but not ecstatic. For those who weren't so keen on the album, the main problem seemed to be that, at seventy minutes in duration, the album was just too long, and that a cut down *Best Of The Information* would have been a much more powerful proposition.

That said, the *Observer* called *The Information* 'a musical delight', while for the *Times*, which gave the album four stars, 'the possibilities— like the conceptual album artwork of blank sleeves and stickers—seem

213

endless for Beck'. *Mojo* awarded a faintly subdued three stars, while for *Uncut*, 'there are plenty of good things here, but there's also a sense of artist and producer operating in default mode'. *Q* magazine's somewhat unfair conclusion was that Beck had 'fused his best albums [and] made something worse', but as far as the *NME* was concerned, 'Beck gets better as he gets madder, this is definitely his best since *Midnite Vultures*—maybe even since *Odelay*.' For the *Guardian*, the album was 'a bracing reminder that Beck's musical imagination has survived his fall from fashion', while for the *Independent*, it marked 'the first time Beck's made two great albums in succession since the heady days of *Mellow Gold* and *Odelay*'.

US critics were generally enthusiastic, with *Rolling Stone*'s David Fricke calling *The Information* 'one of the best albums Beck has ever made' and describing it as 'a compelling overload, combining the sample-delic bloom of Beck's best-loved album, *Odelay*, and the folk-pop introspection of his least understood, 2002's *Sea Change*'. Headier still praise could be found in *Entertainment Weekly*, which awarded its usual A- grade and celebrated 'a swarming, psychedelic set', while noting, 'No one's better suited to shape such a project than Nigel Godrich. ... He and Beck pump bleeps, blips, samples, scratches, voices, telephone noises, and kalimbas into songs soaked in drones and dub reverb. It's a sonic tour de force, and Beck seems comfortable in the info-storm, which he presents not as dystopia or utopia, but as a restless middle ground, like Dante's limbo, or America in 2006.'

On October 2, the day *The Information* was issued in the UK, the BBC's 6 Music radio station had a dedicated 'Beck Day', for which the singer recorded live versions of some of the songs from the new album and then took part in an interview with DJ Steve Lamacq. For the ensuing tour, Beck commissioned a set of puppets to represent each of his band members to 'play' at the shows with him. The shows would typically open with 'Loser', but with only the puppets onstage, before Beck joined them partway through. The puppets' antics would then be projected behind the 'real' band for the rest of the show. A highlight of these shows came during 'The Golden Age', for which the band would sit around a mocked-up dinner table while Beck began the song alone before gradually joining him on improvised percussion using cutlery and other items from the table.

In February 2007 a second deluxe edition of *The Information* was released, including additional tracks, a DVD of all the videos, a disc of remixes, and all four of the sticker sheets given out with the original album. 'We're moving into a time when the song and the imagery and video are all able to exist as one thing,' Beck told *Rolling Stone*, shortly before the album's release. 'It's not even technically an audio thing anymore. It's something else. The conventional ways aren't working like they used to, so now there's a willingness to try new things.'

* * *

Compared to the hectic schedule of the previous three or four years, 2007 was a quieter period for Beck. In May, he and Marissa had a second child, Tuesday, and that summer he released a standalone single, 'Timebomb', a driving slice of pop-rock with minimal lyrics. The song was nominated for a Grammy in the Best Solo Rock Vocal Performance category, but would be his only new release of the year, as he took time off to be with his family.

There was another reason for his low profile, however. In 2005, while filming the video for 'E-Pro', he had been held up in a harness for the duration of the ten-hour shoot, the result of which was a debilitating back injury. 'There was this crazy choreography, where he was in a harness inside this moving wheel, being hit with sticks,' Joey Waronker told *Rolling Stone* in 2014. 'In the footage, it looked like he was floating around. Somehow, he got seriously hurt.'

Beck himself would not even mention the injury in interviews until 2013, when he belatedly explained what had happened and revealed that he hadn't wanted to be 'the guy who won't stop talking about his war wounds at the picnic'. Even as he kept quiet about the injury, however, it was clear that the pattern of his working life was changing.

CHAPTER 17

'You get an idea and go with it. There's no great plan.' (2008-10)

In January 2008, *Odelay* was given the tenth-anniversary deluxe reissue treatment—twelve years after it was originally release. Beck had been so busy recording and promoting *Guero* and *The Information* that the new version of his most famous album had to be pushed back two years. Now, with eighteen months having passed since *The Information* was released, it gave reviewers a chance to reappraise the album and decide whether it still stood up as a classic. And it did.

Beck gave interviews in support of the reissue, but decided against the twenty-first century craze of going on tour and playing the entire album in sequence in front of an audience. 'I've been asked to do *Odelay* live,' he explained to pitchfork.com's Ryan Dombal. 'It didn't feel right for me. I toured that album incessantly for three and a half years straight when it came out, and it's not going to really get better than it was then. It seems a little soon to bring something like that back, too. The window for nostalgia is getting narrower. I feel like I'd need a good couple of decades to be far enough away from it to see it.'

He wasn't too happy with the reissue, either. 'I'm a little conflicted on it,' he continued. 'But they were going to do it with or without my help. I was able to find some things to include that hadn't been heard before, but it was probably a little soon to be doing a special edition. The people who wanted it probably had it. Sometimes, reissues can be revelatory, or put the original record in a different light, but those are rare. Everything that was left behind from *Odelay* was pretty much just scraps and four-track B-sides.'

The two-disc reissue contains the original album, three remixes, a dozen previously issued B-sides, the 'Deadweight' single, and just two previously unreleased songs, 'Inferno' and 'Gold Chains'. Hearing all the tracks in one place does make it easier to see where Beck was heading before meeting up with The Dust Brothers, with the downbeat blues of 'Ramshackle', 'Feather In Your Cap', and 'Brother' sitting well together.

Looking back, Beck spoke of the pressure he felt when he was given a decent budget to record *Odelay*.

I was acutely aware that I was thought of as a one-hit wonder. Through the whole making of [*Odelay*], I thought, *I'm never going to have the money to do something like this again, so I'm just going to go out in a fiery blaze.* That's really how it was received when I turned it in to the record company. I had major people in the music business calling up to tell me, 'Don't release this record. It's gonna be career suicide.'

This is the record that I spent $200,000 making—more money than anybody in my family had ever dealt with in the history of my entire family, probably back to the beginning of time. That was a lot of pressure. But I grew up flipping through the cut-out bins, and you'd see ten copies in a row of a record that obviously didn't sell, and they're all, like, 20 cents a copy. When I was making *Odelay*, I thought, at least I'll try to do something interesting, so that when someone finds it in the bin twenty years later, they'll be like, *This is kind of weird. Hello.*

Beck was also making preparations for his next album. In December 2007, he approached Brian Burton, aka Danger Mouse, with a view to having him producing some of his new songs. Burton had risen to fame in 2004 by mixing Jay-Z's *Black Album* and The Beatles' 'White Album' to create his own *Grey Album*, before cementing his reputation by teaming up with Cee-Lo Green to form Gnarls Barkley. By the time he met Beck, Burtheon had also produced Gorillaz, Sparklehorse, and The Rapture.

Beck wanted to get away from the methods of working he'd followed with The Dust Brothers and Nigel Godrich and try something fresh. The idea behind *Modern Guilt* seemed to be a reaction against the sprawling work Beck had done over the last five years. Instead of containing fourteen or more songs, there would be just ten, and the album wouldn't be seventy minutes long but just half an hour. There would be no band, no assortment of fifteen or more people playing on the album, just Beck and one or two guests to help out. There wouldn't be extravagant packages with DVDs, sticker sets, and special editions, just a simple CD case with a plain booklet listing the lyrics. The differences were marked.

Beck found Danger Mouse easy to work with. 'It felt like we could have been making our fourth record together,' he told *Rolling Stone.* 'It did help that we share a lot of musical references. We spent the first week just talking about different records. His knowledge is pretty deep, especially with some of the obscure late-60s, early-70s rock. I was hoping all the songs would be two minutes long, but then I got rid of all the short songs.'

Convening at Anonyme Studios in Los Angeles, the pair started each new song with Beck playing acoustic guitar over a drumbeat. If they decided it was a 'take', Burton would add bass, and then Beck would go back and record any further instruments himself. 'I write the music first,' he told NPR's *Morning Edition,* 'and I record it. Then, with a song like "Modern Guilt", I just get on the microphone and write something really quick, sort of off the top of my head, so I can remember the melody. And what happens a lot of times is that what I initially sing on there ends up being on the record. A lot of these things, I don't really get to spend too much time figuring out what it is.'

The opening 'Orphans' features backing vocals by Chan Marshall, aka Cat Power, and does a good job of introducing the album's retro feel. Over a stuttering heartbeat of drum and bass (provided by one of the only other guests on the album, Jason Falkner), Beck's dreamlike vocal sets out the overriding themes of the album: guilt, indecision, lack of direction, and a sense of being lost. 'Gamma Ray' bounces along for a furious three minutes and sounds as if it were stripped from an obscure 60s spy movie. While on 'Orphans' he was an abandoned child, on 'Gamma Ray' he's a refugee from a burning house, worried about the melting icecaps.

'Chemtrails' is a desolate tale of watching people drown in the sea outside his window, the music echoing the lyric with haunting mood changes and deathly piano reminiscent of Big Star's *Third*. Joey Waronker was on hand for the drumming and percussion master class, the result of which is an epic and undervalued addition to Beck's catalogue.

The title track picks up the pace again. Here, Beck is feeling shame but he doesn't know why. Is the lyric autobiographical? Beck is unlikely to say either way, but it doesn't take too much of a leap to equate the lyrics to his views on Scientology. He has often said that the public portrayal of the church is very different to the one he has experienced first hand, and how he doesn't recognise the criticisms various journalists have made of the religion. 'Misapprehension is turning into convention,' he sings. 'Don't know what I've done but I feel ashamed.'

'Youthless' takes its title from Beck's shortlived poetry fanzine of the early 1990s, and is musically the closest relative to some of the quasi-rap/drum'n'bass songs on *The Information* and *Guero*. 'Walls' brings back Chan Marshall to great effect as it snakes and swirls around a hypnotic beat, the singers bemoaning a time of war and personal collapse. 'Replica' is possibly the weakest song of the collection, stuttering to nowhere in particular, while 'Soul Of A Man' is a sleazy blues that returns to the theme of confusion introduced on the title track.

Like many of Beck's album closers, 'Volcano' shuffles along in a ramshackle way, with David Campbell's strings and the harmonious vocals lifting us up and away from the volcano into which we have jumped while Beck stands at the edge and warms his bones. It's a melancholy end to what is often a very melancholy album.

For Beck, *Modern Guilt* was also 'a very disciplined record'. 'I feel like I didn't let myself do certain things that were habits for me,' he explained.

'Over the years, you collect all sorts of habits and mannerisms, and I tried to jettison as many of those as I could. It's almost impossible to have any kind of distance from what you're doing. When I hear the songs, I hear all these things I could've done, or that I would've done years ago.'

Modern Guilt continued Beck's recent run of placing in the top ten of the *Billboard* 200, where it peaked at #4. He also broke into the UK top 10 for the first time when the album reached #8. And, finally, with Beck having reached the age of thirty-seven, the man-child references disappeared from reviews of the album. Beck was well into middle age now; his songs were definitely more 'adult' than before, and it was left to Danger Mouse to add a sheen of 'coolness' and modernity to them. *Rolling Stone* gave the album four stars and drew attention to 'Beck's love of 60s psychedelic music … all acid-trip guitars, mod dance-party beats, daisy-chain harmonies, and thundering percussion', while also claiming that the first five songs 'stand among Beck's strongest work'. In the UK, the *Independent* called the album 'a short treat', while the *Observer* bemoaned a lack of 'tunes' and the *Guardian* dismissed it as a 'vanity project'. Despite the somewhat lukewarm critical response, *Modern Guilt* was nominated for Best Alternative Album at the 2008 Grammy Awards, but lost out to Radiohead's *In Rainbows*.

During the summer of 2008, Beck played a series of dates to promote the album, but they were generally seen as some of the weakest he'd played, especially in Europe. His movement seemed to be limited onstage and the band (Scott McPherson on drums, Bram Inscore on bass, Jessica Dobson on guitar, and Brian LeBarton on keyboards) felt more efficient than ebullient.

Of course, what wasn't known at the time was that the back injury Beck had suffered several years earlier had severely limited his ability to perform and even to record. Instead, for the next few years he decided to take a low-key approach to making music, stepping back to concentrate on production work for other acts. 'I stopped touring indefinitely,' he told *Rolling Stone* in 2014. 'I didn't know if I ever would again. I wasn't able to use my guitar and voice in the same way. It altered my life for a long time.'

* * *

When news broke that a deluxe reissue of *One Foot In The Grave* was to be released in April 2009, fans could be forgiven for thinking it would offer little more unheard material than the reissue of *Odelay* had the previous year. How wrong they were. The two-disc set adds sixteen more songs to the album, twelve of which were previously unreleased. The others comprised the three songs from the seven-inch single of 'It's All In Your Mind'; the title track, 'Feather In Your Cap' (which Beck had also been attempted for *Odelay*), and 'Whiskey Can Can', a charming, lively song with fairly odd lyrics about a woman who's 'the old boat in a sewer' and 'the old man with manure'. There was also 'Close To God', a different mix of which had been issued on Calvin Johnson's *Selector Dub Narcotic* compilation. It pits Johnson's incredibly deep voice against Beck's, which is fed through a vocoder, the result of which is that the words are almost impossible to understand. The backing matches a disjointed drumbeat and Space Invader sound effects with occasional wah-wah guitar licks by Johnson, and as such the song stands alone from the rest of the material released from the sessions.

The other 'new' songs are very much in the same vein as the original album, though perhaps with a little more humour running through them. On 'Mattress', Beck references his own hit single with lines like 'I'm a loser, I'm a winner/ I'm a sucker, I'm a sinner'. With its band arrangement and subtle electric guitar, 'Teenage Wastebasket' could have been a single, had one been required, and is another paean to a wacky girlfriend along the lines of 'Nitemare Hippy Girl' (as is 'Your Love Is Weird'). 'Favorite Nerve' is a dour outtake, while 'Piss On The Door' contains snippets of lyrics Beck would later use in other songs, and at one point drifts into 'Electric Music And The Summer People'. 'Sweet Satan', meanwhile, revisits Beck's devil fixation, and is another travelogue in the manner of 'Satan Gave Me A Taco.' Overall, the extra material is more than enough to justify buying the album all over again.

* * *

A few months after releasing the expanded *One Foot In The Grave*, Beck put up another 'new' album on his website for fans to download for free:

an acoustic version of *Modern Guilt*. The idea of putting out an alternate version of his most recent album was just part of his continuing exploration of looking at ways to interpret old material and present it in a different way. He'd moved on from his early days of singing cover songs to reinterpreting his own songs in other styles and releasing an album of remixes.

Now, his latest project would see him record his own versions of favourite albums with his friends. Under the umbrella title of 'Record Club', Beck began posting video clips of sessions on his website. 'I was doing the record club thing for years before I put it out, just for our own amusement,' he later told *FGM*. 'We would all just say, *This is the best time I've had making music in years*. There's something very humanizing about the whole experience, and I just needed some humanizing.'

'The original intention was just to get musicians together,' he added, in an interview for NPR's *All Songs Considered*. 'I just needed an idea to hang it on, because I knew there wouldn't be enough time to really write music—but if there was a record we could cover, that's kind of playtime for musicians. Most bands, they go out and they play a similar set every night. There's a routine, and there's a job aspect to it, and then they create kind of an autonomous space to just kind of go and make a bunch of noise. I finally realized we have to create something where we can just go and mess around.'

Over the course of a few months, Beck would call in an eclectic bunch of musicians and they would set to work recording an entire album in a day—sometimes a very long day—with little or no rehearsal. The first album to be given this treatment was the seminal *The Velvet Underground & Nico*, which Beck recorded with his 2008 touring band plus Joey Waronker. The songs are given an earthy, folk-like quality that breathes new life into the material even if you've already heard it hundreds of times before.

For Beck, some of those takes proved revelatory. '["Black Angel's Death Song"] was toward the end of the night,' he told pitchfork.com. 'Everybody was falling asleep, because there is a kind of triathlon aspect to the whole thing. You get to a point where you're like, *Oh, we still have four left*, and it's 12:30 or 1am. I think for that one, I just grabbed an acoustic guitar and did it. I did a really simple kind of folk version of it. Some of the other ones, we got more ambitious, but some of them you just look around the room and see who wanted to sing and who wanted to play drums.'

To date, Beck has 'released' four more albums in the same vein: *Songs Of Leonard Cohen* (with MGMT, Andrew Stockdale from Wolfmother, and Devendra Banhart), Skip Spence's *Oar* (with members of Wilco and Feist), Yanni's *Live At The Acropolis* (with Tortoise and Thurston Moore), and some radical reworkings of songs from INXS's career peak *Kick* (featuring a guest appearance by Sergio Dias of Os Mutantes and some memorable vocal interpretations by St Vincent).

These group collaborations led Beck into more production work, starting with sessions for an album for Charlotte Gainsbourg in late 2009. The daughter of the legendary French singer and writer Serge and his actress muse Jane Birkin, Gainsbourg had always struggled to emerge from beneath the shadow her late father still cast. One of the ways she tried to do so was to sing in English rather than French.

Gainsbourg had met Beck at a White Stripes concert in 2005, and they talked about working together then, but by the time they eventually came to do it, she was lucky to still be around. In 2007, she hit her head while water-skiing, and it was only six months later that she found out that she had suffered a cerebral haemorrhage. The experience had a deep impact on her psyche. Beck wrote an album's worth of material for her and then agreed to produce it, too, while selecting a band of musicians to play on the record, drawing on his usual core of Joey Waronker, Jason Falkner, Greg Kurstin, Brian LeBarton, and Justin Meldal-Johnsen, among others.

The sessions went well. 'I've never worked with someone who understood what I wanted like Beck,' Gainsbourg told the *Guardian* in 2010. 'We never spoke about the accident but Beck seemed to know what I'd been through.' They named the album *IRM*—the French equivalent of an MRI—in reference to the many brain scans she'd had to undergo. The sounds of medical equipment are sprinkled throughout. 'He'd start with a rhythm and I'd react,' Gainsbourg continued. 'Then he'd gradually build a song, and I came up with a few words and titles.' The actual songs were a little hit and miss, but the project cemented Beck's growing reputation as a producer.

The calendar year of 2010 was perhaps Beck's quietest in almost two decades, but he still managed to collaborate with Tobacco on a couple of songs for his album *Maniac Meat*, produce songs for Jamie Lidell, and record songs for the soundtracks to *The Twilight Saga: Eclipse*, *True Blood*, and *Scott Pilgrim vs The World*. Further production work followed in 2011, including contributions to Thurston Moore's *Demolished Thoughts* and ex-Pavement frontman Stephen Malkmus's *Mirror Traffic*.

In the meantime, Beck's own recorded output remained limited. At one point, he spent some time in Nashville working with Jack White, but the only evidence that these sessions actually happened was the country-tinged 'I Just Started Hating Some People Today', released on White's Third Man Label. For now, he seemed more interested in reappraising his previous work and looking at new ways of presenting it, heading toward the logical conclusion on his path of re-enactment and unusual presentation: *Song Reader*.

CHAPTER 18

'These songs are meant to be pulled apart.' (2011-14)

As the second decade of the twenty-first century progressed, there was still no sign of a new Beck album, but by the middle of 2012, his more attentive fans were beginning to get an idea about what had been going on behind the scenes. That summer, Beck issued 'I Just Started Hating Some People Today', taken from the previous year's Nashville sessions, followed by an ambitious twenty-minute Philip Glass remix, 'NYC: 73–78'.

Rework Philip Glass Remixed was issued as a celebration of the composer's seventy-fifth birthday, with Beck chosen to curate the project as well as contributing its centrepiece. Drawing on elements of more than twenty of Glass's compositions, 'NYC: 73–78' goes through numerous changes of tone and mood, with piano, ghostly voices, and heartbeat-like rhythms taking turns to lead, but what could easily have slipped into the realms of unpleasant cut-and-paste medley is in fact a startling single work throughout.

As he explained to Ryan Dombal of pitchfork.com, Beck was spoiled for choice when it came to starting work on the project, with more than 800 Glass compositions to choose from.

> His music goes through all kinds of eras. A synthesizer era, all kinds of chamber music, symphonic music, scores, ballets. But when you're listening to a vast body of work that somebody has

created, you get this macro view. After a while, you start to realise bigger patterns, that there's this bigger piece of music they're trying to make. That was more noticeable in the classical era, because classical composers were churning out this music that had a certain momentum and rhythm. That's what I wanted to explore with the remix: taking these different ideas from all these disparate eras and seeing how they correspond with each other, and trying to melt it all together.

Back to his own music, Beck reunited once again with Joey Waronker, Roger Manning Jr., Smokey Hormel, and Justin Meldal-Johnsen for a show at the El Rey Theater in Los Angeles, as a prelude to a short series of summer shows. These dates mainly served as 'greatest hits' performances, however, with a heavy dose of *Mutations* and *Sea Change* songs thrown in each night, and gave no clue as to what Beck was planning for later in the year.

Between finishing his work on the Philip Glass album in 2011 and the late autumn of 2012, Beck had been hard at work preparing his most unusual 'album' to date. He had pushed the boundaries of what an album actually was before, most notably on *The Information*, but this time he was to move into even deeper unchartered territory. In an era when the very concept of the album continued to be tested by digital distribution and buying habits, Beck decided to make things even more difficult. Anyone who wanted to hear his latest collection, *Song Reader*, would have to figure out how to perform the music themselves.

Beck had had the idea of releasing a collection of songs as sheet music since the mid 90s, when he'd been sent a copy of the transcriptions for one of his early albums. 'It didn't make any sense,' he told Dombal. 'They were trying to notate for piano, various guitar squeals, feedback, me shouting through a distortion pedal, and instruments and synthesizers not even playing notes that are in any kind of scale. It was very haphazard and ham-fisted. I thought, *It's a shame they're going to put this book out, because people are going to buy it and have a rough time trying to make some of these songs work*. And that's when I thought, *What if I wrote songs specifically for people to learn off of a page?* That's a different kind of songwriting. It makes you think about how you present the song in a different way.'

Back then, however, Beck was too busy recording and touring to spend any time on the project. He didn't start to seriously consider the idea until around 2004, when he began discussing the possibility with Dave Eggers and his McSweeney's publishing imprint.[50] It was then that he recalled hearing how one of Bing Crosby's songs had been so popular that the sheet music of it sold 54 million copies. 'When that song came out, there were maybe 120 million people in the country,' he told Pitchfork.com, 'so that means that about one out of every two people walking down the street had a copy of that song, and their family was playing it after dinner in the parlour. This idea of a mass convergence on a song struck me.'

Beck had first tried to read and notate music when visiting the library back in the 1980s to find out how to play old blues and folk songs from books. 'By no means am I an expert at notating music or music theory,' he continued. 'I'm just making do with what I have. It was something I thought about off and on over the years, and I've also been very interested in that period of time from the 1950s to the late 1960s, when songs were written out, and people just came in and played everything straight through in two or three hours. It was a whole era of music being notated before it was even attempted in a recording studio.'

It was the link with McSweeney's that really got the project rolling—and that led to it becoming a beautifully packaged and presented project that non-musicians would also be drawn to. Beck started collecting and sifting through cases of old sheet music, and was swept along by the company's artwork. 'I realised that it would be a shame to ignore the humour and fun in the medium,' he explained, in an article for mcsweeneys.com. 'Sheet music could be loud, and garish, and completely preposterous. Some of those old songs are relics of a brand of American absurdity, the same absurdity you see in bad 1970s cop shows or 1980s pop videos. I think there's a way to celebrate it all, without reducing it to ironic fodder.'

Song Reader became the opposite of what he had been planning, which was a plain offering in which the music was left to do the talking, with little in the way of direction. Beck wanted people to be completely free to interpret the songs as they wished. But he was torn between that and the idea of also providing something for fans who could not read or play music to engage with, too.

> The initial idea of putting the songs out simply and sparsely ultimately wasn't as engaging as a book. I know most people aren't going to play these songs—they're going to look at the book. So I spent a lot of years going back and forth on the songs. I felt like if I was going to ask people to learn them, they'd have to be really good.
>
> I kept shelving it, thinking, *Who am I to ask people to play these songs?* I realised it would take decades to come around with songs that I thought were good enough to ask people to learn. So the book started incorporating different ideas from old sheet music, and ultimately became a bit more humorous and tongue-in-cheek, though I hope it strikes a balance, and that we didn't go all-out in that direction.

Beck explained that he found completing the book much more challenging than completing the recording of an album, but he was excited to hear what feedback he'd get, and what interpretations of the songs would be made. The songs were set forth, and right away versions of them began popping up on YouTube in a multitude of styles. Learning to play a song from sheet music is very different to learning it by listening to an original performance, where the original is bound to have an effect on how it is subsequently played, and Beck had also tailored the songwriting away from what he might usually do in order to suit his own voice.

'I realised early on that the songs would have to be different,' he explained. 'When you write for your own voice, you have certain constraints you become accustomed to, [but] when you're asking other people to learn songs they've never heard—that puts a different kind of pressure on what the songs should be. I thought a lot about whether these songs should be simple sing-alongs or more esoteric pieces that would make for better reading on the page for non-musicians, whether they should be written in older styles or if that would make them dismissible as a nostalgic whim.'

The songs themselves are as diverse as you'd expect from a Beck project. There's ragtime ('I'm Down'), dance tunes ('They Didn't Believe I Could Do The Foxtrot'), patriotic numbers ('America, Here's My Boy'), love songs ('Why Does A Heart That Longs To Love You Have Two Hands That Won't?'), marches ('Now That Your Dollar Bills Have Sprouted Wings'), and downbeat balladry ('Why Did You Make Me Care?'). Instructions to the player are generally sparse—'Doleful', 'Plaintive', 'Swing'—but the final song, 'Last Night You Were A Dream', comes with the request, 'Please do not hurry this song.'

The titles of 'Rough On Rats' and 'The Wolf Is On The Hill' both date back to the 1870s, with Beck reusing the original sheet-music artwork alongside his versions. 'Old Shanghai' also has arrangements for trombone, tuba, and tenor sax, giving a clue as to what Beck might perhaps have done with the song himself.

These songs are meant to be pulled apart and reshaped. The idea of them being played by choirs, brass bands, string ensembles, anything outside of traditional rock-band constructs—it's interesting, because it's outside of where my songs normally exist. I thought a lot about making these songs playable and approachable, but still musically interesting. I think some of the best covers will reimagine the chord structure, take liberties with the melodies, the phrasing, even the lyrics themselves. There are no rules in interpretation.

Ninety percent of people won't be able to play these songs, but there'll be so many versions to hear on YouTube. In a way, there'll be unlimited versions—it'll be an album with 1,000 tracks.

With tracks from *Song Reader* popping up online at an increasing rate, and reviews of the book package still appearing, Beck moved quietly along to try another new venture. On February 9 2013, he performed at an event titled Hello Again, hosted by the car manufacture Lincoln at 20th Century Fox Sound Studios in Los Angeles. The company was attempting to relaunch its brand by challenging people to reimagine things in new ways. Beck chose to present a radical version of the David Bowie song 'Sound And Vision', but rather than put together an assortment of his usual backing band from the last decade, he brought in Chris Milk— who has made videos for Green Day, Kanye West, U2, Arcade Fire, and others—to cover the 'vision' side of the evening, and no less than 157 musicians to provide the 'sound' side.

On the night, Beck took to a small circular stage alone, surrounded by the largely invited audience and the various musicians. The arrangement had been prepared by David Campbell, with his Orchestra Eclectica among the diverse selection of participants, alongside The Dap Kings, the Millennium Choir, Fred Martin & The Levite Camp Of Urban Entertainment Institute Choir, The LA Samba School, the USC Drumline, Inca The Peruvian Ensemble, and various other musicians credited with Theremin, saw, alpine horn, and yodelling. There can't be many times in musical history that such a diverse range of styles and talents has been employed in a singular musical project.

Using 360-degree cameras, online viewers were able to log in and control the experience and watch whatever part of the show they wanted, using their own webcams to track and then react to their head movements. The result was a mesmerising display of modern technology that allowed remote viewers to take control of the concert experience, while Beck and the multitude of musicians gave a breathtaking performance. 'I never had anything like that come my way,' said Beck. 'And I probably won't again.'[51]

* * *

A couple of months later, Beck began a series of live *Song Reader* events. On May 19, he played a warm-up gig in Santa Cruz that saw Justin Meldal-Johnsen and Roger Manning Jr join him for an acoustic performance of various oldies and half a dozen news songs, including 'Sorry', 'Don't Act Like It Isn't Hard', and 'Heaven's Ladder', plus three brand new tracks, 'Morning', 'Don't Let It Go', and 'Unforgiven'.

The following night, Beck participated in a full-on *Song Reader* event at the Davies Symphony Hall in San Francisco, with McSweeney's and *Pop-Up* magazine acting as hosts. Thao Nguyen opened proceedings by performing 'We All Wear Cloaks', before a host of musicians including Dan The Automator, Devendra Banhart, and The Kronos Quartet came onstage to tell stories and present their versions of the songs. Beck himself sang 'Sorry', 'America, Here's My Boy', and 'Don't Act Like Your Heart Isn't Hard' before returning at the end to play 'Heaven's Ladder' with a collection of NASA musicians dubbed The International Space Orchestra.

On Independence Day at the Barbican Centre in London, England, Beck pulled together the most star-studded of all the *Song Reader* rosters: recently revitalised Scottish pop-rockers Franz Ferdinand, Joan Wasser (aka Joan As Police Woman), singer-songwriter James Yorkston, Jarvis Cocker from Pulp, Guillemots, previous collaborators Beth Orton and Charlotte Gainsbourg, and comedy act The Mighty Boosh, among others. The show demonstrated the very essence of the project when both Franz Ferdinand and Guillemots chose to perform 'Saint Dude', the former presenting it as a country ballad, and the latter playing it as harmony-laden post-punk funk. The raucous night ended with most of the musicians back onstage for an ensemble run-through of 'Rough On Rats'.

Over the next few months, Beck released a series of standalone tracks as downloads and twelve-inch singles, each of which included a lengthy reworking of the title track as the B-side. The first of these, issued at the end of June, was the stop-starting electronic lament 'Defriended'. 'I Won't Be Long'—more in the vein of *Modern Guilt*, with its guitar and retro-beats—came just a week later, with the third, 'Gimme', with its experimental percussion and what sounds like a steel drum, following in mid September.

'For ten years I've been talking about putting out a series of twelve-inch singles, one at a time,' he explained to the *Guardian*. 'I was holding them back because I wasn't sure what I was doing with them. I just felt like I wanted people to hear them.'

The lengthy B-sides were perhaps inspired by the Philip Glass piece he had recently prepared. 'I've always been interested in that idea of being allowed to have unlimited time to go anywhere you want with music, and not being disciplined into a structure,' he told pitchfork.com. 'There's a lot of freedom in those early-1970s Miles Davis records. Being able to take musical ideas through every iteration is attractive to me. Granted, not everyone's going to want to listen to that, but it should exist.'

Each of the three singles contains artwork by Swedish painter Mamma Anderson. 'I like the way she takes domestic scenes and almost stages them,' Beck noted. 'There is a familiarity yet an otherness, which was similar to what I was trying to capture in the songs.' The first of the images, for 'Defriended', shows a group of women sitting around a table, smoking and drinking; the second, for 'I Won't Be Long', is of a wall of pictures, including one of The Beatles and another of the Million Dollar Quartet; the third, for 'Gimme', depicts another slightly surreal table scene.

* * *

After completing a whirlwind tour of South America—four countries in eight days—Beck wrapped up the *Song Reader* series with a third and final event at the Walt Disney Concert Hall in Los Angeles on November 24. This time, the show offered the added bonus of having the Los Angeles Philharmonic Orchestra (conducted by David Campbell) onstage throughout. Jack Black introduced the show, which included spoken segments by Van Dyke Parks and others. Beck sang 'America Here's My Boy' alone and later introduced 'Wave' for the first time, while appearances were also made by Anne Hathaway, Jon Brion, Jenny Lewis, and Jarvis Cocker.

By now, the news was out that there was a new Beck album, *Morning Phase*, in the works. The album was to appear in early 2014, and there was even talk that it might be the first of two new LPs released during the year.

With six years having passed between the release of actual Beck albums—the kind where you buy a CD and listen to it at home—there was bound to be some scrutiny of what he had come up with. Beck himself was more aware than ever before that he should take extra time on the preparation of the songs for the album, and that their production should bring them together as a whole piece. 'I recorded a bunch of things real quick,' he explained. 'Then, I thought, *I need to come back and try this again.*' Those initial sessions date back almost nine years and took place in Nashville. He put those songs on hold but returned to Nashville several years later to record 'I Just Started Hating Some People Today' for Jack White, while at the same time he worked on a trio of other songs, 'Waking Light', 'Blackbird Chain', and 'Country Down'.

If the sessions were slow and somewhat haphazard, then that reflected the way things had been in recent times. 'I didn't have a label anymore,' Beck told *Rolling Stone*. 'I wasn't sure if I was going to put out a record, or if I should put out a record. It felt like I was standing still, while everything else was in such flux.' There was also the back problem he had been suffering with for the past few years. 'I was in bad shape,' he admitted. 'There were a number of years where I couldn't pick up my guitar. Making [*Modern Guilt*] was like doing it with both hands tied behind your back. It hurt to sing. I'm whispering through half of those vocals.'

It was only when he began to revisit some of the older songs back in Los Angeles at the start of 2013 that *Morning Phase* really began to take shape. 'I tried to make this record a few times,' he told NPR's *All Songs Considered*. 'I did a lot of recording [in Nashville], and it was one of those things where it didn't quite come together. That's really the beginning of the record, going to Nashville. But there was something about bringing it back to Los Angeles. I got the band that I did most of *Sea Change* with, and it just felt right. The songs started to work and it started to feel like a record.'

The need to make a cohesive album was something that remained lodged in Beck's mind as he worked on the songs. As he explained to

Mike Diver, in an interview for *Clash* magazine, he wanted to prove that he had improved over time, unlike some bands who start out great but never seem to progress:

> You'd like to think that you can get better with time. That you learn more, and become able to present that a little better. I was probably a little more single-minded in what I was trying to get out of each song. For long periods, stuff just didn't work, songs would sound too sentimental, or too middle-of-the-road somehow. So I worked on them relentlessly, and eventually something began to work about them. Some songs I gave up on, but it was really a matter of putting the time and patience into this record. A lot of my [previous] records were purposefully done in one take, out of tune, really rough around the edges. That was always intentional. It's not that I couldn't have spent time and worked on them, but over time you come to appreciate songs that have that extra time taken on them. On this album, I spent a lot of time making sure the songs were different from each other.

String arrangements play more of a role on *Morning Phase* than on any previous Beck album. As usual, David Campbell was involved with the arrangements, although Beck himself also had a hand in them. As Beck explained to Miranda Freeman of *Rip It Up*:

> He did the orchestrating and conducting, but a lot of times I'd record on a keyboard and we'd expand on it together. I'm actually pretty specific about the strings, and I have strong opinions about using orchestra. There's this whole history of pop music and singer-songwriter music that uses orchestra that goes into easy-listening territory, and it can too often be used as a device to over-sentimentalise a piece of music. I really go for an unaffected style, as I think I like modern-classical music and baroque music when it's played in a very simple, plain way.

The string sections were recorded 'down in the basement' of the Capitol Records building in Los Angeles, where everyone from Frank Sinatra and Nat 'King' Cole to The Beach Boys and The Beastie Boys had recorded. A lot of what was recorded there for *Morning Phase* was never actually used—with only about 20 percent of the string parts making it onto the record, in Beck's estimation. 'There's so many little pieces,' he told NPR. 'At the last minute I had about four or five of these fragments, and I just tried sticking them in different places. So it wasn't really thought out.'

One piece that did fit well, 'Cycle', was chosen to open the album, and right from the opening notes, you know that this is going to be unlike any other Beck album to date, the mournful strings recalling Samuel Barber's 'Adagio'. After that, we're off into 'Morning', and with it the themes are set: reawakening, fresh starts, and optimistic beginnings after a spell of confusion and unease. In musical terms, 'Morning' could be the twin of 'The Golden Age', but the lyrics are far more personal.

While numerous reviews would refer to *Morning Phase* as Beck's 'Californian Album', 'Heart Is A Drum' recalls more of an English folk heritage. That's not to say that there aren't echoes of Laurel Canyon and the early-70s songwriters that David Campbell worked with when Beck was an infant. 'Say Goodbye' treads delicately into that territory, before 'Blue Moon' goes back to Beck's own fingerpicking days.

At the centre of the album comes its real heart, 'Wave'. Foreboding strings lull the listener in to its desolate waters, and then it's too late, as you almost sway slowly along while Beck is carried away into isolation. 'I don't know if I have any perspective on it other than: I sat down to write, and that came out,' Beck later noted, when asked about the song by *Clash* magazine. 'It's one of those things where you sit down with an intention to write something, but it's never exactly what comes out. I just have to accept that is what came out, and it represents something.'

Initially, he hadn't been sure what to do with it, and over time had tried to pass it on to other singers to use (likely Thurston Moore or Charlotte Gainsbourg). 'When I played it for people it always got a reaction,' he told NPR's Bob Boilen. 'You don't want to get in the way of the orchestra. With a lot of the songs on this record, it was like, *how do you keep this mood and not disrupt it, or break the spell of whatever's happening with the music?* On some of them it's singing soft, singing higher, trying different voices. I had songs where I'd try singing it twenty different ways, just beating it into the ground, and then you finally find something.'

'Blackbird Chain' returns to the softly strummed California vibe, though Beck's visions of California are quite different to those an outsider might have. 'I'm not sure what a Californian outlook is,' he said. 'I grew up in East LA. I never saw the sea. All we saw was smog and urban blight. The palm trees had rats the size of cats, [and it] could take two to three hours to get from one side of the town to the other.' Only after getting married did Beck move to a house by the coast, and once he did he found that he was kept awake at night by the sounds of sea lions barking.

After 'Phase', another lush string segment, we are led into the final trio of songs: the Byrds-esque 'Turn Away', the pedal-steel melancholia of 'Country Down', and 'Waking Light', a keyboard-led finale that builds to some nifty guitar work as the song crashes down at the end. 'I think with these particular songs, there was a mood that hopefully the songs convey,' Beck explained to Joseph Stannard, in an interview for thequietus.com. 'I just tried to inhabit that, and work on the songs over and over until that particular feeling started to manifest in the songs. It was coming from trying to find something redemptive about experience and travails, and difficulties, and just general life.'

Despite the sometimes-slow pace of the album, it is certainly one of hope and optimism. While that slowness was often noted in reviews, with the *Observer* calling it 'magma on a go-slow' and *Uncut* reckoning that it was 'too consistent in mood and pace', the album was generally well received. The *Independent On Sunday* named it 'CD Of The Week' and summed it up as 'cheering proof that Beck isn't ready to start repeating himself just yet'. The *NME* gave the album eight out of ten, noting that it 'makes for some of the most affecting comedown folk you're likely to hear all year', while for *Q* magazine Beck had 'properly reacquired his mojo'. In the USA, Will Hermes of *Rolling Stone* cut right to the heart of *Morning Phase* by describing it as 'a record about what to do when the world seems totally fucked'.

There was also the sense that now, having grown up in public, and then gone through the rowdy noise of his early years, through the party albums, the breakup records, and the midlife crisis, Beck had arrived at a safe place. The storm was over, and the six-year wait between albums had been worth it.

'I felt that because of the long gap, I wanted to put out something that had a little bit more of a musical range,' he told thequietus.com. 'I do feel it's a "fresh start" record. I think it sums up something, and for me I've gone through a long period of physical challenges, and that's really been something I've put a lot of time and work into getting through. So, that went into the music.'

He had also come to the realisation that there is still plenty more to come. 'Pop is inherently a young forum. I used to think that I would stop making music when I was forty—it seemed a good point. In fact, I kind of did for a few years, but when I started playing live again, it felt like my body of work still had a lot of holes in it that still needed filling in. Anyway, nowadays The Rolling Stones are headlining festivals at seventy, and you get artists going on into their eighties, just like the old bluesmen used to do. And you know what? I see no reason at all why I shouldn't do that.'

Endnotes

1   Olaf was related to Bibi Lindstrom, a beloved Swedish artist and sometime art director on the films of Ingmar Bergman.
2   Abraham was a labour organiser during a dynamic time of great upheaval and conflict. Born in Russia, he arrived in the United States in 1883. He was a member of the Knights of Labor and secretary of the United Trade Unions of New York and Vicinity. He later served on the Board of Grievances and the Joint Board of Sanitary Control, and published *Memoirs of a Cloakmaker*, an account of the New York City garment industry through 1910. In 1944, a Liberty ship, built to support the American war effort, was named after him.
3   'I've had it confirmed from several sources [that he used those words],' says Bibbe.
4   Jimmy Breslin became a very well known writer and journalist. He was awarded the Pulitzer Prize for Commentary in 1986.
5   After the divorce, Jim Shapiro started another air transit company in North Africa with a character nicknamed Pierre Lafitte. He later remarried and settled in Sweden.
6   In recent years, Beck has been a little more open about his upbringing, but early in his career he would give poor unsuspecting journalists the run-around. Even his buddy Thurston Moore of Sonic Youth, who interviewed Beck for MTV in 1994, received a master class in question avoidance that would have made any politician proud. 'I wanted to ask about who you are,' Moore began. 'I've asked a few people, but I don't seem to be able to get any straight answers. So Beck, is Beck your real name? Were you christened Beck?' Beck stared back at Moore but said nothing. Then he took off

his boot and threw it across the studio, before responding to further questions by holding a Walkman to his microphone and playing back a stream of incoherent noise.
7   LA is home to more Iranians than any city except Tehran; it has the most Armenians outside of Yerevan, and the fastest growing Asian population anywhere in the West.
8   The Masque club, which opened in July 1977, also hosted bands like X, The Germs, and The Go-Go's before being closed down in early 1979 due to fire regulations.
9   Bibbe: 'Once, in a little upstate town, my mother got into a catfight with some woman who started yelling, "The lousy kikes are messing up our town." So my mother hauled off and decked her. I remember getting turned away from hotels back then. They were "restricted", which meant that Jews weren't allowed. So we were Jewish enough to be discriminated against. I was open to different religious ideas. As a teen, I was an atheist. Then suddenly, somewhere in there, I realized I was really Jewish.'
10   Pussy Galore were the band that opened the door to one of Beck's later musical passions: noise rock. From their beginnings in Washington DC, they set about offending as many people as possible with their brand of hardcore punk/noise. They put out five albums and five EPs in a seven-year span, recording songs with titles like 'Dial M For Motherfucker'—an obvious influence on some of Beck's early song titles. After they split up in 1992, guitarist Jon Spencer formed the Jon Spencer Blues Explosion, with whom Beck would later work.
11   Mississippi John Hurt taught himself to play in the 1920s and recorded some material

for Columbia. It didn't sell very well, however, and he returned to farming. Years later, in 1963, he was tracked down at the age of seventy-one and persuaded to record again. He could still sing and play well, and he continued to play live until his death in 1966, having now found a new generation of fans.

12 Eddie James 'Son' House was possibly the most important of the Delta blues innovators. His passionate playing is best represented on his 1930s recordings for Paramount, and he was a great influence on both Robert Johnson and Muddy Waters—both blues greats in their own right.

13 Lightfield Lewis is reported to be putting together a documentary from his own home videos from 1983 until the present day. Beck appears in one clip that has been shown online and further footage is said to exist of him singing Duran Duran songs in 1986.

14 Hall started out as a spoken word artist but later found more widespread recognition with the band King Missile. He initially gained a reputation as an interesting live spectacle while performing as a stream-of-consciousness poet at the Fort on the Lower East Side. He soon began to blend his spoken-word prose with actual songs, but he needed some extra help for that, as his musical expertise began and ended with his playing of the triangle. Formed in 1986, King Missile Dog Fly Religion (later shortened to King Missile) released six albums in seven years—the last three on Atlantic Records—before splitting up in 1994.

15 Stein had founded Sire Records in 1966 and subsequently signed such legendary acts as the Ramones, Talking Heads, and Madonna. Fields, an author and journalist, managed the Ramones, MC5, Stooges, and others, and was a key figure on the New York punk and new-wave scenes.

16 A singer, songwriter, and multi-instrumentalist, Summerhill would go on to work with everyone from A Tribe Called Quest to Bill Frisell.

17 A Silver Lake landmark for many years, Tang's closed down in 2013.

18 Like the rest of the establishments on its block on Hollywood Boulevard, Raji's has since been demolished.

19 Bozulich had been in Neon Vein and then Ethyl Meatplow, perhaps best described as 'pseudo-industrial-alternative-dance-rock'. They cut three singles before releasing their only album, *Happy Days Sweetheart*, in 1993. The Geraldine Fibbers, meanwhile, had originally formed as a side project by the members of Ethyl Meatplow and Glue. 'Carla called me up before *Mellow Gold* out,' Beck recalled. 'She had written some songs with a country flavour; we got together and did some stuff on a four-track at my house. Some of those songs turned out to be Geraldine Fibbers songs.' The band made their recorded debut in 1994 with the mini-album *Get Thee Gone*, on which Beck guests, before releasing their full-length debut, *Lost Somewhere Between The Earth And My Home*, on Virgin in 1995.

20 The band's line-up was completed in 1992 when Anna—at eighteen, even younger than Beck—recruited drummer Tony Maxwell. That Dog signed to Geffen in 1993 and, after getting some college airplay and gigs in the LA area, they joined Beck on his first real tour in support of *Mellow Gold*. Beck would go on to work with the band on a variety of projects that would eventually surface on *Mellow Gold*, *The Poop Alley Tapes*, the *Stray Blues* compilation, *Good To The Last Drop*, and *Guero*, and they have supported him on several subsequent tours.

21 The Silver Lake area had been central to the early movie business, with several silent classics featuring the likes of the Keystone Cops filmed there. So too was Laurel & Hardy's *The Music Box*, in which they try to move a piano up a steep flight of stairs—the kind of job that

Beck himself would be doing more than sixty years later.

22 Rob Zabrecky was also at the Jabberjaw that night. 'Beck opened up the show,' he recalls. 'Come to think of it, Jack Black did a little a-capella number that night as well.'

23 Hill Of Beans had a song called 'Satan, Lend Me A Dollar' that most likely inspired Beck's 'Satan Gave Me A Taco'. Moramarco was also in a 'band' called Mime Crime, who mimed played heavy metal. They were said to rock hard, but they made no noise whatsoever. Moramarco was the 'singer', Steve Hanft 'played' guitar, Mario Prietto was the 'bassist', and Pete Blood was on 'drums'. They appear, very briefly, in the 'Loser' video, while Blood can also be seen in the 'Beercan' promo.

24 In hindsight, he would add, 'I think the best thing to do is to have your own label. I never realised how easy it was to put out your own records.'

25 On the spine, the title is incorrectly listed as A Western Harvest Moon By Moonlight.

26 Stephenson struggled in the years after 'Loser' with an undisclosed form of mental illness. He had trouble staying focused on anything, and became destructively obsessive over minute details. He was hospitalised at one point, but after undergoing treatment was able to complete work on Forest For The Trees. Beck guests on the album, which was released in 1997, and spawned the top 30 hit 'Dreams'.

27 This likening to Dylan could also be stretched to 'Loser': compare Beck's exhortation to not 'believe everything that you breathe' and warning about getting 'a parking violation and a maggot on your sleeve' to the 'Don't follow leaders / Watch your parking meters' couplet in 'Subterranean Homesick Blues'.

28 Some of the other songs Beck wrote around this time, like 'Cold Brains', would later find their way onto the more acoustic environment of his 1998 album Mutations. Another, 'Brother',

would appear as a B-side to the 'Jack-ass' single.

29 An aside to this story is that, while work on the album continued at the PCP Labs, a carpenter by the name of Mark Ramos Nishita came by to fix a broken gate. He ended up playing keyboards for The Beastie Boys, and released two solo albums as Money Mark on their Grand Royale imprint in the late 1990s.

30 Travis left the band at the end of the tour and briefly joined Elastica. She now leads her own band, The Abby Travis Foundation.

31 'I remember the stages being, like, a mile apart. I remember racing on a golf-cart thing— just flying through the mud. It's about as off-road as Lollapalooza got.'

32 In the meantime, The Dust Brothers kept themselves busy by starting their own label, Nickel Bag, while Mike Simpson took an A&R position with DreamWorks SKG (where, among other things, he helped sign Eels). They also worked with some other Hansons (on 'Mmmbop'), and tried again to get that elusive Dust Brothers album back on track—they had, after all, been trying to record it since 1985. ('Something always gets in the way,' Simpson told me. 'We're really fortunate to have all this work, but I can't wait to set aside some time for ourselves. That's when we'll get really busy.')

33 Ocampo's work is also the subject of the 1999 film God Is My Copilot.

34 In a separate interview, Beck claimed the song was 'about industrial waste as a stimulant and actually a delicacy that's marketed in new ways. And every few months [there's] a new angle, a new level of exposure'.

35 'Stagger Lee' is one of the oldest pieces of folklore in African American music. The song was famously recorded by Mississippi John Hurt in 1928, but had already been around for about seventy years even then, known variously as 'Stack O' Lee Blues', 'Stackolee', and 'Stagolee', among other titles. It tells of

the violent acts of a young black man by the name of Stagolee, culminating in his murder of someone who beat him at craps.

36 The song was also remixed by Oasis's Noel Gallagher and The Dust Brothers.

37 Lloyd Price had his finest moments in the 1950s, when his brand of New Orleans R&B gave him a slew of top ten hits in the US (and, on occasion, in the UK). He even reworked 'Stagger Lee', taking it to #1 in the US in 1958.

38 Beck was rather more reserved in his appreciation of Oasis. 'I haven't really been paying too much attention. I thought they were good at the MTV Awards. The remix came about because my A&R guy had been hanging around with Oasis and he asked Noel if he was down with it, and he was. That was as much as I had to do with it. I felt very honoured by Noel's interest—I would never think that he would have the time to do something like that. I mean, I wouldn't have the time to remix one of my own songs, no matter how much I liked it.'

39 As a fifteen-year-old, he had bought a drum machine from Trent Reznor, who was working at the time as a salesman at a local music store. 'Watching Nine Inch Nails get bigger and bigger, seeing Trent come up, that inspired me. It was like, *Wow, this guy who sold me a drum machine when I was fifteen is becoming the biggest rock star in America*. I drove that inspiration into DJing, which was something, I would say, nobody was really doing at that time—using that kind of energy towards turntables.'

40 Manning Jr. had been a member of various bands before landing a job with Beck. He started out with Beatnik Beatch, who put out one album (*At The Zula Pool*) in 1987, before forming the critically acclaimed Jellyfish. Jellyfish may have dressed like psychedelic 60s throwbacks, but their music was not in keeping with their image. Sounding more like Badfinger crossed with Squeeze, they put out two great albums in the early 1990s, *Bellybutton* and *Spilt Milk*. After they dissolved, Manning joined forces with cowriter Eric Dover to form Imperial Drag. After recording a self-titled debut, they set off on tour with an opening slot for Alanis Morissette, and then their own headlining tour of the US and Canada. When Imperial Drag too folded, Manning bounced back again, forming The Moog Cookbook with Brian Kehew. The duo put out two hilarious albums of instrumental cover versions that rely heavily (if not surprisingly) on the old synthesiser. A highlight of the Cookbook's shortlived career was when they played an in-store show in Los Angeles that Michael Jackson inadvertently walked into, whereupon he was given a copy of the duo's CD. Manning Jr. also toured with Justin Meldal-Johnsen as guests of the French band Air.

41 Brown was a long-time friend of Beck's who had played with the likes of The Creatures (Siouxsie Sioux's side-project turned full-time band) and Ben Lee (the twenty-year-old Australian wonder kid signed to The Beastie Boys' Grand Royal label); Ralickie had met Beck through mutual friend Mike Bioto and had previously played with Natalie Merchant, as well as with David Brown's band Brazzaville.

42 Initially, the first verse contained the line 'I heard you moaning', which was eventually replaced by 'You're so helpless'. The chorus wouldn't change at all, but the second verse went through at least three different versions. In 1994, it started with 'You're building momentum / Something you want to avoid doing'; by the time of Beck's 1995 radio appearance on KCRW, it had become 'Stumbling religion / Starting to get annoyed'; he then finally settled on 'Count your blessings / And do the things that you should'. There may have been further in-studio changes. 'I tried to record this for *Odelay*,' he told *Rolling Stone*, 'but it just didn't fit.'

43 The German and Japanese versions of the CD album also carried extra tracks—'Halo Of

Gold' and 'Black Balloon' on the German edition, 'Electric Music And The Summer People' on the Japanese release—that would later appear elsewhere as B-sides. The German CD comes in a gatefold Digipak, while the Japanese version contains an extra booklet with an article about Beck and all the lyrics from the album.

44 *Rolling Stone*'s love for the album continued when it later featured at #436 in the magazine's list of the 500 greatest albums of all time, and at #17 among the top 100 albums of the 2000s.

45 The coroner's report returned an open verdict. 'While his history of depression is compatible with suicide, and the location and direction of the stab wounds are consistent with self-infliction, several aspects of the circumstances (as they are known at this time) are atypical of suicide, and raise the possibility of homicide.'

46 The European and Japanese versions of the album came with bonus tracks attached—the poppy 'Send A Message To Her', the heavy jam of 'Chain Reaction', and the insanely catchy 'Clap Hands'.

47 The leaked version of *Guero* comprises 'Brazilica', 'Guero', 'Go It Alone', 'Chain Reaction', 'Nazarene', 'Black Tambourine', 'Earthquake Weather', 'E-Pro', 'Summer Girl', 'Scarecrow', 'Rental Car', 'Send A Message To Her', and 'Hell Yes'. 'Brazilica' is actually 'Missing', 'Nazarene' is 'Emergency Exit', and 'Summer Girl' was shortened to 'Girl', while 'Guero' became 'Que Onda Guero?'

48 In May, the *Rolling Stone* album chart showed a top four comprised of 50 Cent, Faith Evans, Beck, and *Now 118*. Beck was in unchartered territory, both in terms of the acts around him and the heights he was reaching.

49 Look for the hilarious YouTube clip of Beck playing 'Nausea' on *Late Night With David Letterman* where Borat makes an impromptu guest appearance.

50 Eggers, the author of books including *A Heartbreaking Work Of Staggering Genius* and *What Is The What*, started the literary journal *Timothy McSweeny's Quarterly Concern* in 1998 (with the more mainstream monthly *The Believer* debuting five years later). Each issue is given a theme, often with a distinctly retro slant that showcases the company's eye for design and presentation.

51 At the time of writing, the performance is still available to view at hello-again.com

Discography

A full listing of every Beck release—including promotional issues and compilations—would fill a small book by itself. What follows, then, is a list of all 'physical' Beck records; download-only releases have been omitted, and duplications of albums with the same track listing have been largely left out.

Singles / EPs

MTV Makes Me Want to Smoke Crack / To See That Woman Of Mine / Privates On Parade* / Rock Paper Scissors*

Flipside FLIP46 (USA 7-inch, 1992; clear blue vinyl, limited to 500 copies; tracks marked * by Bean)

Loser / Steal My Body Home
Bong Load BL5 (USA 12-inch, 1993)

Loser / Totally Confused / Corvette Bummer /
MTV Makes Me Want To Smoke Crack (Lounge
Act Version)
Geffen GFSTD 67 (UK CD, 1994)

Loser / Alcohol
Geffen DGCS 7-19270 (USA 7-inch, 1994)

Loser / Corvette Bummer / Alcohol / Soul
Suckin' Jerk (Reject) / Fume
Geffen DGCDM-21930 (USA CD, 1994)

Steve Threw Up / Motherfucker / Cupcake
[unlisted]
Bong Load BL11 (USA 7-inch, 1994)

Beercan / Got No Mind / Asslizz Powergrudge
(Payback 94) / Totally Confused / Spamnking
Room / Bonus Noise
Geffen DGC DM-22000 (USA CD, 1994)

It's All In Your Mind / Feather In Your Cap /
Whiskey Can Can
K IPU 45 (USA 7-inch, 1994; fold-over sleeve on
black or brown vinyl)

Pay No Mind (Snoozer) / Special People /
Trouble All My Days / Supergolden (Sunchild)
Geffen GFST 73 (UK 12-inch, 1994; withdrawn,
but some copies still in circulation)
Geffen GED 21911 (USA CD, 1995)

Where It's At / Make Out City (remix by Mike
Simpson) / Where It's At (remix by Mario C and
Mickey P) / Where It's At (remix by John King)
/ Bonus Beats
Geffen DGC 9180 (USA 12-inch, 1996)

Where It's At (edit) / Where It's At (remix by
John King) / Lloyd Price Express / Dark And

Lovely / American Wasteland / Clock
Geffen MVCZ-15001 (Japan CD, 1996)

Devils Haircut / Dark And Lovely / American
Wasteland / 000.000
Geffen GFSTD 22183 (UK CD, 1996)

Devils Haircut / Devils Haircut (remix by Noel
Gallagher) / Groovy Sunday (remix by Mike
Simpson) / Trouble All My Days
Geffen GFSXD 22183 (UK CD, 1996)

The New Pollution / Richard's Hairpiece (remix
by Aphex Twin) / Electric Music And The
Summer People
Geffen GFSTD 22205 (UK CD, 1997)

The New Pollution / The New Pollution (remix by
Mario C and Mickey P) / Lemonade
Geffen GFSXD 22205 (UK CD, 1997)

Sissyneck / Feather In Your Cap
Geffen GFS 22253 (UK 7-inch, 1997)

Sissyneck / Burro / Dark And Lovely / Devil Got
My Woman / Brother
Geffen GEFDM 22310 (Australia CD, 1997)

Jack-Ass (Butch Vig remix) / Jack-Ass (Lowrider
mix) / Burro / Strange Invitation / Devil Got My
Woman / Brother
Geffen GFSTD 22276 (UK CD, 1997)

Deadweight (edit) / Erase The Sun / SA-5
Geffen GFSTD 22293 (UK CD, 1997)

Clock / The Little Drum Machine Boy / Totally
Confused
(UK promo CD, 1997; given away free with
December 1997 issue of *Select* magazine)

Tropicalia / Halo Of Gold / Black Balloon
Geffen GFSTD 22365 (UK CD, 1998)

Cold Brains / Electric Music And The Summer People / Halo Of Gold / Runners Dial Zero / Diamond Bollocks
Geffen INT5P-6561 (US promo CD, 1999)

Cold Brains / One Of These Days / Diamond In The Sleaze / Halo Of Gold / Electric Music And The Summer People
Geffen INTDM-97093 (Australia CD, 1999)

Nobody's Fault But My Own / One Of These Days / Diamond In The Sleaze
Geffen MVCF-12015 (Japan CD, 1999)

Sexx Laws / Salt In The Wound / Sexx Laws (Wiseguyz remix)
Geffen 4971812 (UK CD, 1999)

Sexx Laws / This Is My Krew / Sexx Laws (Malibu Mix)
Geffen 4971822 (UK CD, 1999)

Mixed Bizness / Mixed Bizness (Cornelius mix) / Mixed Bizness (DJ Me DJ You remix) / Mixed Bizness (video)
Geffen 497300-C (UK CD, 2000)

Mixed Bizness / Dirty, Dirty / Sexxlaws (video)
Geffen 497301-2 (UK CD, 2000)

Mixed Bizness / Mixed Bizness (Cornelius remix) / Mixed Bizness (Les Rythmes Digitales remix) / Mixed Bizness (DJ Me DJ You remix) / Mixed Bizness (Bix Pender remix) / Dirty, Dirty / Sexxlaws (Night Flight To Ojai)
Geffen MVCF-14002 (Japan CD, 2000)

Nicotine & Gravy / Midnite Vultures / Zatyricon / Nicotine & Gravy (video)
Geffen 497389-2 (UK CD, 2000)

Lost Cause
Geffen Sea003 (UK promo CD, 2002)

Guess I'm Doing Fine
Geffen 'acetate' (UK promo CD, 2002)

E-Pro / Venom Confection / Ghost Range / E-Pro (video)
Interscope 988 00522 (UK CD, 2005)

Girl / Girl (Octet remix) / Girl (Paza remix) / Girl (video)
Interscope 988 246-9 (UK CD, 2005)

Ghettochip Malfunction Hell Yes / Hell Yes / Gucci Bag in Flames Hell Yes
Interscope Hellyes1 (UK CD, 2006)

Timebomb / Timebomb (instrumental)
Interscope (US promo 12-inch, 2007)

Chemtrails / Vampire Voltage No. 6
XL Recordings XLS370 (UK 7-inch, 2008; glow-in-the-dark vinyl)

Gamma Ray / Gamma Ray (Jay Reatard version)
Geffen B0012115-21 (USA 7-inch, 2008)

Youthless / Half and Half
XL Recordings (USA promo 7-inch, 2008)

Defriended / Defriended (extended mix)
Fonograf (USA 12-inch, 2013)

I Won't Be Long / I Won't Be Long (extended mix)
Fonograf (USA 12-inch, 2013)

Gimme / Gimme (Instrumental) / Gimme (Georgic Mix) // Gimme (Extended Version, Part 1) / Gimme (Extended Version, Part 2)
Fonograf (USA 2x12-inch, 2013)

Blue Moon / Blue Moon (edit)
Capitol (US promo CD, 2014)

Albums

Golden Feelings
The Fucked Up Blues / Special People / Magic Stationwagon / No Money No Honey / Trouble All My Days / Bad Energy / Schmoozer / Heartland Feeling / Super Golden Black Sunchild / Soul Sucked Dry / Feelings / Gettin' Home / Will I Be Ignored By The Lord / Bogus Soul / Totally Confused / Mutherfukka / People Gettin Busy
Sonic Enemy (USA cassette, 1993)
Sonic Enemy (USA CD, 1999)

Mellow Gold
Loser / Pay No Mind (Snoozer) / Fuckin With My Head (Mountain Dew Rock) / Whiskeyclone, Hotel City 1997 / Soul Suckin Jerk / Truckdrivin Neighbors Downstairs (Yellow Sweat) / Sweet Sunshine / Beercan / Steal My Body Home / Nitemare Hippy Girl / Mutherfuker / Blackhole / Analog Odyssey [unlisted]
Geffen DGCD- 24634 (USA CD, March 1994)

One Foot In The Grave
He's A Mighty Good Leader / Sleeping Bag / I Get Lonesome / Burnt Orange Peel / Cyanide Breath Mint / See Water / Ziplock Bag / Hollow Log / Forcefield / Fourteen Rivers Fourteen Floods / Asshole / I've Seen The Land Beyond / Outcome / Girl Dreams / Painted Eyelids / Atmospheric Conditions
K KLP28 (USA CD, 1994)

One Foot In The Grave (Deluxe Edition)
As above, plus: It's All In Your Mind / Whiskey Can Can / Mattress / Woe On Me / Teenage Wastebasket (electric & band) / Your Love Is Weird / Favorite Nerve / Piss On The Door / Close To God / Sweet Satan / Burning Boyfriend / Black Lake Morning / Feather In Your Cap / One Foot In The Grave / Teenage Wastebasket (acoustic) / I Get Lonesome (alternate version)
XL Recordings LC 05667 (USA 2CD, 2009)

Stereopathetic Soulmanure
Pink Noise (Rock Me Amadeus) / Rowboat / Thunder Peel / Waitin' For A Train / The Spirit Moves Me / Crystal Clear (Beer) / No Money No Honey / '8.6.82' / Total Soul Future (Eat It) / One Foot In The Grave / Aphid Manure Heist / Today Has Been A Fucked Up Day / Rollins Power Sauce / Puttin It Down / '11.6.45' / Cut 1/2 Blues / Jagermeister Pie / Ozzy / Dead Wild Cat / Satan Gave Me A Taco / '8.4.82' / Tasergun / Modesto / Ken [unlisted] / Bonus Noise [unlisted]
Flipside FLIP60 (USA CD, 1994)

A Western Harvest Field By Moonlight
Totally Confused / Mayonaise Salad / Gettin' Home / Blackfire Choked Our Death / Feel Like A Piece Of Shit (Mind Control) / She Is All (Gimme Something To Eat) / Pinefresh / Lampshade / Feel Like A Piece Of Shit (Crossover Potential) / Mango (Vader Rocks!) / Feel Like A Piece Of Shit (Cheetos Time) / Styrofoam Chicken (Quality Time)
Fingerpaint 02 (USA 10-inch, 1994; first 2,000 copies c/w unique finger-painting)

Odelay
Devils Haircut / Hotwax / Lord Only Knows / The New Pollution / Derelict / Novacane / Jack-Ass / Where It's At / Minus / Sissyneck / Readymade / High 5 (Rock the Catskills) / Ramshackle
Geffen DGCD-24823 (USA CD, 1996)

Odelay (Deluxe Edition)
As above, plus: Computer Rock [unlisted] / Deadweight / Inferno / Gold Chains / Where It's At (U.N.K.L.E. remix) / Richard's Hairpiece / American Wasteland / Clock / Thunder Peel / Electric Music And The Summer People / Lemonade / SA-5 / Feather In Your Cap / Erase The Sun / 000.000 / Brother / Devil Got My Woman / Trouble All My Days / Strange Invitation / Burro
Geffen B0010262-02 (USA 2CD, 2008)

Mutations
Cold Brains / Nobody's Fault But My Own /
Lazy Flies / Canceled Check / We Live Again /
Tropicalia / Dead Melodies / Bottle Of Blues / O
Maria / Sing It Again / Static / Diamond Bollocks
/ Runners Dial Zero
Geffen GED 25184 (USA CD, 1998)

Mutations
As above, plus: Halo Of Gold / Black Balloon /
Electric Music And The Summer People
Geffen MVCF-24047 (Japan CD, 1998)

Midnite Vultures
Sexx Laws / Nicotine & Gravy / Mixed Bizness
/ Get Real Paid / Hollywood Freaks / Peaches &
Cream / Broken Train / Milk & Honey / Beautiful
Way / Pressure Zone / Debra
Geffen 4905272 (USA CD, 1999)

Midnite Vultures
As above, plus: Arabian Nights
Geffen MVCF-24060 (Japan CD, 1999)

Sea Change
The Golden Age / Paper Tiger / Guess I'm Doing
Fine / Lonesome Tears / Lost Cause / End Of The
Day / It's All In Your Mind / Round The Bend /
Already Dead / Sunday Sun / Little One / Side
Of The Road
Geffen 0694933932-A (USA CD, 2002)

Guero
E-Pro / Qué Onda Guero / Girl / Missing / Black
Tambourine / Earthquake Weather / Hell Yes
/ Broken Drum / Scarecrow / Go It Alone /
Farewell Ride / Rental Car / Emergency Exit
Interscope B0003481-02 (USA CD, 2005)

Guerolito
Ghost Range (E-Pro remix by Homelife) / Qué
Onda Guero (Islands remix) / Girl (Octet remix) /
Heaven Hammer (Missing remix by Air) / Shake

Shake Tambourine (Black Tambourine remix
by Ad-Rock) / Terremoto Tempo (Earthquake
Weather remix) / Ghettochip Malfunction (Hell
Yes remix by 8-Bit) / Broken Drum (Boards Of
Canada remix) / Scarecrow (El-P remix) / Wish
Coin (Go It Alone remix by Diplo) / Farewell Ride
(Subtle remix) / Rental Car (John King remix) /
Emergency Exit (Th' Corn Gangg remix) / Clap
Hands / Fax Machine Anthem (Hell Yes Dizzee
Rascal remix) / Qué Onda Guero
Interscope B0005650-02 (USA CD, 2005)

The Information
Elevator Music / Think I'm In Love / Cellphone's
Dead / Strange Apparition / Soldier Jane /
Nausea / New Round / Dark Star / We Dance
Alone / No Complaints / 1,000 BPM / Motorcade
/ The Information / Movie Theme / The Horrible
Fanfare-Landslide-Exoskeleton
Interscope B00076700 (USA CD+DVD, 2007)

The Information
As above, plus: Inside Out / This Girl That I Know
/ O Menina // Cellphone's Dead (Ellen Allien
remix) / Nausea (Bumblebeez remix) / Dark Star
(David Andrew Sitek remix) / Nausea (The Chap
remix) / Cellphone's Dead (Jamie Lidell Limited
Minutes remix) / Cellphone's Dead (Ricardo
Villalobos remix)
Interscope B0008341-00 (USA 2CD+DVD, 2007)

Modern Guilt
Orphans / Gamma Ray / Chemtrails / Modern
Guilt / Youthless / Walls / Replica / Soul Of A
Man / Profanity Prayers / Volcano
Geffen B0011507-02 (USA CD, 2008)

Morning Phase
Cycle / Morning / Heart Is A Drum / Say
Goodbye / Blue Moon / Unforgiven / Wave /
Don't Let It Go / Blackbird Chain / Phase / Turn
Away / Country Down / Waking Light
Capitol B001983802 (USA CD, 2014)

Index

After School Special, 103
Al's Bar, 61, 65
Anderson, Mamma, 232
'anti-folk' scene, 44–8, 50–1, 52–4, 56, 58–9, 68, 77, 151
Atwell, Martha, 65–6

Ballew, Chris, 89, 99–101, 106
Banham, Reyner, 17
Banhart, Devendra, 223, 231
Banjo Story, 52
Bateman, Bill, 102, 134
BBC Radio 1, 108, 121, 140
Beale Street Music Festival, 106
Beastie Boys, The, 110–11, 126, 140, 197, 202, 207, 235, 242
Beatnik Beatch, 243
'Beautiful Way', 180
Beavis & Butthead, 87
Beck, Like The Beer, 68
'Beercan', 60, 94, 96, 107, 109, 117, 242
Berg, Tony, 82
Berrol, Bill, 86
Berry, Bill, 176
Berryhill, Cindy Lee, 46–7
Bertram, James, 89, 90
Big Star, 160, 189, 219
Bioto, Mike, 92, 114, 243
'Blackbird Chain', 233, 236
Black Fag, 24
'Blackhole', 94–5
Blasters, The, 102, 134
Boat, the (studio), 201–2

Bong Load Custom Records, 71, 72, 78, 92–3, 96, 97, 128, 162–3, 167, 170, 171, 181
'Bottle of Blues', 159, 168
Bozulich, Carla, 66, 241
Brass Menagerie, 151, 177, 179, 185
Breslin, Jimmy, 10, 240
Brion, Jon, 169, 232
'Broken Drum', 203
Brown, David, 151, 243
Burnette, Don ('Dallas Don'), 78, 82

Café Troy, 7, 61, 65, 74, 82, 103
Cage, John, 14
Caldato Jr, Mario, 10, 207
Campbell, David, 15, 18, 20, 23, 30, 37, 143–4, 156, 178, 187, 200, 203, 219, 230, 232, 234, 235
Campbell, Noreen, 19
Campbell, D. Warren D, 19
'Canceled Check', 110, 143, 154–5, 164, 172
Carrillo, Sean, 25, 30, 61
Carter Family, The, 33, 34, 66, 68
Cash, Johnny, 110, 118, 154
'Cellphone's Dead', 211, 212
Chameleon, the (club), 44, 47, 48, 52, 56
'Chemtrails', 219
Clark, Dick, 183
Club Spaceland, 65
Cobain, Kurt, 34, 61, 83, 94

Cocker, Jarvis, 231, 232
Cohen, Leonard, 15, 26, 188, 223
'Cold Brains', 138, 148, 152, 153, 157–8, 161, 165, 168, 174, 194, 242
Cole, B.J., 108
Coleman, Wanda, 69
Cooley, Ben, 106
'Corvette Bummer', 97, 106
'Countess From Hong Kong', 180
Coyne, Wayne, 192–5
Crash, Darby, 24
Crosby, Bing, 227
'Cut 1/2 Blues', 49, 71
'Cycle', 235
Cymbala, Scott, 65, 69
Cypress Hill, 115

D., Mike, 98
Danger Mouse, 217–18, 220
'Dark Star', 211, 212
Davis, Vaginal Creme, 24
'Dead Melodies', 110, 148, 152, 157
'Deadweight', 147, 156, 161, 217
'Death is Coming to Get You', 82
'Debra', 139, 165, 172, 176, 180
'Defriended', 231, 232
Depp, Johnny, 70
'Devils Haircut', 116, 120, 121–2, 123, 130, 131, 136, 137, 140, 142, 145, 146, 172, 202

de Wilde, Autumn, 163, 198
'Diamond Bollocks', 125,
  158–9, 161, 163, 172,
  175, 204
Diaz, Paulo, 128
DJ Swamp, 8, 138, 141,
  142–3, 153, 171, 178
Domino Records, 109–110
Don't Get Bent Out of Shape,
  68
Douridas, Chris, 82, 99, 132
Dover, Eric, 243
Downs, Bertis, 176
Duchamp, Marcel, 14
Dust Brothers, the, 65,
  111–12, 119, 124, 125,
  131, 149, 173, 198–9, 201,
  203, 205–6, 217, 218,
  242, 243
Dylan, Bob, 45, 48, 93, 94,
  124, 148, 157, 191, 242

'Earthquake Weather', 203,
  207
Eggers, Dave, 212, 244
Elastica, 138, 140
'Electric Avenue', 169, 172
'Electric Music And The
  Summer People', 116, 121,
  153, 161, 221, 244
'Elevator Music', 211
Elliott, Ramblin' Jack, 45,
  51, 98
Empire, Kitty, 123
'E-Pro', 202, 204–5, 215, 244

Factory, the, 12–13, 14, 36
Falkner, Jason, 186, 218, 223
Farm Aid, 147
Farrell, Perry, 114, 115
Fats, Hollywood, 134
'Feel Like A Piece Of Shit', 88
Field Day Festival, 197

Fields, Danny, 45, 241
Fingerpaint Records, 65, 87
Flaming Lips, The, 192–6, 198
Flipside Records, 73, 104
Fluxus movement, 14–15
Forest For The Trees, 72, 242
Franz Ferdinand, 231
Fresh Meat And Old Slabs, 49,
  52, 746
Fricke, David, 191, 214
'Fucked Up Blues, The', 49
'Fuckin' With My Head', 93,
  97, 117, 137, 138
'Fume', 68, 75, 116, 126, 143

Gadson, James, 186, 210
Gainsbourg, Charlotte, 223–4,
  231, 235
Gallagher, Noel, 140, 243
'Gamma Ray', 219
Geffen, David, 84
Geffen Records, 84–6, 88,
  91, 93, 94–5, 98, 99, 100,
  114, 162–3, 167, 170–1,
  181, 241
Geradine Fibbers, The, 66,
  241
'Get Real Paid', 178–9, 192
'Gimme', 231, 232
Ginsberg, Allen, 47
Glass, Philip, 225–6, 232
Glastonbury Festival, 145–6
Godrich, Nigel, 151–4, 155,
  156, 158–60, 163, 186,
  187, 209, 210, 212–3,
  214, 218
'Goin' Nowhere Fast', 49, 50
'Golden Age, The', 187, 214,
  235
Golden Feelings, 52, 76, 89,
  168, 175
Gold Mountain, 86
Gomez, Dave, 100

Grammy Awards, 142–4, 169,
  204, 215, 220
Green Day, 65, 230
Greenstein, Paul, 134
Grimley, Tom, 92, 104
Guero, 7, 199, 201–8, 209,
  212, 216, 219, 241
Guerolito, 207–8
'Guess I'm Doing Fine', 187
Guthrie, Arlo, 33
Guthrie, Woody, 7, 32–4, 48,
  50, 51, 55–6, 75, 82, 142

Haden, Charlie, 67, 125, 129
Haden, Petra, 67, 88, 92
Haden, Rachel, 67
Hall, John S., 44
Hansen, Alfred Earl 'Al', 10–15,
  19, 21–2, 23, 25, 37–8, 40,
  116, 121, 122, 125, 190
Hansen, Bibbe, 12–13, 15,
  19, 22, 23, 24, 25, 30, 37,
  63, 240
Hansen, Channing, 18, 21, 22,
  59, 63, 68, 110
Hansen, Cosimo, 199–200
Hansen, Gordon, 10
Hansen, Katherine, 10
Hansen, Nicholas, 10
Hansen, Nicholas Jr., 10
Hansen, Tuesday, 215
Harris, Ross, 63, 96
Harte, David, 92
HBO (TV network), 172
'Heartland Feeling', 41, 77,
  122
'Hell Yes', 203, 207, 244
Hell Yes EP, 207
Herouvis, Valerie, 12
'High Five (Rock The Catskills)',
  119, 121, 129–30
Highland Grounds, 65
Hoffer, Tony, 174–5, 178

'Hollywood Freaks', 165, 179
HORDE tour, 146
Hormel, Greg 'Smokey', 8,
  101, 114, 133, 134, 152,
  154, 156, 175, 192, 203,
  210, 226
House, Son, 33, 34–5, 167
Hurt, Mississippi John, 31,
  33, 34, 35, 83, 135, 168

'I Just Started Hating Some
  People Today', 224, 225,
  233
'Information, The', 212
Information, The, 7, 209–15,
  216, 219, 226
INXS, 223
'It's All In Your Mind', 91, 100,
  108, 187, 221
'I Won't Be Long', 231, 232

Jabberjaw (venue), 61, 65,
  71, 242
'Jack-ass', 120, 123, 124,
  132, 142, 145, 146, 169,
  242
Jane's Addiction, 114
Jayne, Sam, 89–90
Jellyfish, 243
Johnson, Blind Willie, 32, 34
Johnson, Calvin, 82, 83,
  89–91, 221
Johnson, Kristin, 46
Johnson, Robert, 34, 203,
  241
Johnston, Daniel, 44–5, 56,
  68
Jonze, Spike, 212

Kates, Mark, 85
KCRW (radio station), 7, 78,
  94, 99, 132, 165, 192, 243
Kehew, Brian, 243

Kelly, Kirk, 46
Kelly, R., 179
Kerouac, Jan, 12
Kick, 223
King, Carole, 18
King, John, 111, 120, 198
KOME (radio station), 132
Kool Keith, 167, 169
Kraftwerk, 179
KROQ (radio station), 78, 132,
  140, 160
Kurstin, Greg, 210, 223
KXLU (radio station), 78, 83,
  100

Lach, 44, 46, 47, 52
Lamacq, Steve, 214
'Lampshade', 89, 172
Later with Jools Holland (TV
  show), 145
Leadbelly, 33, 34, 35, 47,
  51, 56
Lebarton, Brian, 210, 220,
  223
LeBlanc, Leo, 118
Lee, Ben, 243
'Lets Go Moon Some Cars',
  49
Letterman, David, 139, 146,
  244
Lewis, Jenny, 232
Lewis, Lightfield, 37, 241
Life Less Ordinary, A (film),
  147
Limon, Leigh, 110, 144, 147,
  152, 184, 189
Lindstrom, Bibi, 240
Lipscomb, Mance, 34
Lipton, Bart, 173
List, Daniel, 14
Lollapalooza, 113–15, 117,
  119, 123, 125, 130, 134,
  146, 242

'Loser', 7, 31, 35, 70, 72–3,
  75, 78–80, 81, 82, 84, 92,
  93, 95–6, 97, 98, 103,
  106–7, 109, 110, 112,
  116, 117, 122, 135, 138,
  141, 143, 161, 190, 194,
  214, 242
Loser, 140
Louvin Brothers, 66
Love, Courtney, 94
Luffman, Mark, 123
Lync, 89–90

'Magic Stationwagon', 77
Malkmus, Stephen, 128, 224
Maness, Jay Dee, 172
'Mango Vader Rocks', 88
Manning Jr., Roger, 8, 151,
  154, 157, 185, 203, 210,
  226, 230, 243
Manning, Roger, 46, 55, 56–7
Marr, Johnny, 167, 179
Mason, Harvey, 210
Masque, the (club), 23, 240
Maxwell, Tony, 241
Maxwell's (club), 138
Meldal-Johnsen, Justin, 8,
  37, 126, 133, 152, 156,
  157, 171, 172, 175, 185,
  186, 203, 210, 223, 226,
  230, 243
Mellow Gold, 7, 76, 88–100,
  106, 107, 108, 109, 112,
  116, 118, 122, 123, 124,
  125, 126, 128, 132, 163,
  214, 241
Midnite Vultures, 125, 126,
  159, 173–83, 184, 188,
  196, 198, 214
Milk, Chris, 230
'Milk & Honey', 179
'Minus', 107, 110, 116, 121,
  208

Mittleman, Margaret, 71
'Mixed Bizness', 176, 178, 182
'Modern Guilt', 218
Modern Guilt, 7, 218–22, 231, 233
Modern Rock Live (radio show), 126, 132
Mondle, Theo, 133, 150
Moog Cookbook, The, 243
Moramarco, Steve, 73, 75, 242
Moore, Thurston, 81, 83, 100, 199, 223, 224, 235, 240
Morning Phase, 7, 232–7
MTV, 34, 86, 117, 141, 161, 213, 240; Video Music Awards, 146
'MTV Makes Me Want To Smoke Crack', 73, 82
Mutations, 7, 84, 107, 125, 136, 139, 147, 148, 154, 155–65, 168, 169–72, 174, 175, 177, 180, 181–2, 185, 186–7, 209, 226, 242
'Motherfucker', 76, 94, 97, 116, 240

Nelson, Willie, 147, 169
Neuman, Jon, 71
'New Pollution, The', 120, 123–4, 128, 129, 136, 145, 146, 182, 194, 204
'Nicotine & Gravy', 178
Nirvana, 34, 86, 98
Nishita, Mark Ramos, 242
'Nitemare Hippy Girl', 94, 221
'Nobody's Fault But My Own', 148, 158, 161, 168, 170, 174, 186
'No Money, No Honey', 76, 77, 122, 137

Oar, 223
Oasis, 140, 151, 243
Ocean Way (studio), 152, 186, 210
Ocampo, Manuel, 122, 242
Odelay, 7, 67, 94, 107, 108, 110–14, 119–30, 132, 136–7, 139, 140, 143, 148, 150, 151–2, 161–2, 163, 164, 170, 175, 176–7, 181, 196, 201, 202, 204, 205, 208, 214, 216–17, 221, 243
'One Foot In The Grave', 138, 139, 146
One Foot In The Grave, 68, 90–1, 100, 163, 188, 204, 207, 221
120 Minutes (TV show), 81
Ono, Yoko, 14
'Orphans', 218–19
Orton, Beth, 167, 169, 174, 180, 231
Ostlin, Audrey, 9, 10, 11–14, 30
Ostlin, Olaf Gabriel, 9, 240
Ostlin, Robert, 9

P., Mickey, 131
Paleface, 44–5, 47, 53–6, 57–8
'Paper Tiger', 187
Paul's Boutique, 54, 111, 128
Pavement, 104, 115, 126, 160, 224
'Pay No Mind', 49, 68, 76, 82, 93, 97, 116, 138
PCP Labs (studio), 111, 174, 201, 242
'Peaches & Cream', 179
Petralia, Mickey, 174
Phoenix Festival, 137
Pik-Me-Up (club), 65, 67

Playing With Matches (exhibition), 37
Plouf, Scott, 89
Poop Alley (studio), 87, 89, 104
Poop Alley Tapes, The, 241
Possum Dixon, 66–7
Presidents Of The United States Of America, 101, 133
Prietto, Mario, 89, 242
Price, Lloyd, 131, 243
Primer Of Happenings & Time Space Art, A (book), 14
Prince, 139, 145, 177, 178
Pussy Galore, 31, 44, 65, 240

'Que Onda Guero', 202–3, 205, 244

Radio Ranch Straight Shooters, 101, 134
Radiohead, 160, 197, 220
Ralickie, David, 151, 243
'Ramshackle', 110, 124, 125, 129, 138, 211, 217, 219
Reading Festival, 117
Record Club, 222
Reinhart, Sunny, 114
R.E.M., 108, 150, 173, 176, 186
Reznor, Trent, 243
Ribisi, Giovanni, 198
Ribisi, Marissa, 198, 199, 200, 215
Ricci, Christina, 203
Rodgers, Jimmie, 34, 108, 145
Rolling Stones, The, 15, 189, 193, 211, 237
Rosenthal, Abraham, 9, 240
Rosenthal, Charlotte, 12
Rosenthal, Sadie, 9

Rothrock, Tom, 71, 72–3, 78, 96, 105–6

'Runners Dial Zero', 160, 163, 211

Saturday Night Live (TV show), 142, 168

Schnapf, Rob, 71, 92

Scientology, church of, 30, 200–1, 212, 219

Sea Change, 7, 186–92, 194, 197, 198, 209, 214, 226, 233

Sedgwick, Edie, 12

'Sexx Laws', 176, 177, 182

Shapiro, Jimmy, 13, 240

Shelley, Rachel, 212

Shelley, Steve, 126

'Ship In A Bottle', 188

Shocked, Michelle, 46, 47

Simon, Carly, 17

Simpson, Mike, 111–13, 198, 202, 242

Solanas, Valerie, 14

'Soldier Jane', 214

Song Reader, 224, 226–9, 230, 231, 232

Songs From A Room, 26

Songs of Leonard Cohen, The, 223

Sonic Enemy (label), 76, 175

'Soul Suckin Jerk', 93, 94

'Sound And Vision', 230

Spacey, Kevin, 142

'Special People', 76

'Stagger Lee', 130, 168, 242, 243

Star Wars (film), 31, 61

'Steal My Body Home', 73

Stein, Seymour, 45, 241

Stephenson, Carl, 35, 72–3, 88, 92–3, 111, 128, 224, 242

Stereopathetic Soul Manure, 68, 104, 106

Stern, Arthur, 55

'Steve Threw Up', 75

Stubbs, David, 127

Sub Pop (label), 79, 103

'Sucker Without A Brain', 49, 50

Summerhill, Julian, 50, 54–5, 241

'Supergolden (Sunchild)', 76

'Tasergun', 74–5

Ten Ton Lid, 66

10 Years Of Mellow Gold (film), 71

Terry & The Pirates, 130

Terry, Sonny, 93, 108

TFI Friday (TV show), 145

That Dog, 67, 88, 92, 101, 104, 241

Tibetan Freedom Concert, 125–6

'Timebomb', 215

Top Of The Pops (TV show), 98, 100

'To See That Woman Of Mine', 73

'Totally Confused', 49, 76, 89, 138, 149

Travis, Abby, 114, 115–16, 117, 242

'Tropicalia', 147, 156, 161, 168, 171, 174

'Trouble All My Days', 75, 76–7

'Truckdrivin' Neighbors Downstairs', 97, 137, 138

True, Everett, 108

Tyson, Mike, 66

Ultimate Akademie (art school), 37

Unplugged (TV show), 34

Veloso, Caetano, 174, 199

Velvet Underground, 36, 180, 196, 222

Velvet Underground & Nico, The, 36, 222

Verve, The, 108, 161

VH1 Fashion Awards, 147

'Volcano', 219

'Waking Light', 233, 236

Walker, Charlie, 13

Walker, Scott, 157

Walt Mink, 102, 136

Warhol, Andy, 12, 14, 36

Waronker, Anna, 67, 88, 101

Waronker, Joey, 8, 67, 100, 101, 102–3, 106, 108, 113, 133, 134–5, 136, 142, 150, 152, 157, 160–1, 169, 171, 173, 175–6, 186, 187, 203, 210, 215, 219, 222, 223, 226

Waronker, Lenny, 101

'Wave', 232, 235

'We Live Again', 156–7

Western Harvest Field By Moonlight, A, 65, 68, 87–9, 212, 242

'Where It's At', 116, 117, 119, 120–1, 123, 125, 131, 139, 142, 143, 149, 161, 194

White, Jack, 204, 224, 233

Yanni, 203

Yanni Live at The Acropolis, 223

Yauch, Adam, 125–6

Zabrecky, Rob, 67, 94–5, 242

Zinder, Jac, 118

ROB JOVANOVIC

Acknowledgements

I started the first version of this book more than fifteen years ago, and along the way a lot of folk have helped out in many different ways. Below is a list of people who made this book possible: Chris Barlow, Brian Bauer, John C. Book, Tim Bourneman, Cathy Brillon, Erika Y. Brinda, Lee Cannon, Mr Chonk, Marie Cox (if you read this, drop me a line), Carolyn, Mary D. Decicco, Wendy Diplock, Luke Eygenraam, Dustin Patrick Fitzgerald, Adam Flaherty, Ben Goldberg, Carlos D. Giffoni, Deborah Gilmore (if you read this, drop me a line too), Ian Gittins, Penny Guyon, Dustin Harjo, Paul Hellier, Cathy Illman, Levi Klau, Tony Linkin, Doreen Lobelle, Ehren Meditz, Joseph Milbury, Sitar Mody, Deirdre Mullins, Hunter Neisler, Shauna O'Brien, Graham Palmer, Mark Paytress, Chris Quigley, Tom Reed, Lily Simonson, Paul Smernicki, Geoff Snack, Wietze Spjikerman, Toni Stickroth, Pete Tognetti, Abby Travis, Truck, Todd M.R. Tue, Keith Zehr, and Flo—thanks for the tour on your day off.

I would also like to give special thanks to Tom Seabrook and Nigel Osborne at Jawbone for their faith (and patience!) with this project.

If anyone ever wants to chat about this book, or about Beck in general, you can reach me at robj@innotts.co.uk.

Bibliography and sources
The sources used in preparing this book were many and varied. I perused Beck's myriad radio and TV interviews, as well as the hundreds of newspaper and magazines articles, features, reviews, and interviews. These were gathered from *Alternative Press*, *The Big Issue*, the *Daily Telegraph*, the *Guardian*, the *Independent*, the *Los Angeles Times*, the *New York Times*, *Magnet*, *Melody Maker*, *Modern Drummer*, *Mojo*, *NME*, *Notion*, the *Observer*, *Q*, *Record Collector*, *Rolling Stone*, *Select*, *Spin*, the *Times*, *Uncut*, *Vanity Fair*, *Village Voice*, *Vox*, and *Word*, among others.

I also interviewed Beck myself in 2002, and was kindly given access by Ian Gittins to use his interview from 2013. I was also fortunate enough to be granted new interviews with the following, specifically for this book: Cindy Lee Berryhill, Mario Caldato Jr, Rebecca Gates, Sam Jayne, Roger Manning, Paleface, Julian Summerhill, DJ Swamp, Anna Waronker, and Rob Zabrecky. To those who wish to remain anonymous—you know who you are—thank you!

Photo credits
Jacket: Dan Tuffs/Getty Images; 2–3: Martyn Goodacre/Getty Images; 238–9: Wendy Redfern/Getty Images.

254

ALSO AVAILABLE IN PRINT AND EBOOK EDITIONS FROM JAWBONE PRESS

The Resurrection Of Johnny Cash: Hurt, Redemption, And American Recordings
Graeme Thomson (978-1-906002-36-7)

Crazy Train: The High Life And Tragic Death Of Randy Rhoads
Joel McIver (978-1-906002-37-1)

The 10 Rules Of Rock And Roll: Collected Music Writings 2005–11
Robert Forster (978-1-906002-91-6)

Just Can't Get Enough: The Making Of Depeche Mode
Simon Spence (978-1-906002-56-5)

Glenn Hughes: The Autobiography
Glenn Hughes with Joel McIver
(978-1-906002-92-3)

Entertain Us: The Rise Of Nirvana
Gillian G. Gaar (978-1-906002-89-3)

Adventures Of A Waterboy
Mike Scott (978-1-908279-24-8)

She Bop: The Definitive History Of Women In Popular Music (Revised Third Edition)
Lucy O'Brien (978-1-908279-27-9)

Solid Foundation: An Oral History Of Reggae (Revised and Updated Edition) David Katz (978-1-908279-30-9)

Read & Burn: A Book About Wire
Wilson Neate (978-1-908279-33-0)

Big Star: The Story Of Rock's Forgotten Band
Rob Jovanovic (978-1-908279-36-1)

Recombo DNA: The Story Of Devo, or How The 60s Became The 80s
Kevin C. Smith (978-1-908279-39-2)

Neil Sedaka, Rock'n'roll Survivor: The Inside Story Of His Incredible Comeback
Rich Podolsky (978-1-908279-42-4)

Touched By Grace: My Time With Jeff Buckley
Gary Lucas (978-1-908279-45-3)

A Sense Of Wonder: Van Morrison's Ireland
David Burke (978-1-908279-48-4)

Bathed In Lightning: John McLaughlin, The 60s And The Emerald Beyond
Colin Harper (978-1-908279-51-4)

My Bloody Roots: From Sepultura To Soulfly And Beyond
Max Cavalera with Joel McIver
(978-1-908279-63-7)

What's Exactly The Matter With Me? Memoirs Of A Life In Music
P.F. Sloan and S.E. Feinberg (978-1-908279-57-6)

Who Killed Mister Moonlight? Bauhaus, Black Magick, and Benediction
David J. Haskins.(978-1-908279-66-8)

Million Dollar Bash: Bob Dylan, The Band, and The Basement Tapes (Revised and Upated Edition)
Sid Griffin (978-1-908279-69-9)

Lee, Myself & I: Inside The Very Special World Of Lee Hazlewood
Wyndham Wallace (978-1-908279-72-9)

Confessions Of A Heretic: The Sacred And The Profane, Behemoth & Beyond
Adam Nergal Darski with Mark Eglinton
(978-1-908279-75-0)